Cornerstone
Colony

Thomas Douglas, 5th Earl of Selkirk
(from a portrait believed to be by Raeburn)
Manitoba Archives

Cornerstone Colony

Selkirk's Contribution to the Canadian West

Grant MacEwan

Western Producer Prairie Books
Saskatoon, Saskatchewan

Cover design by Warren Clark

Printed in Canada by
Modern Press

Saskatoon, Saskatchewan

Canadian Cataloguing in Publication Data

MacEwan, John W. Grant, 1902-
   Cornerstone colony

   Bibliography: p.
   Includes index.
   ISBN 0-919306-80-2

   1. Red River Settlement, Man.* 2. Selkirk,
Thomas Douglas, 5th Earl of, 1771-1820.
I. Title.
FC3372.M24   971.27'01   C77-002205-7
F1063

43,898

To the memory of a great historian and gentleman,
one to whom the author
has a huge debt of personal gratitude,
Arthur Silver Morton of Saskatchewan.

Contents

Preface

This writing task has been approached with a conviction that the Red River Settlement in its first twenty-five troubled years made a deeper and more lasting imprint upon what was to become Western Canada than the Fur Trade made in 200 years. The Colony should be presented as the Cornerstone upon which western agriculture in all its enduring greatness was founded. It was the pioneer effort forced to face all the danger and make all the mistakes. And whether the Founding Father, Lord Selkirk, was in it for reasons of charity or personal gain, or a combination of the two, is beside the point at this moment. Whatever his inner motives, he deserved to be remembered as the leading colonizer in Canadian history and the first developer with a clear vision of the goodness of western soil.

A Canadian may be pardoned for wishing that Selkirk had been a permanent resident here. His stay in the West was very brief — less than three months — but for the faith he displayed when nobody in public life was ready to stand with him, he earned the Westerner's undivided admiration.

Contemplating the extent to which his zeal changed the West of Canada — or all of Canada — can be an intriguing exercise, likely to lead to the conclusion that nobody in or out of public life did as much to give shape to our destiny. And if at some point he had the idea of adding to his wealth, it need not be held against him. He helped hundreds of needy people; he was the first to engage in a fight against eastern and overseas interests which would have kept the West as a private fur preserve; he introduced techniques and ideas which were decades ahead of their time; he colonized in three widely separated parts of British North America, and instead of making a fortune, his program cost him dearly and exhausted his financial resources. During his lifetime, he received more opposition than praise, an added reason for some belated payments in recognition.

Selkirk, of course, is not a stranger to Canadian historians and writers. But certain aspects of his contribution have received less than adequate attention. In embarking upon this book, therefore, it was with the hope of placing more emphasis on the Selkirk role in blazing trail for agriculture. If the Red River Settlement was so important as a starting point in a new industry or if it could be fairly regarded as the first real Experimental Farm in half a continent, the fact deserves more attention than it has ever received. Hence, while this book gives minimum treatment of some aspects of Selkirk's life which would hold interest for Canadian readers and scholars, it attempts to do more for the struggles that made him Western Canada's Founding Farmer.

As is always the case in producing a book of this type, the author owes gratitude to various institutions and individuals. As source material commanding gratitude, nothing can equal the Selkirk Papers, a truly fabulous store of relevant information inviting further study in the Public Archives, in Ottawa. The papers offer research resources which no writer is likely to exhaust.

Worthy of special mention, also, is that collection of official correspondence tabled in the House of Commons in London in 1819, at the instigation of Sir James Montgomery, member of parliament and brother-in-law of Lord Selkirk.

There are the numerous workers in archives and libraries across the country who have been helpful. And finally an expression of appreciation which is long overdue; it dates back more than thirty years to a time when it was the author's good fortune to be a frequent traveling companion of the late Arthur Silver Morton, professor of history at the University of Saskatchewan. He was at that time bringing his masterpiece, *A History of the Canadian West to 1870-71*, to completion and trying to locate the exact sites of many ancient trading posts in the West. It demanded many expeditions into remote countryside and hazardous river-crossings by not-very-skillful canoemen. The younger man was the self-appointed chauffeur and packer, and the elder reciprocated handsomely by being the self-appointed private tutor in western history. To have sat at his feet beside many bedtime campfires was a rare and memorable experience.

He was well aware of the younger man's interest in the Red River Settlement and especially in its singular role in western agriculture at its birth. In his patient and kindly way, he was constantly making withdrawals of Red River and Selkirk information for transfer to the still-humble files of the younger man. He seemed to be authorizing his admiring fellow-traveler to pursue that particular chapter in western history — or was it wishful thinking on the part of the latter? In any case, his contributions were most useful and most appreciated.

CHAPTER ONE

The Founding Father

A tall thin man wearing expensive clothes grown shabby from constant use paced nervously back and forth at the west side of Red River where a city to be known as Winnipeg would someday arise. Counting steps, he was obviously measuring ground for some purpose but he was soon interrupted. After coming into view, he was quickly surrounded by curious and anxious settlers from the log-hut homes built at intervals of about 200 yards along the river front to the north of Point Douglas.

His arrival in the settlement on June 21, 1817 — one day after his forty-sixth birthday — was an event of unusual interest because he was the one and only person the settlers could thank or blame for their presence in this new land and the one upon whom their fortunes seemed to depend.

From other years in depressed Ireland and the Scottish Highlands, these people had grown to regard noblemen and other rich and powerful men with suspicion if not with scorn. But this man with quiet and gentle mien, Thomas Douglas, 5th Earl of Selkirk, appeared to be an outright contradiction of all their preconceived notions. If he had selfish motives in bringing evicted families across the Atlantic to settle on the fresh and untried soil of Rupert's Land — not yet Western Canada — he managed to conceal them well.

"There he is," a Highlander whispered to his wife, "but ye'd no ken he was the Earl o' Selkirk."

"Aye," the woman replied. "He's got a gude face but he looks frail an' ev'n ill. He's no' lang for this warld I'd be thinking."

More settlers gathered and crowded in upon him to catch his soft-spoken words and touch his woolen jacket. He talked in simple and friendly terms, quite enough to dispel many of the quaint superstitions about titled gentry. These people knew they had a debt to him. Now, almost instantly, they were finding an affection for him. The admiring Irish were wishing they could claim him as a Roman Catholic and the Scots were wishing he were Highland instead of Lowland. But it didn't really matter because his slow and clear expressions of friendliness were dissolving those differences which too often breed prejudices.

To be within chatting distance of a living Earl was something these people could not have imagined, especially this one who was already one of the most controversial figures of his time, a wealthy aristocrat with an apparent concern for less fortunate people, one who would spend his own money to assist emigration from the Old Land, one who would take on the powerful North West Company, almost single-handedly, and promise to return blow for blow. And adding to the sense of astonishment, here was the man who was described as the biggest owner of land in the world, the proprietor of the District of Assiniboia, a Rupert's Land property totaling more than twice the area of Scotland.

It was almost beyond belief. With his wealth and rank and influence, he might have been spending his years in pursuit of Old World comfort and luxury, as many high-born Britishers were doing. Instead, he had become obsessed with a North American hinterland he had never seen and a colonization scheme big enough to frighten a professional promoter. This overseas venture in settlement was not his first; actually, it was his third — and last — also the most ambitious and costly and frustrating.

As settlers continued to press in upon him on that bright June morning in 1817, he took opportunity to reassure them of his continuing support. After glancing in all directions as if to verify his directions or catch a vision of the emergence of a thriving and prospering community, the Earl raised his voice to reach all who were nearby: "I'm sorry you had so many troubles but we will not allow the attacks on this colony to be repeated. You have my word for that. It is my highest hope that you will find security such as you deserve and for which you have longed. Before I leave, I will do all in my power to ensure for you the opportunity to gain a contented way of life in this new land. May I suggest that this Parish be called Kildonan, to preserve the memory of the district from which many of you came. And here I offer you a site of ground for your school, and over there another for your church and manse. We shall take steps at once to see that you get roads and bridges, and seeds and cattle."

Primitive and still-untested Red River Settlement was six troubled years old, each of its years more troubled than the one preceding it. Who save the possessor of great faith could believe the local fortunes would change now? It was little wonder that the man upon whom the main burden had fallen looked worn and sad. Repeatedly he had heard both friends and foes saying his scheme was an adventure in folly, assured only of failure. "Preposterous," rival fur traders had shouted every time his undertaking was mentioned. "This is fur country. What stupidity to expect settlers to succeed in this land of ice and snow! Didn't somebody warn that the country is doomed to eternal sterility? What nonsense is Selkirk dreaming up?"

Now, astonishingly, the man was assuring his people of better days ahead.

In making a prophecy of better times, Selkirk was partly right. There were better days ahead for his colonists, but not for him. Much as he might have wished to remain with these people with a childlike dependence upon him, he was under the disagreeable compulsion to return to Montreal or Toronto or Sandwich — or all three — to face the courts in a long and depressing series of trials in which he would be alternately plaintiff and defendant. It would be the cruel sequel to those warlike acts in the long strife between men who believed the good soil of the Northwest could and should support agriculture and settlement, and others who held fanatically to the idea that the country should be kept exclusively for wild furs.

There in the East where the North West Company had succeeded in creating a political climate favorable to itself, Selkirk would stand alone, or almost alone, arguing for his right to test the fur country for settlement and then fight if necessary to protect the innocent homemakers against savage attacks. Hounded almost to death in Montreal, he was the first person to stage a battle of words on behalf of the West against the Eastern interests.

He promised the colonists he would return to spend more time among them. The thought made him happy. Gladly he would have spent half of his time at the Red River Settlement, correctly called Assiniboia at that time, sharing frontier food and hardships with his people, and half in Scotland and England where his responsibilities were of a demanding kind. He had farming interests at home and political obligations in the House of Lords. But, although still in middle age, the Earl of Selkirk would never again see Red River. Only one who could peer into the future could know that the next year and a half would hold him brutally to the exigencies of the courts and his enemies; and then, after paying a high price in time and money and health, he would be going home — to die.

It is easy to understand why the settlers loved him, and why men in sections of the fur trade hated him and entertained thoughts of murder. It is not so easy to know why the Selkirk role in nation building did not receive more recognition. Granted, he made himself most unpopular in Montreal where the North West Company was powerful, and elsewhere in the East, and this might have damaged the man's lasting national image; but there was no reason for Westerners failing to honor the man of so many distinctions. There might have been serious errors in judgment or indiscretions in the seizure of Fort William and the arrest of North West Company officers in 1816, but there was provocation and there was much to offset the mistakes. The magnitude of his aid to the peasant folks who came as his settlers placed him among the leading philanthropists of his time, or all time.

Even the extent of his land holdings, embracing an ownership which has never been equaled and will probably never be equaled, should have been enough to make him memorable. Any person who could mount a claim to 116,000 square miles of fertile western land — some 74 million acres — would scarcely need to look further for distinction. And no less distinctive were the circumstances of the purchase, including price. The acquisition of this land, mainly in what was later Manitoba, on May 29, 1811, for a consideration of ten shillings and an undertaking to bring a specified number of men to the country each year for ten years, must surely qualify as the best land purchase in history. That the purpose was colonization did not make the deal any less stupendous. There was a Believe-It-Or-Not quality about it.

Fortunately, land taxes were still unknown in the country and Selkirk's vast expanse could be carried at no cost except in terms of worry. He could afford to be generous in making land gifts. When he chose to recognize a friend or a debt, he might do it by making a simple gift of a township — thirty-six square miles. In recognition of long service or special feeling of friendship, the token of appreciation could and did consist of from five to ten townships, as shown in his instructions in November, 1811: ten townships for Miles Macdonell, five for Ronald McDonald, five for Thomas Clark, and so on. A letter of November 8, 1811, preserved in the Selkirk Papers, itemized land grants totaling more than fifty townships, mainly in parcels of five townships each.

Nor was it just ordinary land; much of it was Red River Valley soil which inherited its unusual richness from the ancient Lake Agassiz and was destined to occupy an important place in western agriculture.

As viewed from the vantage point of 160 years later, the Selkirk performance which overcame powerful resistance to found the first agricultural enterprise in the Canadian West, must be seen as one of the outstanding acts of faith in the history of a nation. It had to be faith because there was no such thing as a soil survey or economic report or feasibility study — not even a good map or a clear external expression of optimism about the outcome. Indeed, most of the Earl's friends at home saw as sheer madness his dream of drawing upon evicted and displaced Britishers to start a colony on an untried frontier.

But was it madness or was the scheme backed by vision and judgment more penetrating than anybody of that period realized? True, the colony came close to complete failure on different occasions. Twice local enemies believed they had effected total destruction of the settlement; once the Red River, rampaging in flood, dealt a destroying blow; several times grasshoppers attacked voraciously and on one occasion there was a major exodus of discouraged settlers hoping to improve their fortunes in Upper Canada or back in Scotland. But instead of collapsing as the critics said it must do, the Selkirk Settlement survived and staggered on to become the very cornerstone of Western Canada's monumental agricultural industry.

Perhaps it was luck more than judgment that led the settlers for that initial farming experiment to locate on soil which ranks with the most fertile in the world. Perhaps it was more than luck; perhaps it was something in the hidden Selkirk wisdom but, in any case, the man was a leader far ahead of his time. Of course he made some serious mistakes, of which more will be said, and he paid dearly for them, but who, from his generation — or any generation, made a more crucial and courageous impact upon the destiny of the country to become Western Canada? If Canadian agriculture, through which the nation made its finest contribution to world needs, were to choose a Patron Saint or Founding Father, what candidate would have an equal claim upon the high honor? It would seem to belong to Thomas Douglas, 5th Earl of Selkirk, who started not one but three farming colonies in widely separated parts of the country and who practically stood alone in declaring faith in the soil of the fur country.

What emerged at Red River was a gigantic pilot plant or experimental farm. Indeed, the first project to carry the name of Experimental Farm between the Atlantic and Pacific oceans was the one started at Red River in 1818 at Selkirk's direction. That the undertaking known as the Hayfield Experimental Farm was not a great success is beside the point; Selkirk recognized the need and deserved full credit for the effort to meet it. Had the Earl lived longer, his experimental farm — Canada's first — no doubt would have survived.

A few years after the Hayfield Farm lost its special status, a second farm was set apart for experimental purposes, and then a third one. All were short-lived. But present-day citizens who find pride in Canada's Experimental Farm System, started in 1886, should take notice of the fact that Selkirk's initial plan to provide the benefits of planned experimentation preceded the government program by more than sixty years.

Even before 1818, the Earl's Red River undertaking was making the entire colony appear like a testing ground. The money and the ideas came from him and many of his schemes and projects would have seemed timely half a century later.

If the agricultural colony had the character of an experimental farm, Lord Selkirk was like the director of research, and was the author of nearly every facet of the experimental program. Even before Miles Macdonell reached Red River, he had instructions from the Earl to make careful observations of the soil and study all crops grown with the idea of determining the ones possessing the greatest degree of genetic suitability. In the hope of finding products for export and sale on world markets, he urged the testing of flax and hemp; and hoping that wool might be an appropriate item for shipment overseas, he instructed that individual fleece records be kept for the Merino sheep sent in 1812. Every fleece should be marked with the identity of the particular ewe or ram from which it came and thus be submitted to the wool experts overseas in order to secure a proper assessment of individual breeding worth. The technique was enough to brand this man as a scientist as well as a pioneer colonizer.

It was Selkirk's idea that Miles Macdonell should capture buffalo calves and test the practical problems in raising them in captivity. He offered several proposals for domesticating the wild things and suggested a buffalo park for the colony. There should be a hybridizing experiment involving the buffalo and domestic cattle, he told Miles Macdonell, and he demanded reports on progress. He wanted information about the possibility of domesticating the muskox — "muskbuffalo" as he called those wild creatures of the North — and speculated about the feasibility of developing an export trade in muskox wool. Likewise, he wanted test data about the relative economy and worth of water power and windmill power for the colony, and he ordered a report on the kinds of tools and machines most needed by his people. Such questions raised prior to 1820 seem strikingly mature.

Although his residence in the West was brief — only a few summer months with a promise to return — his influence gave direction to a completely new ecomonic and social shape for nearly half a continent. Without him and his ambitious undertaking in settlement, the country would have remained in the selfish embrace of the fur trade much longer. Western Canada would have waited additional decades before realizing a successful agriculture; and railroad construction in the West would have been delayed substantially. It does not require much imagination to identify the reasons.

The most intriguing question of all has rarely been raised: Without the pioneer demonstration of agricultural settlement would the government of the new Canada have been interested in 1869 in buying the lands of the West which traders insisted were unfit for any other industry except furs? And if Canada had not acted to acquire the West at that time, would the United States, caught up in the spirit of Manifest Destiny, have succeeded in buying it from the Hudson's Bay Company, as that neighboring country had bought Alaska from Russia just two years before?

It becomes obvious that the West of Canada — or all of Canada — has a debt to Selkirk. Fittingly, the Earl's family names were perpetuated in western features — Forts Selkirk and Daer, the Manitoba town of Selkirk, the Selkirk range of mountains, and Fort Douglas and Point Douglas beside Red River. Appropriate as these names will seem, they are but minimum recognition and the debt has remained, a debt that was never paid and rarely recognized.

CHAPTER TWO

In the Beginning

"A Douglas! A Douglas!" workers and tenants shouted gleefully on the morning of June 20 in 1771, when it was known that another son had been born to the 4th Earl of Selkirk and his lady in residence at beautiful St. Mary's Isle at the mouth of the River Dee in Kirkcudbrightshire, Scotland's southwest. Such was the jubilation that a visitor from Dumfries remarked to a servant: "Gawd mon, ye'd think ye'd faithered the bairn yoursel. Why all the hilarity? This is not ev'n the furst; this'n they're callin' Thomas Douglas is the seventh son, no less, an' wi six aheed o' heem, he'll no' hae ev'n a wee chance o' ever inheriting the Selkirk name or the family baubies."

Nobody could argue; six elder brothers and almost as many sisters could certainly affect an inheritance but assets nobody could ever deny the newcomer were the Douglas pedigree and family traditions — and the pride engendered by them. Members of the Clan, on occasions of reckless exuberance, were known to argue that Noah's last name was Douglas and his ark carried the family crest on its bow. In more serious moments, they told of Sir William Douglas who stood gallantly with William Wallace in the thirteenth century campaigns, and Sir James Douglas who was a close companion of Robert the Bruce and fought at Bannockburn in the fourteenth century. It was Sir James, ancestor of Thomas Douglas, who vowed to carry out the dying wish of his friend and fighting companion and carry the Bruce heart in a silver casket to the Land of the Bible, to be interred in the Holy Sepulchre. Apparently Sir James tried to fulfill the promise and carried the heart as far as Spain where he paused to indulge in the pastime of war with the invading Moors and there, in 1330, lost his life. The king's heart was returned to Scotland.

No less valorous were the deeds of another ancestor, Archibald Douglas, known as "Bell-the-Cat" Douglas because he, at the time of James III of Scotland, was the one who volunteered to confront the tyrannical ruler with the protests and demands being voiced by the less courageous noblemen.

Lovely St. Mary's Isle, refreshed by spray from the Irish Sea, offered the best of all environments for growing boys and Thomas Douglas found pleasure in the fields and byres and along the shoreline lapped by tireless waves. He loved the tales of the Isle, said to have been the one-time abode of freebooters and pirates. Even in the years of his boyhood, the Isle was the object of an attack by John Paul Jones, one of Scotland's native sons who gained a niche in history by giving support to the revolutionary American Colonists and taking to brigandage on the high seas. One of his escapades took the form of an attack in 1783 upon St. Mary's Isle, taking it without trouble. The purpose, presumably, was to capture members of the Douglas family and hold them for ransom, but they were absent at the time and the roguish John Paul found nothing better to do than some assorted looting.

The young Thomas Douglas, like most of his six brothers and six sisters, was not a robust person and never became a great athlete. But he was a serious student and with only the remotest chance of ever inheriting the Selkirk title and fortune, it seemed especially important that he obtain a useful education, perhaps preparation for the practice of law.

It was an eventful time in world history. The lad was five years old when the American Colonies climaxed their revolution with a Declaration of Independence, and when he was eighteen years of age, the French Revolution was capturing public attention and leading to the flight of the French aristocracy, the execution of a king, and the rise of Napoleon. The French turmoil did not escape the serious attention of Thomas Douglas and with considerable sympathy for the revolutionists, he visited France to make his own assessments.

In due course, he attended the University of Edinburgh and was identified there as one of the quiet and earnest young men with high ideals. By this time he was above average height and lean, pallid in complexion and slightly withdrawn. But he was a friendly fellow, ready to engage in conversation, and he formed lasting fraternal bonds with various young men who were to win national and international distinction. Philosopher Dugal Stewart, for example, who would become professor of both mathematics and moral philosophy — a strange combination — and Walter Scott, whose pen would win world acclaim, were his close university friends. Members of the group or "Club" were considered slightly radical in their views but their interests were literary and humanitarian more than political.

These friends or members of the "Club" formed lasting loyalties to each other and years later when Lord Selkirk was mortally ill after having been distressingly entangled in litigation in Upper and Lower Canada, Sir Walter Scott offered a glowing compliment, saying: "I never knew in my life a man of a more generous and disinterested disposition, or one whose talents and perseverance were better qualified to bring great and National schemes to conclusion."[1]

Another of Scotland's distinguished sons, Robert Burns, would be twelve years older than the young Douglas but moderately well known to him and his family. Burns was generally cynical towards Britain's "bluebloods," saying that "The rank is but the guinea's stamp," and expecting to find them distant and snobbish. But to his acknowledged surprise, he found members of the 4th Earl's family to be humble and likeable. He was a guest at the Selkirk seat on at least one occasion and in various other encounters with the Douglas people, they won his admiration — some of it in verse as on that autumn day in 1786 when the bard was dining at the home of Dugal Stewart, near Mossgiel. Among the guests was Basil William Hamilton Douglas, second son of the 4th Earl and at that time, as the oldest living son, he was known as Lord Daer. Burns would be nursing some deep-seated hostility toward the high and mighty young nobleman whom he was meeting for the first time, and may have been ready to pen a stinging poetic rebuke such as other "belted knights" had received. But instead of being irritated, the poet was favorably impressed and the spontaneous verses, "On Dining With Lord Daer," were the confession of a pleasant surprise on this "ne'er to be forgotten day":

> I sidling sheltered in a nook,
> An' at his Lordship steal't a look
>   Like some portentous omen;
> Except good sense and social glee,
> And what surprised me moderately,
>   I marked nought uncommon.
>
> I watch'd the symptoms o' the Great,
> The gentle pride, the lordly state,
>   The arrogant assuming;
> The fient a pride, nae pride had he,
> Nor sause, nor state, that I could see,
>   Mair than an honest ploughman.
>
> Then from his Lordship I shall learn,
> Henceforth to meet with unconcern
>   One rank as weel's another;
> Nae honest worthy man need care
> To meet with noble, youthful Daer,
>   For he but meets a brother.

A few years later, 1793, while accompanying his friend John Syme, distributor of stamps at Dumfries, and riding a gray Highland pony, Burns was traveling to pay a visit at St. Mary's Isle.[2] The circumstances of the morning — a nagging headache, a sick stomach, and the ruination of a pair of new shoes in the Kirkcudbrightshire mud — left the poet in an ugly mood. Then, to add to the Burns displeasure, he was obliged to pass close to the residence of the Earl of Galloway, with whom the poet had been angry. It was enough to excite Burns' scorn:

> Spare me thy vengence, Galloway;
> In quiet let me live;
> I ask no kindness at thy hand,
> For thou hast none to give.

Syme was worried about the poet's ill temper at that moment, but there was no need to fear because the fulminations directed at Galloway seemed to dissolve all other traces of acrimony and Burns, although now bootless, was in a jovial state of mind for his arrival at the Douglas home. Two Douglas daughters — both beautiful — were present, and visiting there also was Pietro Urbani, an Italian musician from Edinburgh. There was Scottish song and Burns recited from his ballads and nothing more was needed to make it an evening of delight.

It was on this occasion, too, that Burns, when asked to say grace before dinner, offered extemporaneously what became known as the Selkirk Grace:

> Some hae meat and canno' eat,
> An' some wad eat that want it;
> But we hae meat an' we can eat,
> An' sae the Lord be thankit.

Next day, as the two travelers made their way homeward along the gentle River Dee, Burns was deep in thought and Syme had the good sense to remain silent, thereby to avoid breaking a chain of thoughts. The outcome was a draft of the immortal poem, "Scots Wha Hae wi' Wallace Bled," described as one of the noblest war songs in English literature.

The Burns influence upon Thomas Douglas may have been much greater than was generally recognized. Certainly the younger man came to share many of the Burns ideas about society and its needs. Douglas, too, saw Man's Inhumanity to Man making countless thousands to mourn, especially in poverty-stricken Ireland and in northern Scotland where small tenant farmers and crofters were being uprooted from their holdings.

At the time of Burns' death in 1796, Douglas was twenty-five years of age, traveling extensively and becoming more and more critical of social conditions as he found them. He was taking a bold stand in opposition to the slave trade in which there was British participation, also to the use of liquor in the North American fur trade dealings with native people. Gradually, he was taking a bigger interest in the North American scene, even though his travels had not taken him far in a westerly direction. Long before he had any proprietary connection with British North America, he was exercised about the fur trade, particularly as it was conducted by the North West Company. His critical views about the Montreal-based concern seemed to stem from his associations with one Count Andreani, whom he met in Switzerland in 1794. Andreani's prejudiced opinions about the North West Company could be recognized in Selkirk's *Sketch of the British Fur Trade*, published in 1816.

One by one the sons of the 4th Earl of Selkirk died, until Thomas, the youngest, was the only survivor. As the only remaining son, he became Lord Daer and then, in 1799, death claimed Dunbar Douglas, the 4th Earl of Selkirk, and the title passed to Thomas, then twenty-eight years of age. The inheritance of both title and family fortune might have changed the young man greatly, sending him in search of the pleasures his money would buy. It would not have been the first time sudden wealth had bought riotous living. But his ideals remained unchanged, the only difference in his life being the resources with which he could now carry out his charitable dreams. Re-examining the state of poverty in parts of Ireland and the callous "clearances" of the crofter folks in the Scottish Highlands, he resolved to do something about the unhappy situations. Visiting the Highlands, he saw very clearly the forces which were working to drive people from the lands they had occupied for generations. The small farms were failing to return enough to keep the tenant operators and also pay a dividend for the landlords and the latter concluded that they would make more or lose less money with the lands converted to sheep ranges. The crofters were being ordered to vacate the only homes they had ever known. The evicted people might move to Glasgow or London and hope to obtain employment but they were totally unfitted for anything except life on those small Scottish farms.

One other possible alternative was not being overlooked; parts of the United States were calling for settlers and offering inducements. Bold and risky as any adventure beyond the Atlantic might appear, some of those discouraged Britishers were going to the Carolinas. Selkirk saw emigration to North and South Carolina as a double misfortune because it represented a drain on Britain's human resources and left colonial lands unoccupied. His anxiety led to the idea of moving people from the troubled spots of Ireland and Scotland to new lands in the colonies. Such a movement could prove beneficial to both the settlers and the Empire. The challenge gripped him; but how was this high purpose to be carried out?

Needing the backing of government, Selkirk began pestering people in authority in London for measures which would allow him to carry out his plan. But his appeals to the Colonial Secretary for land reservations in the western part of British North America, on which distressed Scots and Irish could be helped to make a new life for themselves, were received with polite indifference. The idea was impractical, the authorities contended, and then proceeded to search for reasons which would justify their stubbornness. The big country of Rupert's Land belonged to the Hudson's Bay Company — it was theirs by Charter — and even if the rival North West Company refused to acknowledge the validity of that Charter, the Imperial Government would not intrude. The country produced good furs and perhaps the traders were correct in contending that any land with such an inhospitable climate should be left for beavers and other fur-bearers.

If Selkirk was rebuked, he didn't show it. His moral fiber was growing tougher. Behind a mask of nonchalance were a bold spirit and a streak of stubbornness. This apparent conflict in his personality made it difficult for some people to understand him. Friends recognized courage and imagination in his demeanor, but the British public generally accepted him simply as another rich man's son who was not to be taken seriously. Those who knew him as a quiet and retiring fellow were surprised to discover the determination and complexity he possessed, especially when it came to matters of social reform.

But how the British ladies and gentlemen appraised him did not faze the young Earl; he knew what he wanted to achieve and he would be difficult to restrain. After traveling widely in England, Scotland, Ireland and Wales, making notes about poverty and oppression and hardship, his desire to help unfortunate people became a preoccupation.

But how could he, working single-handedly, hope to perform an effective service in the rehabilitation of needy Britishers? The victims of poverty and rebellion in Ireland and selfish land-use planning in the Highlands might have seemed to require totally different remedial treatments, but Selkirk's reasoning led to a conviction that a program of assisted emigration with the opportunity to fashion new lives on lands in the colonies would meet the needs of both groups. A wisely devised policy would help all concerned, the downtrodden people who could be expected to grasp the chance of making a fresh start, the Mother Country which would be relieved of a heavy social responsibility, and the colonies which needed serious settlers. It might even enrich the Earl in whose mind the profit motive was never really overlooked.

There was unoccupied land in the colonies, lots of it, and yet those dispossessed Scottish crofters who refused to drift to city slums were accepting invitations to take land in the Carolinas and other parts of the United States. Selkirk fumed about the British failure to counsel and help these people. Why not new colonies for Scottish families in British North America? Why not colonies for the unhappy people of Ireland? If it would make the change in their way of life less frightening, Selkirk would plan colonies which would be exclusively for Scottish Protestants and separate colonies for Irish Catholics.

And having set his hand "to the plow," Selkirk was not one to turn back.

CHAPTER THREE

The Great Canadian Colonizer

In official British circles, emigration was a dead issue. There was no public interest in exporting any part of the population, even though the people involved might benefit. It was a London viewpoint that if France and Britain became embroiled in another war, manpower at home would take on a new importance. And as for those who had taken part in the recent rebellion in Ireland, members of His Majesty's government believed that resort to emigration would only serve to spread the existing Empire troubles over a larger area.

But undaunted by public indifference, Selkirk prepared a written submission, calling it "A Proposal."[1] Actually, this thesis-like production was more than a Proposal. It and the correspondence which followed afforded a rather good insight into the mind of the Earl and might even have given backing to those who contended that His Lordship's motives encompassed more than benevolence, that unless there was at least a moderate chance of financial reward sooner or later, the Earl's interest could wane. It could be interpreted more compassionately as meaning that even a philanthropist must consider his own survival. Anyway, it was the cold hand of economics — high costs and only slight chance of returns that caused the Earl's rejection of at least one settlement, the one proposed for Sault Ste. Marie.

To give his plan the benefit of a formal introduction to the government, a copy of the memorial, "A Proposal, Tending to the Permanent Security of Ireland," was submitted to His Majesty's Secretary of State on April 3, 1802. Possibly the author was being somewhat presumptuous by following immediately with a statement about "The Choice Of A Situation For The Colony Suggested In My Memorial."

Lord Pelham, who read the submission, might have had some prejudiced views and was at the outset unimpressed by the principle of finding overseas homes for the Irish troublemakers. He conveniently transferred the file to one of his colleagues, Lord Hobart, attaching a memorandum in which he acknowledged Selkirk's idea for what it was worth, without praising any part of it. Grants of land were already being made in both Upper and Lower Canada, he wrote, "To all British subjects who go there as settlers. But I think I see great difficulties and objections to government undertaking to transport and settle people from Ireland or elsewhere in either of the Canadas."

The proposal was idealistic, to be sure. Nobody would suggest that the Irish problem could be removed by emigrating a few people. Unfortunately, the unhappy state of Ireland would be a lasting danger to the Empire and coercion and military force would only make a bad situation worse. The only hope, pleaded Selkirk, was in a "gradual diffusion of wealth and commerce and the pursuit of active industry, assisted by a better system of education" which might in time "obliterate the unhappy divisions."

The first step, Selkirk submitted, should be effected by emigration. "Where the leaven of disaffection is so strong, a great advantage would result from the removal of those who in times of trouble would be likely to become leaders of sedition and . . . dangerous if they remain." Accordingly, it would contribute to the tranquillity of Ireland if "an alluring field for the enterprize and ambition of such characters could be opened in a different part of the world. For this purpose, the Memorialist begs leave to suggest that a colony should be established expressly for Irish Catholics in some unoccupied part of North America." Everything should be arranged "to suit their religious and national prejudices," and the arrangements should include assistance from the public purse to meet the cost of passage.

The Earl, as author of the program, offered to give from his personal resources to ensure success. "Deeply impressed with the importance of these views, the Memorialist would not hesitate to devote his personal exertions and the best years of his life to the service of his country in carrying them into execution. If this plan should be adopted by government, he would undertake to settle the proposed colony in America, provided he were assured of effectual support and that a situation were chosen possessed of those natural advantages which are requisite for success. Such, he trusts, may be procured in a climate where the attention of the colonists may be directed to objects of cultivation." He would even "pledge the expense of passage" and undertake to obtain as many settlers as might be thought advisable.

Anybody reading the Proposal would be impressed by the Selkirk generosity and would then wonder, naturally, if the Earl were prepared to suggest a location for the big experiment. Of course he was ready to make a recommendation; the area of his choice was the Valley of the Red River, draining into "Lake Winnipeck" and, without waiting for the question to be put to him, he was appending the all-important Supplement.[2]

In expressing confidence in the suitability of that area far west from Lake Superior for the purposes of agriculture and settlement, Selkirk was following a hunch and standing virtually alone. Granted, there was only the flimsiest reason to suppose that the country would support his scheme but his faith never wavered.

Students may well inquire about the origin of this strange infatuation with the Red River country which the Earl had never seen. It may have started with his reading of Alexander Mackenzie's *Voyages From Montreal*, first published in 1801. Although Mackenzie was a staunch opponent of settlement anywhere in the fur country, he dropped a few complimentary remarks about the soil in certain parts. Probably he regretted his words but about Red River he wrote: "There is not, perhaps, a finer country in the world for the residence of uncivilized man, than that which occupies the space between this Red River and Lake Superior. It abounds in everything necessary to the wants and comforts of such people. Fish, venison and fowl, with wild rice, are in great plenty."[3]

Going as far inland as Red River would, Selkirk admitted, be an inconvenience but he believed the advantages would outweigh the disadvantages. Here was territory with fertile soil and a climate more temperate than on the shores of the Atlantic and not more severe than that of Germany and Poland. "The soil and climate are similar to those of the Russian Provinces which supply most of Europe with hemp." Settlers could expect to find many new crops which would grow and thrive in that part, perhaps even vines.

Selkirk did not let it be overlooked that he possessed some qualifications to speak on agricultural matters and assess agricultural potentials. "I flatter myself," he said, "I am qualified to form an opinion from the attention I have paid to agriculture for a considerable number of years and the opportunities I have had to study it."

Even though it was a self-appraisal, it was perfectly correct that Lord Selkirk was a serious student of agriculture in the broadest sense and operated his farm properties at St. Mary's Isle with studious care.

One of the obstacles confronting an inland colony, Selkirk noted, would be transportation or "the expense of carriage." The cost from Red River would be too high to allow for the export of grain, but, he suggested, such an apparent handicap could turn out to be an advantage because the colonists would direct their search for other commodities having greater value in relation to weight. Selkirk saw great promise in hemp, a crop which had been "neglected in the Maritime Colonies."

He had another proposal for the support of his plan, Free Trade with the termination of Hudson's Bay Company monopoly. Having no connection with the old Company at that time, he could speak objectively and boldly — and did, saying: "The greatest impediment to a Colony in this quarter [meaning Manitoba of later years] seems to be the Hudson's Bay monopoly which the possessors cannot be expected easily to relinquish. They may, however, be amply indemnified for its abolition" without loss of revenue. His technique would have remodeled the fur trade completely and changed the whole course of western history. The scheme would require a license from every person trading with the Indians and the revenue so raised would be used to compensate the Company for the loss of the monopoly. Settlers would be free to trade and carry their goods to overseas markets by way of Hudson Bay. Moreover, the revenue from licenses might be sufficient to pay the added cost of providing police and military protection for the colonists. There would be other side benefits; with less competition between the two old Companies, the use of liquor in Indian trade could be reduced or eliminated. And the traders would show more responsibility even to the point, perchance, of giving proper attention to the conservation of beavers and other sources of their business. It was not too much to suppose, Selkirk said, that the Indians would react to the new system by accepting "civilized and peaceful habits."

It sounded well but nobody except Lord Selkirk could see how the proposed changes could bring so many benefits to the settlers. Nor was Lord Pelham convinced, as his comment to a colleague in government showed; he could agree with Lord Selkirk's criticism of the fur trade but would be loathe to interfere in "that trade which takes good care of itself. There is such a thing as Salutary Neglect which in such cases beats all the care in the world."[4]

The Selkirk plan might have found more support from Lord Hobart than from Lord Pelham — at least up to a point. But the wheels of government grind slowly and after waiting a month or so for a decision, the impatient Earl wrote to invite the Minister to return his manuscript. After another month, July 6, Selkirk wrote again. Sensing government reluctance to interfere with the Hudson's Bay Company's land claims as set down under the Charter, Selkirk asked if he might obtain for the proposed settlement "a grant of land in Upper Canada adjoining the falls of St. Mary, between Lake Superior and Lake Huron, and also of the mines and minerals I may discover on the North Coasts of these two lakes. In case His Majesty is pleased to bestow these grants, I will make very considerable exertions to render them productive. . . ."

Nor did the Earl's request end there. He was not hesitant about asking. "Your Lordship hinted also that some lands might soon be open in the Island of Prince Edward, for a grant of which I should also apply and would make similar exertions for their cultivation."

Sarcastic critics might have inquired why he didn't ask for all the unoccupied land in British North America and be done with it. Like a good salesman, he pointed out that possession of lands and an interest in settlement in both areas would enable him to devote the principal part of his time to the program, thereby bringing more benefit "both to myself and the public."[5]

The Sault Ste. Marie property, if granted, would be for Irish Catholic settlers, Selkirk promised. But Lord Hobart was not prepared to approve grants on a lavish scale and invited Selkirk to reconsider the scope of his requests. The Earl in turn wrote to emphasize a point of national importance which, he suspected, might have been overlooked. That neck of water at the juncture of the lakes would always possess peculiar importance in the internal commerce of the country. It was the only avenue of communication between the Canadas and the Northwest. Selkirk's point was a valid one: "If that territory is at any time to be colonized by His Majesty's subjects, it seems of importance to secure this pass and be before hand with the Americans in establishing a respectable settlement there."

At the same time, Selkirk was not going to let the Minister of the Crown forget about the minerals and added that because the land in the region was rough, far from the sea and in a colder climate, it would not have the appeal of similar land on Lake Ontario and Lake Erie and would require a bigger promotional effort to obtain settlers. To furnish the extra inducement, Selkirk would need the grant of mineral rights "as a compensation for the expense I must incur to induce the settlers to go beyond their usual range."

Hobart, in the letter to which Selkirk was making reply, had expressed doubts and some fear about the idea of starting such a colony with the Irish. Instead of debating the reasons for the doubts, however, Selkirk accepted the idea of "beginning with people more tractable than the Irish." It is possible that the mineral opportunities had suddenly appeared so tremendously valuable to him that he could not afford the risk of antagonizing or arguing. Any smart person might see it as a time to be agreeable. And so, the Earl was reversing some earlier contentions and saying that the Irish "ought, no doubt, to be engrafted on a better stock." Now he would make it his business to find German settlers instead, and he knew he could always fall back on the Scots and get enough of them to occupy the land.

Many Scots had gone in that very year to the Carolinas and he was confident that with the "grant of minerals" to underpin his program, he could offer their countrymen a better settlement proposition than they could obtain in the United States. He could in the course of a few years attract between 500 and 1,200 families to that region.

In hinting again that the plan depended upon the granting of the mineral rights, the man was exposing a side to his personality that had not been so evident before. If anybody up to that time had wondered if the humanitarian dedication were really sufficient to overshadow all else in personal gain, the doubts would have been strengthened.

As it turned out, the government, in its wisdom, was not willing to grant all the mineral wealth to be discovered on the long and challenging coastline of two great lakes and the Earl concluded that the cost of the proposed project was too much for him to carry alone. "I have not a fortune sufficiently ample. . . . Prudence requires me to pause . . . ." The events invited many spectators to wonder if, without the chance of gaining rich mineral wealth, there would have been any interest in colonizing that particular part of British North America — or any part — at the beginning of the last century. But Selkirk made it clear that he was still ready to become the colonizer if a grant of land were obtained on Prince Edward Island.

Men in government who doubted that emigration would be sufficient to convert Irish belligerents to peaceful and loyal citizens were relieved when Selkirk was seen to be backing away from the Sault Ste. Marie plan. Instead of converting rebellious people, wasn't there the chance that emigration would simply spread the Irish capacity for making trouble?

The opportunity to colonize Prince Edward Island came in 1803 and the Earl bought 80,000 acres of land once occupied by French colonists in the southeastern projection of the island. This time there would be no mineral wealth to blur or distort the issue and the settlement area would be easy of access. At once the Earl authorized recruitment in the Highlands and the response was instantaneous, just as he had expected it to be. Many families with plans for emigration to the United States welcomed most enthusiastically the chance to remain with their own flag and go to Prince Edward Island. In keeping with the Earl's dislike for delay, 800 men, women and children in three ships — the *Dykes*, the *Polly* and the *Oughton* — were sailing to establish new homes beyond the ocean at midsummer. In the new land, these immigrants became known as the Skye Pioneers although many of them were from other parts in the Highlands, Ross-shire, Inverness-shire, Argyllshire and Uist. Qualities they had in common, however, were hardiness and resourcefulness and these would prove their worth.

The Earl, ever a man of the people, was accompanying, traveling on the *Dykes*, and hoping to be among the first to land on the new soil. But sailing vessels crossing the Atlantic would find it difficult to travel on schedule, and the *Polly*, after encountering a series of hazards, ice floes, storms and even an encounter with pirates, was the first of the three ships to land passengers, having dropped anchor in Orwell Bay, east of Charlottetown, on August 7. Selkirk's ship arrived two days later and the Earl promptly erected his tent alongside the tents of his settlers.

As the sun went down, according to Selkirk's Recollections, the scene was enlivened by campfires and lazy curls of smoke arising from them.[6] Additionally, the Earl saw the assembled "groups of figures, whose peculiar national dress added to the singularity of the surrounding scene. Confused heaps of baggage were everywhere piled together beside their wild habitations; and by the number of fires the whole woods were illuminated. At the end of this line of encampment I pitched my own tent, and was surrounded in the morning by a numerous assemblage of people, whose behaviour indicated that they looked to nothing else than a restoration of the happy days of Clanship."

Eighteen days later the *Oughton* arrived and discharged its cargo of settlers, largely from the Island of Uist, bringing the immigrant total to 800 able and eager people of all ages. Among them, according to one writer, Lorne C. Callbeck, was Mary Halliday, illegitimate daughter of Lord Selkirk.[7] Now there was a scramble to obtain land allotments in that isolated area stretching far along the shoreline. To this, Selkirk gave his personal attention. The allotments were not gratuitous but were offered at "scarcely equivalent to one-half of the current rate of the island."

Time was short enough. There was much for the newcomers to do before the icy grip of winter; they had houses to build, trees to clear where they hoped to cultivate for spring planting; furniture to make, bed ticks to fill with feathers or hay, candles to create from tallow, and food supplies to gather. Many of the pioneer tasks, such as log work for making houses, would be new to them but they were versatile with their hands and soon mastered the use of the ax. Winter diets would not be handsome — mainly porridge, potatoes and fish — but the Highlanders were accustomed to humble fare and they were thankful for what the island would afford.

Homes were built in clusters, with four or five families in a group, and the log structures varied only slightly in size and shape. The prevailing size was 14 feet by 18 feet which meant that a family of five or six would be slightly crowded. Moss and clay served to chink the awkward spaces between logs, and poles tied down with pliable twigs and overlaid with bark and a thatch of long aquatic grass provided the roof. In the absence of glass, windows were either omitted or the openings in the walls were fitted with a semi-transparent rawhide.

Having attended to housing and other urgent chores, the men turned to building boats to aid them in fishing, and when winter set in, the newcomers were ready for it. They did not escape troubles and setbacks and the first winter brought an epidemic of fever but there was a medical man among them — one of Selkirk's long-standing friends — and the disorder passed.

The Earl left the island in September, satisfied that his people were adequately prepared for winter. He had reason to go to New York and from there he made his way to Montreal. It was while journeying from New York to Montreal that he met Miles Macdonell who was living in the district of Cornwall. Here was a Scot born in the Highlands but who emigrated with his family to New York and then following the War of Independence, elected to move northward to be on the British side of the border. Selkirk was impressed by this man with a military bearing and apparently made a mental note that he was one who might be extremely useful in some future colonization undertakings.

On this, the Earl's first visit to Montreal, the reception was most cordial, almost overwhelming. Simon McTavish and William McGillivray, leaders in the North West Company and among the most influential people in Montreal society, showered him with attention and the halls of the famous Beaver Club where the Nor'Westers entertained lavishly, rang with merriment in the distinguished visitor's honor. Having no connection with the fur trade at that time and presenting no threat to the powerful North West Company, Selkirk could still be accepted without prejudice. Nobody lacking the gift of prophecy could have foreseen the cruel snubs directed at Selkirk by some of the same Montrealers a few years later. Instead of entertaining him with wine and lobster, they were hauling him to court to face charges resulting from the conflicts between the fur trade and an attempt to establish an agricultural settlement close to the western fur country.

Exactly twelve months after leaving his infant Prince Edward Island colony, Lord Selkirk returned to it and found reasons for "the utmost satisfaction." The people were taking their first harvest, a small crop of grain and a bigger one of potatoes — enough of the latter to meet the total needs of the colony. By this time, too, some of the settlers were building better houses, with foundations of stone and roofboards and shingles to take the place of bark and grass.

"I will not assert that the people I took there have totally escaped all difficulties and discouragement," Selkirk wrote, "but the arrangements for their accommodation have had so much success, that few, perhaps, in their situation have suffered less, or have seen their difficulties so soon at an end."[8]

The secret of the Prince Edward Island success was Lord Selkirk's personal attention, something he was unable to offer the two settlement projects which followed. But fired by encouragement from the island undertaking, he wanted to get on with the next one, in Upper Canada. In seeking a reservation of land in the townships of Chatham and Dover, beside Lake St. Clair, Selkirk was undertaking to move the emigrants from Scotland at his own expense. He would buy the land but was asking that the government accept part of the payment in produce, mainly hemp. As part of his contract, he would, within ten years, settle a family of Highlanders for every 400 acres obtained.

The purchase was made and as a nucleus for the settlement, twenty families of Highlanders were moved from the Prince Edward Island colony, and Alexander McDonell was appointed to be in charge. The name of the settlement would be Baldoon, taken from that of an ancestral holding in Scotland.

It represented another earnest effort but Selkirk was unable to supervise it adequately and the misfortunes and reverses were many. The location might have been a poor choice in the first place, much of the land being low and marshy. It proved to be unhealthy for the residents and livestock. The poorly drained ground appeared to breed disease and malaria was said to be one of the troubles. Many settlers died. Crops failed and cattle and sheep did poorly and dissatisfaction soared. McDonell's services were less than satisfactory and, altogether, Baldoon was an unhappy experience.

When failure was imminent, Selkirk proposed driving the Baldoon cattle and sheep by way of Chicago to the Red River where the need was great and where the animals would have a better chance of surviving, but war intervened. The climax to a chain of Baldoon troubles came with the War of 1812, when United States troops overran the settlement, slaughtered cattle and sheep to furnish army provisions and added chaos to depression. A statement of war losses made a claim for 78 sheep, "some of them full blooded and ¾ and ½ marrinnoes @ £2-10 each," also expenses in returning 838 sheep apparently taken by the invading army and recovered by General Brock.

Selkirk acknowledged failure and disposed of his land holdings. But if Baldoon was a failure — and it was — Selkirk did not allow it and the attendant financial losses to deter him in his next and bigger venture, away to the west, at Red River, actually his "first love" as a site for settlement. There the potential would be the greatest, also the grief and ultimately — long after his death — the reward.

Perhaps it was as an agricultural colonizer that Lord Selkirk wanted to be remembered. If so, he qualified with distinction. An exact count of the immigrants to three widely separated Canadian frontiers, for whom he could take direct and almost full responsibility, has not been made but the total would certainly exceed 2,000. And colonizing to him meant much more than merely furnishing transportation to the new land; it meant information campaigns and persuasion; it meant physical aids by land and sea to reach the destinations; it meant the assembling of land on which hopeful people would carve new homes and new lives; it meant battling with the enemies and keeping up the help until the settlers were securely established.

Granted, his colonizing objects were called into question by many who had private reasons for opposing. An examination will show, however, that most influential figures in history suffered the same sort of criticisms at one time or another. But whether Selkirk was the great philanthropist or the common capitalist; whether he was the dedicated Empire builder or simply one with an obsession to be the Land Baron of the World; whether he was loyally working for the Mother Country or the Canadian colonies or just for himself, it is impossible to deny him the distinction of being the most extensive colonizer in Canadian history and the one who, in promoting and opening up the frontiers, did more than any other in imparting the agricultural image for which many parts of the nation became famous. His was the sort of dream that came to William Penn, although Penn was more successful in gaining recognition for his contributions. On some points, Selkirk may never be extricated from controversy, but there should be no hesitation in according him the highest honors as an effective colonizer.

CHAPTER FOUR

The Threat of Farmers in Fur Country

Selkirk's purchase of shares in the Hudson's Bay Company was not to be interpreted as a sign of dedication to the fur trade. On the contrary, he held a secret revulsion to it, particularly as it was carried on by the aggressive and sometimes ruthless North West Company. That trade, as he admitted in a letter to his wife, was something "I hate from the bottom of my heart."

His knowledge of the practice of taking and marketing wild furs was academic more than practical but in any case, the practice failed to win admiration. He took exception to the commonplace use of trade liquor in dealing with native people, and rebelled at the thought of two big trading organizations trying to outbid each other with intoxicants in order to win Indian favor. An act of parliament that would prohibit or restrain the sale of spirituous liquors to the Indians of British America would have had his enthusiastic support.[1] In the use of spirits as a trading inducement, the North West Company was probably the greater offender, and the Earl believed that the Hudson's Bay Company, with its "honourable views," would have accepted a restricting order quite readily. But one business concern could not be expected to abandon a profitable trade practice unless its rival did the same.

Foreign to Selkirk's gentle but stubborn nature, also, were the rough and brutal ways of the fur trade, violence among the traders, for example, and torture inflicted upon fur-bearing animals. The steel trap was at the best of times a cruel invention, unworthy of a race claiming moral conscience.

But good behavior and high ideals did not seem to bring benefit back there where men made their own laws to suit their convenience. The robust and domineering Montreal traders were getting the bigger share of the furs, especially in the rich Athabasca region where the waters drained to the Arctic and trapping and trading opportunities were the best on the continent. There the servants of the two big companies were continuously at each other's throats. In assessing the situation, Selkirk was trying to be impartial but it was not easy and he saw more that he considered objectionable in the North West Company conduct, and said so in his treatise on the fur trade published in 1816 and prepared, presumably, prior to becoming a landowner in the West, while he could still count men in both companies among his friends. Very well did he know William Mainwaring, Governor of the English Company from 1807 to 1812, and he could not forget the lavish welcome at the Beaver Club in Montreal where the North West Company Lords of the Fur Forest dispensed hospitality on a grand scale. But Selkirk's interest was in the country of the West rather than in furs or fur-trade hospitality. The greatest challenge of his life was to dignify that soil of the far West with something bigger and more noble than trapping.

Various sins were laid at the doors of the big trading companies but one of the most serious, in Selkirk's view, was the selfish opposition to any suggestion that western soil had a potential for agriculture and should be tested. It was the traders' right to condemn the land and the climate and declare them useless for the purposes of cultivation and settlement; but such would be a prejudiced view and it demanded the immediate attention of those in a position to test it. But strange as it must seem, Selkirk was the only person of his time who had the judgment and courage to proclaim faith in the suitability of the Northwest for settlement and agriculture.

In answering those who believed that Rupert's Land and the territory beyond should remain as fur country, inviolate, Selkirk succeeded in deflating many of the best arguments. In the first place, as he pointed out, the fur trade did not merit the aura of importance that had been allowed to grow around it and because of which the traders contended for exclusive use of territory.

"And what is this Fur Trade for which [such] sacrifice is to be made?" the Earl asked, and then with a touch of ridicule proceeded to give the revealing answer: "... A trade to which the gross returns never exceeded £300,000, and often not £200,000. A branch of commerce which gives occasion to the exportation of £40,000 or £50,000 of British manufacture! A trade in which three ships are employed! This is the mighty object for which not only the rights of private property are to be involved but a territory of immense extent possessing the greatest natural advantages is to be condemned to perpetual sterility."[2]

What he was writing about was the future farm belt of western Canada, insisting that the vast soil resources should not be suppressed for the sake of a trade to the gross amount of £200,000 or £300,000 per year. He began to emerge as a man of unusual vision, qualifying as the first person to have taken a stand on the West's behalf, and at the same time, becoming the first to warn that the neglect of conservation practices could be serious. If left to itself, he said, the system the traders had embraced would soon destroy itself because its object "is to obtain a great immediate return of furs without any regard to its permanent continuation .... A war of extermination is therefore carried on against all the valuable fur-bearing animals."[3]

By 1807, the Prince Edward Island colony was judged a success, and the Baldoon undertaking as less than a success. But with the experience gained in the two initial ventures, the Earl believed that good soil, wise supervision and enterprising settlers would ensure a happy outcome for the next project of the kind. The Highlanders appearing to need relocation and assistance were as numerous as ever and emigration seemed still to be the solution to the Irish problem of unrest. He could and would help the people in both categories by establishing a settlement at or near Red River — the area of his original choice — if given opportunity. The principal obstacle was still the fur traders' selfish and whimsical determination that the country was divinely created for trapping furs and settlement should not be permitted.

He might be the only person saying that it could be done. He might be the only one speaking out against a multitude, repeating that this western land was not "a wild and uninhabitable region bound up in perpetual snows . . . . not only in the Territories of the Hudson's Bay Company but even in Athabasca, and still more in New Caledonia, beyond the Rocky Mountains, there are most extensive tracts of fertile soil, lying under climates perfectly capable of advantageous cultivation."[4]

The time was at hand for the Earl to do something about his convictions in this matter. In buying into the Hudson's Bay Company, therefore, this staunch advocate of a land he had not yet seen but about which he was speaking with singular accuracy was ready to bet his fortune and reputation that the western soil was good, that the pessimists like Jacques Cartier who, following the north shore of the Gulf of St. Lawrence in 1534, had pronounced what he saw as "the land that God allotted to Cain," were wrong. In buying shares in the Company, Selkirk would be buying a voice in shaping Hudson's Bay Company policy and the destiny of Hudson's Bay Company territory.

How was it to be achieved? Circumstances combined to help him. Marriage in 1807 to Jean Wedderburn — sometimes Jean Wedderburn-Colvile, sometimes Jean Colvile — brought her wealthy brother, Andrew Colvile, and cousin, John Halkett, a prominent and well-to-do lawyer, to the support of Selkirk's purposes and schemes. Then, to set the stage more effectively, the Hudson's Bay Company was reeling from financial depression and hoping to find relief in reorganization.

Company returns and profits had fallen sharply, the result of the depletion of furs coupled with crushing competition created by the North West Company. Interest on Hudson's Bay Company shares declined from the customary eight per cent to four per cent, and then in 1809, it disappeared. With such a drop in Company fortunes, the market price of shares plummeted also. Shares which had traded for as high as £250, declined to £60 and members of the committee were worried. The state of depression was enough to bring them to search for economies within the organization and some fresh policies were born.

Henceforth, Company servants in Rupert's Land and beyond would be instructed to be more aggressive — more like the Nor'Westers — in the eternal contest to obtain furs. It did not mean that Hudson's Bay Company workers were to forget their legal responsibilities. Neither were they to allow themselves to be pushed around by bullies employed by the other Company. "Forbearance must not be carried so far as to invite aggression," the letter from London instructed. No longer were the Company servants to yield to threats leading to pillage of property. The letter hinted broadly, too, that the manner of standing up to the competing traders could be a factor in deciding wages and promotions. "We shall consider as undeserving of our favour any officer who shall betray weakness or timidity in defence of the Company's just rights. We expect you will defend like men the property that is entrusted to you and if any person shall presume to make a forcible attack upon you, you have arms in your hands and the Law sanctions you in using them for your own defence."

As an added inducement, Company servants would be able to qualify for a percentage of trade profits. It was another idea borrowed from the other Company which traced much of its success in the field to the position of its "wintering partners" working with the incentive of personal gain when trade volume was high. And to a spectator like Lord Selkirk, the most significant innovation of all was the resolution to produce more of the Company's food needs right at the posts, thereby reducing the high cost of buying supplies in the Old Country and transporting them across the ocean and far inland. Traders in charge of the posts would be encouraged to plant gardens for vegetables and plots with wheat in the hope of obtaining grain for gristing. Thus, the usual money and shipping space normally set aside for flour could be used for other needed articles.

Of course it made good economic sense to strive for a better measure of self-sufficiency on the far-flung fur frontier and anyone familiar with Selkirk's request of earlier years to start an agricultural colony would realize that Company leaders had themselves to blame for the recent high costs for imported food supplies. Now, the new policy aimed at finding more of the Rupert's Land food needs in Rupert's Land, along with the greatly reduced price of Company shares, gave Lord Selkirk the opening for which he had been waiting.

He began buying Company shares in July, 1808. In the next year, Andrew Colvile and John Halkett began buying. Certain other well-known personalities were buying also but for quite different reasons. Strange to say, one of Selkirk's buying companions and confidants at that time was Sir Alexander Mackenzie of the North West Company, and correspondence which passed between them survives. There should have been no secret about Mackenzie's motive; his hope for many years was to gain shipping privileges for his Company via Hudson Bay. It was something the English Company had refused stubbornly. Mackenzie's only remaining hope was for members of the North West Company to buy enough Hudson's Bay Company shares to command a strong voice in shaping policy. Mackenzie and Selkirk had no mutual interests in furs and no mutual interests in the shares except that both wanted to acquire them. Nor were there antagonisms at that time because the significance of Selkirk's purpose in settlement had not been fully comprehended by the Nor'Westers. Mackenzie, on good terms with Selkirk, would have transferred his stock as a sort of loan to Selkirk, to be returned after it had served the Earl's purpose. Writing from London on June 27, 1808, Mackenzie, trying to be helpful, reported to Selkirk on his inquiries about Hudson's Bay Company stock.[5] He had hoped, he admitted to the Earl, to raise £10,000 for his own purchases but recent losses had limited his funds for investment and delayed his plans. In a later letter to the Earl, October 29, 1808, Sir Alexander regretted his inability to report any further progress in obtaining shares and hinted at some executive resistance to his admittance as a shareholder, and wondered if he should at once transfer the £800 of stock then in his name "to make up the qualifications which your Lordship will recollect must have been held twelve months previous to the Election. . . ."[6] Regardless of any estrangement which followed, there was certainly collusion between the two famous figures at this point.

Andrew Colvile, whose advice was especially pertinent in the recent reorganization of the Company, was elected to the Committee on November 28, 1810. Quickly he had become a man of influence. No doubt there were private conferences between Colvile and his brother-in-law and many of the new ideas being brought to the Committee may have originated with the Earl. One can only speculate about the real origin of the resolution approved by the Governor and Committee on February 6, 1811 — a complete reversal from earlier Committee policy: "that Mr. Wedderburn be desired to request Lord Selkirk to lay before the Committee the terms on which he will accept a Grant of Land within the Territories of the Hudson's Bay Company and . . . what Security he may think fit to offer the Company against any injury that may eventually arise to the trade of the Company or any of their Rights and Privileges."[7]

Selkirk received the message with glee. He understood the Company's problems and needs and knew the form of proposition which would appeal to the directors. The Company was in urgent need of workers for Rupert's Land. At a meeting on the previous December 5, it was reported that seventy-two men had returned home by the ships and six others had died in the fur country, leaving a staff which was said to be "quite inadequate to carry on the trade of the Company." The Committee was recommending that 200 men should be recruited from "Scotland, Orkneys or Canada."

In accepting a grant of land, Selkirk would undertake to provide annually for ten years, "200 effective men in each and every year of the said ten years to be ready to embark at such time and place in Scotland as the Governor and Committee may appoint between the first day of May and the first day of July. . . ." Men would be expected to serve for at least three years as either servants or laborers and wages would not exceed £20 per year. In the event that the Earl was unable to furnish the number of men for which he had contracted, he would pay the Company £10 for each of those in deficit.

As for his own settlers, the Earl would guarantee that they would be no threat to the Company's precious trading monopoly but there should be one minor concession; without impinging upon the trading rights and privileges held so dearly by the Company, Selkirk proposed that the settlers be permitted to export their produce through York Factory, using Company ships and paying no more and no less than the customary rates. Such exports would be forwarded to the Company's warehouse in London, there to be sold by auction and subjected to a five per cent export tariff, collectible by the Company for use in policing the area of the settlement and improving communications between the settlement and the Bay, but not to be used to enhance Company profits.

Selkirk judged accurately the concerns and wishes of the Company officials and as an added inducement, he declared his willingness to make a grant of 200 acres in the colony area to any of the Company people recommended by the Governor and Committee, presumably with the idea of taking up residence there.

The proposal satisfied those in the governing body and at the next meeting, on March 6, 1811, it was "resolved that the conditions agreed upon by the Earl of Selkirk, the Deputy Governor and other members of the Council be finally approved and that such conditions be the ground work of the future agreement. And that the Deputy Governor do prepare the necessary instructions to lay before a conveyancer after they shall have been submitted to the Earl of Selkirk for his perusal."[8]

In the meantime, the affairs of the Company continued at a low ebb. The total amount of fur sales in February of that year was reported to the Committee to be a disappointing £12,656 - 2 - 11, and costs were rising. A note from Graham, Simpson and Wedderburn informed the Board of the purchase on its behalf of "100 puncheons of Leeward Island Rum from Messrs. Scott Burn and Co., to be put free on board at 11/11 per gallon, also 6 puncheons of Good Jamaica Rum at 5/6 per gallon payable by cash in one month."[9]

At a meeting on April 24, members of the Committee recessed to visit the sale room and witness the selling of "lots of otter, marten, mink, cat, fox, bear, swan and rabbit skins and bed feathers," then to resume one week later to consider the probable receipts from furs remaining in storage and, finally, to resolve "that no dividend on the General Joint Stock shall this year be paid to the proprietors."[10]

Came the great day of decision, May 30, 1811. Proprietor shareholders had been notified by the secretary that the terms proposed for the Rupert's Land grant were available for their inspection at his office. Interest was running high. On the day before the meeting at which the decision would come to a vote, the secretary reported three applications for the transfer of stock, all to Edward Ellice of the North West Company, whose purpose quite obviously was the same as that of Sir Alexander Mackenzie. But this stock along with £1,000 held by another North West Company man, John

Inglis, and £100 held by Capell Cure, being in the names of the new owners for less than six months, did not qualify the proprietors to vote.[11]

"THURSDAY the 30th of May, 1811

At a General Court Held by an Adjournment From The 22nd Instant for the purpose of Taking Under Further Consideration certain proposals Made to the Committee by the Right Hon'ble the Earl of Selkirk.[12]

For The Question	Present	Against the Question
£1800	William Mainwaring, Esq. Governor In The Chair	
£1800	John Henry Pelly, Esq.	
£1800	Benjamin Harrison, Esq.	
£1800	Thomas Langley, Esq.	
	Carsen Elers, Esq.	
	John Fish, Esq.	
£1800	John Webb, Esq.	
£3300	Thomas Pitt, Esq.	
£1800	Joseph Berens, Jun'r, Esq.	
£4087-10	The Earl of Selkirk	
£4474-3-4	Andrew Wedderburn, Esq.	
	William Thwaytes, Esq.	£9233-6-8
	Robert Whitehead, Esq.	£3000
£1315	Samuel Jones Machell, Esq.	
£1800	Job Mather Raikes, Esq.	
*	Capell Cure, Esq.	£100
	Sir Alexander Mackenzie	£200
*	John Inglis, Esq.	£1000
*	Edward Ellis, Esq.	£1290-13-3
£1821	Charles Smith, Esq.	
	Joseph Bird, Esq.	
	Isaac Currie, Esq.	
	Mathias Lucas, Esq.	
£2339-6-8	Henry Hinde Pelly, Esq.	
£29,937		£14,823-19-11"

N.B. Those marked thus * having not been in possession of the stock six calendar months are not entitled to vote.

As shown by the minutes of the General Court, the Selkirk proposal received the support his Lordship needed although the vote was not unanimous. Shareholders with £29,937 of stock gave their approval while three shareholders with £13,133 - 6 - 8 in stock registered disapproval. Of those favoring the land grant, the proprietor with the most shares was Andrew Colvile with £4474 - 3 - 4 and the one ranking next to him in volume of holdings was Lord Selkirk with £4,087 - 10. John Halkett was not present and apparently did not exercise a proxy vote. The two brothers-in-law, Selkirk and Colvile, together represented £8,561 - 13 - 4, which contradicted effectively the story circulated widely that Selkirk's personal investment had exceeded £40,000, sufficient to dominate the meeting and voting — in other words, that he had voted the big land grant to himself. Actually the combined holdings of Selkirk and Wedderburn (Colvile) were less than those of one of the proprietors, William Thwaytes, an older shareholder, who placed his £9,233 - 6 - 8 of stock in opposition to the proposal. Others in opposition were Robert Whitehead, also a long-time shareholder, with £3,000, and Sir Alexander Mackenzie with £200. Selkirk did acquire larger amounts of the stock at later dates.

The resolution passed quite convincingly but those who opposed it — mainly the North West Company men — were not satisfied to merely register contrary votes. Signed by William Thwaytes, Robert Whitehead, John Fish, Edward Ellice and Alexander Mackenzie, a formal protest was delivered to the Governor and read to the court by the secretary. Addressed "to the Hon'ble Governor and Company of Adventurers of England Trading Into Hudson's Bay," it was a lengthy submission, listing the memorialists' objections to the granting of a part of the Hudson's Bay Company territory to the Earl of Selkirk and his heirs forever in fee simple. "Your memorialists have taken the same into their most serious consideration and . . . submit to your Honourable body the grounds and reasons upon which they dissent to any such grant or alienation of the Company's property."

And what were the "grounds and reasons"? First, there did not appear to be an adequate price consideration. In estimating the area concerned at about 45 million acres, the petitioners were grossly under-estimating its size. It must have hurt the North Westers to admit that the land was "most valuable and fit for cultivation and constitutes no inconsiderable portion of the Company's capital stock."

The second point of objection was in the method of sale; the land, if it were to be sold, should have been offered to the public. The objectors were probably correct in assuming that a public sale would have brought the Company a bigger return.

In their third point, the dissidents warned that there was no assurance that the Earl would ever establish a colony or produce any benefits to the Company.

The fourth point was a warning that the Earl's motive could be simply to enrich himself at the expense of the stockholders, and the fifth point — no doubt the most important to the men of the North West Company, "because it has been found that colonization is at all times unfavorable to the Fur Trade."

There were other fears listed: the Colony could become "an asylum for deserters": there would be danger in the colony's proximity to the United States border, and the Company could expect to be called upon to make various sacrifices on account of a settlement in the years ahead. "These reasons and many others," the signers believed, should put an end to all talk of a land grant to the Earl of Selkirk.

The petition raised some valid questions, to be sure. The payment of a token sum of ten shillings for 116,000 square miles of land possessing virgin fertility must have made this the best land purchase in history; and there would have been decidedly less chance of criticism if the land had been offered publicly before being confirmed to an individual. It should be remembered, however, that if the extensive lands had been offered in some other way, Selkirk might not have been able to buy them; there would have been no Selkirk Settlement in the West and Western Canada would have been immeasurably poorer.

There could be no doubt that for three of the signers, Alexander Mackenzie, Edward Ellice and John Inglis, the real reason for their concern and indeed their involvement was relegated subtly to the fifth clause of the petition, namely the incompatibility between an agricultural settlement and the fur trade. To men like William McGillivray and those around him, the mere mention of agricultural settlement in the fur region was infuriating.

But the vote of the majority prevailed and at a meeting of the committee exactly two weeks after the balloting, it was resolved that: "A Deed granting to the Right Honourable, the Earl of Selkirk, in Fee, certain lands situated . . . as are now particularly described in the said Deed with a map of the said lands affixed to the same was Signed, Sealed and Delivered by the Secretary for and on behalf of the Governor and Company of Adventurers of England Trading Into Hudson's Bay by affixing the corporate seal of the Company thereto."[13]

What the Earl had brought upon himself would have brought most men to despair. It was not in him to retreat. His only questions: What now? Where do we begin?

CHAPTER FIVE

The Vanguard Party

It would be easy to imagine the Earl of Selkirk awakening in a cold sweat on the morning of June 14, 1811, realizing the overwhelming truth that he was now the confirmed proprietor with all the attendant responsibilities for 116,000 square miles of untamed Rupert's Land, more than 70 million acres, more than five times the size of Nova Scotia, more than the combined area of England, Scotland and Wales. A less courageous individual would have entertained some second thoughts about the trouble he was courting. Would such an expanse of country turn out to be an asset or a liability? What were the hidden dangers in this colossus to which he was now chained? Had he acquired an unmanageable monster capable of turning upon him and destroying him? Time alone would tell.

The great tract of land — mainly in what was to become Manitoba, but partly in Saskatchewan, Minnesota and North Dakota — was still something his Lordship had not seen except in his dreams. If there was an apparent familiarity with it, the explanation would have to lie in what he had been able to learn from people who had been there and the limited unbiased reports written on the area.

It was a strange infatuation. Whatever the guiding or compelling force in his unsuccessful request for this land in 1802, and then the successful application nine years later, it deserved credit for perseverance and survival. Now the time had come for action. At the middle of June, as Selkirk realized very well, he must either move quickly to send workers to his distant property or allow another year to be lost. It was not in his nature to accept needless delay with composure. He might be shy and timid in meeting people but in addressing himself to tasks of a useful kind he was bold and forthright. He could and would press forward with all possible dispatch, hoping to have men on the Rupert's Land ground before winter set in.

The first move, wisely, was to verify his legal position in accepting this huge concession. He wanted to be sure that the property was really his in law. The answer he received from some of the best legal minds in Britain was reassuring; the Hudson's Bay Company, as "Lords and Proprietors" under the famous Charter signed by King Charles II, could indeed transfer land and authority. Both civil and criminal jurisdiction could quite properly be passed on to a new owner and a sheriff appointed for his Colony could call men to arms, if it were deemed necessary for defense or the enforcement of law.

As for the Canada Jurisdiction Act of 1803, which was to allow the Courts of Canada to exercise legal jurisdiction in the Indian Territory, Selkirk was again assured — possibly incorrectly — that its application did not reach into Rupert's Land where the English Company operated on Royal Prerogative. It was a point of grave importance to the Red River Settlement a few years later when the conflicts between the settlers, the North West Company and the halfbreeds erupted in violence and criminal charges and countercharges were numerous.

In anticipation of a favorable decision from the shareholders in the Hudson's Bay Company, Selkirk had already sought discussions with certain outstanding individuals he hoped to employ as agents and he had invited Miles Macdonell to come to England from his farm home near Cornwall, close to the St. Lawrence, perhaps to assume special responsibilities in the proposed colony.

As things turned out, Macdonell's role in shaping the destiny of the Red River Colony was second only to that of the Earl. There were troubled times ahead for both. Macdonell was a Scot born at Inverness in 1767. As a child, he accompanied parents to New York and at the end of the Revolutionary War, moved north to live under the British flag. Lord Selkirk, when traveling to Montreal in the winter following the establishment of his new Colony on Prince Edward Island, had met Captain Miles Macdonell where he was farming at St. Andrews, near Cornwall. The Earl's entry in his diary for January 19, 1804, tells of the meeting.[1]

Selkirk had been immediately impressed by this man of good appearance and a military bearing. He had obtained his military commission while serving with the Canadian Volunteers and as the Earl saw him, he was "very much of a gentlemen in manners and sentiment." His Lordship may have resolved at once that he would need this man in some of his future settlement enterprises. "The Captain," the diary noted, "has cleared a considerable tract, built a part of a good house, a large barn. . . . Capt'n M. proposes to clear on about 100 acres more — laying down to grass as soon as cleared — to keep little tillage, and a considerable stock of cattle which he reckons more profitable!"

Selkirk did not forget Macdonell, although the latter, before departing from Stornoway, may have been so moved by frustration to wish that the Earl's memory had not been so good. What he could not know, of course, was the magnitude of the change he was making, from a life of comparative peace beside the St. Lawrence River, to one of turmoil and danger on the far-western frontier.

The Earl's immediate objective was to recruit 200 clerks and workmen to be sent forward as soon as possible for service in Rupert's Land. Most of these helpers would be assigned to the needs of the Hudson's Bay Company, while about thirty of them would be selected to go with Miles Macdonell to Red River and there, at a site to be chosen, make preparations for the settlers and families to follow. The settlers would require shelters, cultivation and an accumulation of food supplies and to furnish these was the purpose of the vanguard party or "advance guard" as it has been called at times.

For the transport of the recruited men and supplies as far as York Factory, the Hudson's Bay Company was making three ships available. They were boats which in the ordinary course of events would sail for the bay not later than the beginning of July. This year, haste would be more important than usual.

Hoping to engage the needed clerks in Glasgow and the workmen in the depressed parts of Ireland and the Scottish Highlands, Selkirk was sending Captain Roderick McDonald to Glasgow, Miles Macdonell to Sligo and Killaloe in western Ireland, and Colin Robertson to the Highlands of Scotland. Robertson was a former employee of the North West Company but retained no loyalty to that organization. He was muscular and bold and vigorous and had another advantage in being familiar with all the tricks of the North Westers.

They were able men but were soon to discover that recruiting for Selkirk's purpose was difficult, due mainly to the subtle efforts of those Montreal traders with predominantly Scottish names who seemed to be perpetually opposing what the Hudson's Bay Company was promoting. The men of the North West Company who were present on May 30 to vote against the Selkirk scheme were not giving up. Indeed, they were only starting their campaign of opposition and their performance made it rather convincing that they believed in the rightness of their cause. Certainly they believed that there was not room in the fur country of the Northwest for both a program of agricultural settlement and their industry as it was carried on. It is probably correct to say that many of the silent men in the Hudson's Bay Company shared the view. The Selkirk plan was especially repugnant to the Montreal men because as rumored, the settlement would straddle one of the important river highways, perhaps two, over which the traders moved their principal supplies of pemmican for the brigades traveling east and west.

On the very day after the meeting at which a majority of shareholders voted to approve the land grant, Simon McGillivray, Sir Alexander Mackenzie, Edward Ellice and other Nor'Westers who happened to be in England, met in London to plot a course of action. Sir Alexander, who had been most friendly with Lord Selkirk, was now hostile. He was also critical of his friends; he could remind them that if they had taken his advice and invested £20,000 or £30,000 of North West Company money in Hudson's Bay Company stock, they might have been in a position to reverse the crucial vote and "it would have been money well spent." His personal pledge, proclaimed "in the most unequivocal and decisive manner," was to oppose the establishment of the colony by "any means in his power."[2]

The weapon to be used in fighting the settlement scheme would be propaganda. If that failed, something else would have to be tried. First, those who were dedicated to opposition would have to ruin Selkirk's chance of obtaining workers and settlers. Two avenues of opportunity were open: one was to bring the Earl's motives into question and the other to warn and frighten all interested parties about the hardships and dangers awaiting them in Rupert's Land.

Rumors derogatory to Selkirk and his plan were soon in circulation, among them that while giving an impression of sympathy and compassion for the downtrodden people, he was really in this venture for the fortune he expected to make through the rising value of the land, also that he would soon own so much stock that he would have the Hudson's Bay Company completely under his control.

Neither allegation was true. The Earl did possess a keen business sense and was not averse to the taking of a profit, but as time was to prove, his concern for the unfortunate people he tried to assist was very genuine. One way of answering the charge when repeated in later years was to point out that Selkirk made no money on his Red River enterprise but lost much. It has been estimated that the great venture, one way and another, cost him not less than half a million dollars. He was not a scheming capitalist, as those who knew him could testify, and there is no reason to believe that he aspired to become another William Penn, friend of King Charles II from whom he obtained a big grant of land which became Pennsylvania and on which he settled large numbers of persecuted people of the Quaker sect.

On the second point, it was true that Selkirk increased his inventory of Hudson's Bay Company shares and became prominent among the proprietors, but he was not at any time an officer or even a member of the administrative Committee. Quite properly, he concerned himself with Company affairs and made proposals for the improvement of general efficiency. Ironically, he was familiar at that time with a confidential Montreal proposal aimed at a more peaceful working arrangement in the fur country; it would have provided for a partitioning of the trading ground with the North West Company, in a general way, retiring from the eastern area and the Hudson's Bay Company retiring from much of the west. But that would not do at all because the eastern section was already overtrapped and exhausted and, besides, the Hudson's Bay Company held already a primary claim to much of the western area by Royal Charter and would not consider surrendering it. A short time later, Selkirk was advancing a confidential suggestion; admitting that the Athabaska district could produce "more profit than the rest of the fur trade put together,"[3] he suggested Hudson's Bay Company retirement from the area outside of Rupert's Land and North West Company abandonment of Rupert's Land. But as might be expected, neither plan was mutually acceptable and those who longed for peace in the fur country would have to wait for the union of the two big companies.

The direction of the anti-settlement campaign was unchanged and the most effective missile was in the form of a letter published over the signature of "A Highlander," actually from the pen of Nor'Wester Simon McGillivray, brother of William McGillivray who succeeded his prudent uncle, Simon McTavish, as the head of the Montreal company. The letter was prepared for reading in the Highlands where Colin Robertson was working to make the projected settlement appear attractive. To ensure the widest possible circulation, the letter was printed in the *Inverness Journal* and proved enough to fill most Highland candidates for Rupert's Land with fear.

Addressed to the Editor, the letter, carefully written, was like a benevolent warning:

Sir — I observed in your Journal of the 19th April last an advertisement holding out various inducements to a few young men to engage 'for the service of the Hudson's Bay Company at their factories and settlements in America,' and among other things, promising such persons as choose to remain at these settlements 100 acres of land at the end of three years service. I have lately been informed also that considerable numbers of young men and families have been engaged in different parts of the Highlands and of the Hebrides, not merely for the service of the Hudson's Bay Company, but to emigrate to Hudson's Bay with a view to settling in and cultivating the country; and I understand that a large embarkment of these intended emigrants is to take place from Stornoway in the course of the present month. I am therefore induced to warn these persons of the delusion which I suspect has been practiced upon them and to give them some description of the dangers and distresses which they are ignorantly going to encounter. The advertisement referred to contains several misrepresentations which I shall hereby point out. It speaks of settlements being already formed, where none exist, and where it is impossible, from the nature of the country and the severity of the climate, that settlement ever can be established. It asserts a positive falsehood in ascribing the climate to be the same as that of Canada, and especially Montreal which has one of the pleasantest climates in America. In fact it is a misrepresentation to state that a settlement is at all practicable on the shores of Hudson's Bay. ... The proposed settlement is, however, intended to be formed about 2,000 miles inland from the Bay and where the climate is rather milder, but still much more rigorous than that of Canada and Nova Scotia, which is described as reasonable. To reach this comparatively mild climate, however, the emigrants must first traverse the inhospitable regions in the vicinity of Hudson's Bay, and perform a voyage of near 2,000 miles of inland navigation, stemming strong currents, and dangerous rapids, and carrying their boats and cargoes over numerous portages. That voyage I do not think they can possibly perform in the present season, for the frost will be approaching before they can reach York Fort, where I fancy they must pass the next winter; and if so, Mr. Editor, it is my firm belief that many of them will perish before spring, from excessive cold and from want of food, if a sufficient supply of provisions is not shipped with them. ...

Supposing, however, that they survive the winter, and overcome the difficulties of the inland voyage in the spring; supposing they safely reach the country where the settlement is intended to be formed, and carry with them a sufficient stock of provisions to subsist until they can raise corn in the country; they will then find themselves at a distance of two thousand miles from the sea, and about the same distance from any other settlement of civilized inhabitants. They will be more effectively separated from their native country than felons who are transported to New South Wales; and in fact they may be considered as totally secluded from intercourse with the rest of civilized mankind. In addition to this, they will be surrounded by warlike savage nations who subsist by the chase and who will consider them as intruders come to spoil their hunting ground, to drive away the wild animals and to destroy the Indians as the white men have already done in Canada and United States. When a savage feels jealousy or resentment, he becomes an active and dangerous enemy; and if the animosity of the Indian tribes is once roused, it is more than probable that the poor settlers will soon become its victims. Or even if they escape from the scalping knife, they will be subject to constant alarms and terror. Their habitations, their crops, their cattle will be destroyed, and they will find it impossible to exist in the country. It is therefore almost a certainty that the proposed settlement cannot succeed, and I must believe that the projector of it is not aware of the dangers and difficulties into which he is leading the poor deluded emigrants who have been engaged to embark in the undertaking. . . .

I have purposely abstained from any reflection on the political expediency of preventing emigration and punishing those persons who endeavor by false statements and from interested motives to induce our countrymen to emigrate to foreign lands. . . . In my present remarks I may aim at warning the persons who are now about to emigrate to Hudson's Bay of the dangers and difficulties in which they are likely to be involved. . . . If this letter should be the means of preserving any of my countrymen from the distresses which await these emigrants, or should be the means of restoring any of them to their native land, I shall be amply repaid for my trouble in writing you, and they will have abundant cause to be grateful for the information now given them by

A Highlander[4]

The author who accused others of misrepresentation was certainly guilty of the same sin. The letter grossly exaggerated the dangers and the difficulties. Instead of the 2,000-mile journey from Hudson Bay to destination, a more correct figure would have been 700 miles. The writer was correct in presuming failure on the part of the group going out in 1811 to reach the Red River end of the journey in that season, but wrong in supposing that many "would perish before spring." In various other respects, the writer was neither completely right nor completely wrong. Danger did indeed exist and it would have been folly to dismiss it just as it was unfair to magnify it. As time was to prove, there was an element of truth in McGillivray's warning that even if the settlers escaped the scalping knife, they would "be subject to constant alarm and terror." Their habitations, their crops and their cattle were destroyed and they almost admitted the impossibility of existing there, but what McGillivray might not have known at that time was that the dangers to which he alluded would be largely inspired by himself and his friends.

To the other obstacles encountered by Lord Selkirk's agents in England and Scotland could be added the annoying delays in the departure of the ships. Instead of leaving the Thames River early in June as planned, the three Company vessels were two weeks late in being ready to sail. But Company men saw to it that the glamour of leaving was not curtailed. Following a long-standing custom, Company officials and officers of the ships gathered at Falcon Inn at Gravesend to dine and mark the moment with toasts and speeches. On this occasion, the first formal departure of the ships since the changes in Company policy, there was something extra and Miles Macdonell was duly invested by Deputy Governor Berens with a commission making him the Governor of "Ossiniboia." Later in the season, Macdonell was one of those in Rupert's Land to be named a Justice of the Peace by the Governor General of Canada, acting under the provisions of the controversial Canada Jurisdiction Act.

Formalities completed, the three ships, the *Edward and Ann, Prince of Wales* and *Eddystone,* drew away and up the east coast, with the wartime precaution of a man-of-war escort from the British Navy. There was further delay at Yarmouth and after leaving the *Prince of Wales* to complete loading at Stromness in the Orkneys, the other two ships reached Stornoway on the island of Lewis on July 17.

Miles Macdonell, traveling on the *Edward and Ann,* was discouraged by the repeated delays, but the stay at Stornoway to take on the remaining workers provided much added reason for exasperation. Moreover, the stop there to take more men aboard was scarcely worth while because the desertions almost equaled the additions.

This was Mackenzie country. Sir Alexander Mackenzie was born within a couple of miles from Stornoway and as might be expected, the North West Company influence was strong. As Macdonell told it, Mrs. Reid, wife of the collector of customs, was Sir Alexander's aunt and her husband official became a genius in finding technicalities which would delay departure.[5] All the while, the men committed by contract to go to Rupert's Land were being pestered by the Mackenzie friends warning them of the dangers ahead and reminding them that they were still in a position to change their minds and quit the ship. Many did desert. Some of the men were induced to join the army and then, having signed up, were required to leave Macdonell and his plan. Even at the hour of departure, a few men were seen to go over the side of the ship and into the water in order to reach shore.

Only on July 26, nine days after the *Edward and Ann* and *Eddystone* arrived at Stornoway, the ships sailed for Hudson Bay. But instead of carrying 200 men for the various services, the total was only 105, roughly half of the number recruited. The North West Company campaign had been effective. Of the total, ninety had been hired to be laborers and fourteen as writers. Also accompanying was an Irish priest, Father Charles Bourke, and one who was supposed to know something about medicine, Mr. A. Edwards.

From this moment of departure, the burden of responsibility for the success of Lord Selkirk's Colony fell upon Miles Macdonell. That he was the proper man for the task was still to be proven and many people were going to be hard to convince.

Meanwhile, the Selkirk motives were inviting a new wave of questions. It was to be expected that men of the North West Company would place the worst possible interpretation on the land grant and the person who had contrived to get it. But now, questions were arising from other quarters: What's behind this colossal land acquisition? What does any individual want with 116,000 square miles of country he has never seen and much of it country which nobody except the North American natives has ever seen? Is benevolence really the purpose or is there a more commonplace reason like a possible fortune from land speculation? Is the alleged philanthropy simply a disguise, or has the Earl found a way by which he can, without conflict, combine a plan for helping needy people and a scheme for advancing personal wealth?

It becomes fairly evident that Lord Selkirk believed that the two goals were not incompatible. His sincerity in trying to bring assistance to poverty-stricken fellow-countrymen can scarcely be doubted, but he chose to believe that his charities could be made to largely pay their own way; the more money he made in business, the more he would have for his benefactions. It could be no sin to conduct business operations in such a way that they would support a program of generous giving and still leave the entrepreneur with a personal profit.

In any case, there was not the slightest chance of putting all the land in the grant to use, so what was to be done with it? His critics chortled when they discovered that he had issued one of those instruments of the business world, a prospectus, a statement intended to arouse the interest and gain the support of investors.

"So that's it," skeptics said, with the satisfaction of having made a great discovery. "His real motive is money. Here is proof that the man is a common land grabber and speculator with the familiar lust for profit."

Whatever the interpretation, here was a real prospectus with the author sounding like a glib salesman, announcing the chance for somebody to buy a portion of the land grant consisting of some millions of acres which in point of soil quality and climate was "inferior to none of equal extent in British America." In the land grant of 116,000 square miles or more than 74,000,000 acres, the exact position of the portion being offered was not stated. But it would be sold "extremely cheap on account of its situation which is remote from present settlement."

If such a tract of land were offered "in Lower Canada and Nova Scotia, purchasers would be eager to obtain it at an hundred or perhaps two hundred thousand guineas," at which price it would make an ample profit in the course of some years by "retailing it in small lots at an advanced price to actual settlers." Herein, the Earl might have disclosed an obvious personal hope for "an ample profit .. by selling small lots at an advanced price."

For anybody seeing fit to invest, the "some millions of acres" being offered could be obtained for £10,000. Only for reasons of its remoteness from populated areas was it being offered "for so inconsiderable a price." And to further overcome obstacles, the prospectus suggested a plan by which the purchasers would bring settlers into the country. The proposal was for a joint-stock company with 200 shares to be sold at £100 each, thereby raising on behalf of the promoters a sum of £20,000, part of which would be used in paying the Earl for the land and part in meeting the cost of bringing the settlers, "thereby rendering the land valuable."

The property owners could then sell outright or lease in perpetuity on terms very encouraging to the settlers, "at the same time abundantly advantageous to the proprietors."

The author of the scheme did not hide his anti-American prejudice, carried over from the Revolutionary War about the time of his boyhood, saying there were "objections against receiving into the proposed settlement any Americans of the description of those who are likely to offer themselves." The proprietors would look mainly to the United Kingdom for their settlers. In this way, emigrants who might otherwise look to the United States for new homesites would be saved for the Empire.

In the area of the new Company-sponsored settlement, the prospectus promised, Protestants and Catholics would have equal and total religious freedom. Perhaps it was to win the blessing of the church leaders that an allotment of land would be set aside in every parochial district for "the perpetual support of a clergyman" of the persuasion to which a majority of the inhabitants were adherents.

The sponsoring patrons would undertake to transport the settlers at reasonable rates to their destinations, certainly at no greater cost to them than if they were about to settle in Nova Scotia. The long distance from the seacoast to the site of the colony would create an additional cost which the settlers could not be expected to pay if they were buying land; this expense would have to be borne by the proprietors and could be expected to average £10 per family. But for this, the promoters would be "amply reimbursed" in the price of the land.

The suggested price for land was ten shillings per acre which was said to be the minimum being asked in the Maritime part of the country. At that rate, the prospectus pointed out, the cost to the settler would be £50 for 100 acres, providing "a net advantage of £40 to the proprietors."

There was not much charity about the price differential. To overcome the handicap of great distance from the sea, the settlers would be advised to grow hemp because it "is so valuable in proportion to its weight that it can bear the expense of a considerable inland navigation." For the same reason, the production of fine wool would be encouraged. The country with its expanses of grasslands and favorable climate would be well suited to sheep, far better than in the Maritime areas, it was mentioned. If the proprietors would contribute a "good breed of Spanish Merino sheep," the settlers would never have any difficulty in making their land payments. Why, "the fleeces of 10 or 12 sheep will pay the rent of 100 acres and with the produce of a very small flock, the price of a lot of land may be paid off in three or four years."

It sounded well. It had the ring of a professional promotion. With such advantages both settlers and proprietors would prosper. There was a word of caution for investors who might be in a hurry: it might be a few years before settlers were sufficiently numerous to ensure dividends to the proprietors but ultimately the reward would be generous. "The amount to which the profits may rise seems almost to baffle imagination . . . it might appear like exaggeration to state it. But the difference between buying land at 1 d. or 2 d. per acre and selling it at 8 s. or 10 s. is very palpable and does not seem to require much comment."

The scheme failed to mature but from his own prospectus, Lord Selkirk borrowed some ideas for the Red River Settlement. And as a money-making scheme offered to the public, it did seem to answer some of the questions about motives, yet it did not deny the probable desire on the part of the Earl to do something for the Empire, something for certain groups of unfortunate people in Scotland and Ireland, and something for himself, all in one grand flourish.

CHAPTER SIX

Into the Stream of New World History

When the tired old ship, *Edward and Ann,* carrying members of the vanguard party for Lord Selkirk's bold experiment in settlement, limped into the estuary of the Nelson River and dropped anchor on September 24, 1811— sixty-one long and monotonous days out of Stornoway — nobody was thinking about history. Considerations bearing on survival could be expected to come first and nobody present would remind the newcomers that this area at the mouth of the Nelson and the nearby mouth of the Hayes could even then claim a long and exciting connection with British American history. It was already 141 years since "The Governor And Company Of Adventurers Of England Trading Into Hudson's Bay" had received its Charter from King Charles II, making them "the true and absolute Lords and Proprietors" of the vast domain known as Rupert's Land and granting monopolistic trading privileges forever.

It was almost 130 years since the Company built its first York Factory, destined to become the most important trading post on the Bay and the one to witness the most vicious naval battles for possession. The most important naval engagement to take place within the Bay and one of the most important in Canadian waters was fought just outside the estuary in 1697, with British and French warships battling for the immediate prize of York Factory. The French, that day, were the victors.

And it was almost exactly 200 years since the English explorer, Thomas Button, had come to the Bay and wintered right there at the mouth of the river which he named Nelson. Button had two reasons for the expedition, the first being a continuation of the long search for the elusive Northwest Passage holding the hope for a shorter shipping route to the rich markets of China. The second reason for being in that unknown part was the hope of finding Henry Hudson who had come in 1610 in pursuit of the same Northwest Passage and experienced tragedy. After wintering at or near the mouth of Rupert River, the Old Man of the Sea whose name is perpetuated in a North American river, a strait and a bay, had a serious disagreement with members of his crew who were in a hurry to return home, and was brutally placed in a small boat along with a few loyal friends and cast adrift on the cold northern waters, never to be seen again.

Button, wintering at the mouth of the Nelson, could qualify as the first European to see the site of York Factory — unless Leif Ericsson's Norsemen came that way in their time. For Button, it was a bad winter and so many members of his crew were lost from scurvy that he was obliged in the spring to abandon one of his two ships.

For Miles Macdonell and his workers, caught in the jaws of harsh reality, any discussion of local history would have seemed frivolous. But as men who were assuming much of the responsibility for the success or failure of the first serious attempt at settlement and agriculture in what would become Western Canada, they were making history to an extent which nobody could have imagined.

The scene which greeted them at York Factory was more primitive and more forbidding than they had expected, and the sub-Arctic autumn was already casting its chilly spell over the tundra and the bleak coastal region marked by stunted forests and a reputation for savage storms. Ice was forming wherever there was fresh water and Company servants were repairing stone fireplaces and diligently dragging firewood into the fort compound to improve their chance of surviving the coming cold.

"So this is York!" men might have been heard to exclaim in tones betraying astonishment. The scene fell far short of the image they had formed. The stockade walls with 400 feet of frontage, 300 feet of depth and reaching 18 feet above the ground, were imposing enough but there was not much else; the buildings within were small and poorly constructed and the location was flat and lacking in drainage. The local record for scurvy was frightening, "except where spruce juice is taken." Nobody had bothered to plant a garden and as a place at which to spend a winter it had little to offer except walls to break the Arctic blasts.[1]

As the newcomers stepped ashore, surveying the coastal landscape as they advanced, two strong-willed personalities — Captain Miles Macdonell as leader of the Vanguard Party, and William Auld, the Master of York Factory and unofficial ruler of the Hudson's Bay Company's North — met for the first time and greeted each other with cool civility. There was much to discuss but Auld, with a special fondness for gossip and bad news, gave Macdonell an immediate opportunity to relate his rather numerous complaints. There were the headwinds, the storms at sea and ice in the strait, combining to make this the slowest voyage on recent record. The circumstances of the ship, *Edward and Ann,* with its old sails and inadequate crew — "only 16 persons including the Captain, mates and three small boys" — were high on the list of grievances. And of course, the unpleasantness and desertions at Stornoway still rankled in the Highland heart; instead of the 200 men Macdonell expected to have on board at leaving the Hebrides, the total was little more than half, with some of them recruited near the last moment in the Orkneys. Auld, having no love for the opposition anyway, appeared secretly grateful for this latest report of North

West Company sins. He agreed with Macdonell that they could expect more trouble from the Montreal men.

"I have reason to suspect, " Macdonell said to Auld by letter a short time later, "every means the N.W. Co. can attempt to thwart it [the settlement] will be resorted to; to what extent their influence may direct the conduct of the natives is to me uncertain and justifies being on our guard at all points."[2]

Nor was Madonell entirely happy with the men who remained after Stornoway, fifty-three of whom were with him on the *Edward and Ann.* No doubt the weeks of close confinement with them on the ship made him overcritical and no doubt the same period of enforced association served to reveal to them the streak of arrogance and autocracy in him.

It was Selkirk's order that Macdonell would have the right to choose the particular men to accompany him to Red River. If the recruits at Stornoway totaled 200 or more, Macdonell could take 40 for his purposes; if the total fell below 200, the group for Red River would be smaller but not less than 30. The long voyage offered one advantage; it gave Macdonell an opportunity to study the men and choose discriminately, keeping in mind, of course, Lord Selkirk's wish to effect a fair balance between Scots and Irish, "with a view of establishing an extensive local connection . . . for this purpose people should be taken from a variety of districts rather than from one in particular."

Captain Macdonell made his selection but his general reaction to the recruits was not flattering. Some were ill during the journey. Scurvy in the course of such a long absence from fresh foods would be inescapable and some of the men were sick from causes of their making: "in consequence of imprudence on shore,"[3] one man, "a Mr. Stevens" would have to be sent home "on account of venereal complaint."   Macdonell had other criticisms about his men. Instead of using their idle hours on the ship for some lofty purpose like studying the Gaelic and Irish languages as he advised, they made no progress. And his efforts to impart some simple military discipline in drill and the use of arms were a failure. Selkirk suggested such simple exercises, mainly to instill habits of subordination and "principles of obedience."

Probably Macdonell expected too much but he had to conclude that there was never a "more awkward squad. Not a man knew to put a gun to his eye or ever fired a shot." And as for the young priest, Father Charles Bourke, who accompanied after committing the indiscretion of departing Killala without the permission of his Bishop, Macdonell added as a sort of a notice of intention to do something, that he was not satisfied with this man.

If Macdonell enjoyed relating his complaints as much as Auld enjoyed listening to them, both men were having a good experience, but there was a major decision which had to be made without delay. It was Selkirk's hope and Macdonell's intention to press on to Red River in the current season but the delays had been serious and plans demanded review. But the question was answered quickly; Macdonell and Auld agreed about the hopelessness of the immigrant party reaching Red River before the lakes and rivers were frozen over. The alternative, only slightly less appealing than a dangerous trip on the ice, was to remain at or near York Factory for the winter, and travel southward after the river breakup in the spring.

There would be local problems and Macdonell and Auld knew it. Space inside the cheerless fort buildings was limited and there is no indication that Macdonell was being invited to move in anyway. He was probably wise enough to realize the advantages of complete separation from the post and the direct rule of William Auld. His decision was to take his men — now twenty-three of them — to build winter shelters for themselves at some point inland where there would be isolation and a better chance of getting wild meat. The spot chosen was on the north side of the Nelson, about twenty-two miles from York Factory.

The selected site was named Nelson Encampment and the men were put to work at once to build log cabins. Macdonell considered his men to be awkward with guns but when he saw them wielding axes, he might have taken a less extreme view of their performance with arms. For some of them, the ax was a completely new experience and the workmanship was not perfect. But with the application of clay for chinking between the logs and poles and sods for roofs and rawhide for windows, the structures promised to be just as protective as York Factory would have been. Using stones and clay, the men made fireplaces and found plenty of dead wood for fuel.

Then there was the matter of provisions. Had Macdonell arrived in time to travel to Red River, he could have drawn, with Selkirk's authority, upon supplies at the fort. Mentioned particularly among the provisions available to him were "25 kegs of rectified spirits" which seemed like a generous allotment for men who might be short of oatmeal. Now it was presumed that the necessity of remaining near the Bay did not nullify the right to draw provisions and Auld appeared moderately cooperative. He warned about scurvy and promised to forward to the winter camp a supply of cranberries which "are equal to oranges and lemons as a specific" for scurvy. "I have also a quantity of crystalized lemon juice which may help in some small degree," he added. Auld had further advice for Macdonell: Keep the men busy at something, anything, and he suggested cutting firewood beyond the camp needs, running races, playing football in the snow or anything for the "employment of the mind."

Perhaps Macdonell did not take Auld's advice and aids sufficiently seriously because the two disorders about which Auld warned became serious. In January, he was writing to report that the "scurvy has at last made its appearance among us." The cranberries and malt were late in arriving and it was only when "spruce beer" or "spruce tea," the old Indian remedy, was prepared and issued that the trouble was arrested.

On January 21, Macdonell acknowledged the delivery from the fort of foods he had requested: 9½ gallons of peas, 81 pounds of oatmeal, an undisclosed quantity of "Brimstone flour," 72 pounds of essence of malt, 52 pounds of cranberries and a "keg of Scotch barley."[4] In acknowledging delivery, Macdonell had one complaint of a most legitimate kind: the barley sent to the encampment was part of a supply intended for seed at the new settlement. "I am obliged to send it back," he wrote reprovingly, "as it cannot be safe here from the insufficiency of our roofs should rain happen to fall in the spring. The Red River Settlement stores are not for consumption here, there being nothing among them of the eatable kind except what is intended for seed. It is best not to molest them."

The standard winter rations among Macdonell's men consisted of one pint of oatmeal and two pounds of meat per man per day. This was considered more satisfying than the usual diet at York Factory which, on a weekly basis, was ten pounds of oatmeal per man, one pound of peas, one pound of barley, two pounds of meat, one and a half pounds of molasses and one pound of fat.[5]

The Nelson Encampment had the advantage of proximity to wild game, especially deer, and late in the winter, Macdonell estimated that "no less than 3,000 deer crossed the river below the Seal Islands from North to South." Most of the deer taken for food in the camp were caught in snares although a few were shot.

But food was not Macdonell's only worry, nor even his biggest. With close confinement and less than enough to keep the men busy, they grew restless and quarrelsome. The Scottish Presbyterians and Irish Catholics argued and fought until the only point about which they seemed to agree was their dislike for Macdonell. They were all seeing too much of each other and Macdonell's domineering ways invited trouble. The only man who seemed to have the sense to make the best of the circumstances was a certain John McLeod whose name was to gain fame at Red River. He was not above some prejudicial opinions about "Irish miscreants and honest Highlanders" with whom he was wintering, but while others were complaining to no purpose, he was writing that he "was never better used in my life."

Apart from McLeod's conciliatory ways, the resentment toward Macdonell grew until it resulted in virtual insurrection. Macdonell threatened to send all the insurgents back to England in the spring, there to face charges of mutiny. But Auld cautioned against such measures, pointing to the act of parliament which placed crimes committed in the so-called Indian Territory under the jurisdiction of the provinces. The truth was that Auld blamed Macdonell for much of the trouble; it was due to his "parsimony"; he did not feed his men enough, and he was needlessly domineering. Anyway, it was the blunt but resourceful Auld who brought the insurgents to order by simply cutting off their rations. As a result, Macdonell was able on June 19 to report to Lord Selkirk that the men "have come to terms and acknowledged their guilt. . . . Mr. Auld refused them rations until they surrendered their arms."[6]

It was a long winter and not very productive. Nobody longed for spring with open water and the chance to be moving more than Miles Macdonell.

CHAPTER SEVEN

The Big Push to Red River

Fifty million northbound birds hurrying to make nests and lay eggs in favorite places confirmed the arrival of the sub-Arctic spring at York Factory and Nelson Encampment. The only contrary force was the river ice which Captain Miles Macdonell watched with the eagerness of a hungry cat gazing at a bird on a low branch. Came the middle of June and the ice was still holding stubbornly. After waiting ten months in the vicinity of York Factory and thinking about the numerous jobs and chores awaiting him at Red River, Macdonell was growing impatient.

It would be no less disturbing to Lord Selkirk to receive Macdonell's letter written on June 19, 1812, just forty-eight hours before the longest day of the year, reporting the Hayes River ice still in place with all the solidarity of a layer of granite.[1] But three days later, on June 22, the great crust heaved and fragmented with cracks like cannonfire and began to move out into the Bay. Macdonell called excitedly for greater haste in making ready the four new boats.

This, hopefully, would end the long controversy about boats best suited to the expedition and boats for the settler folks who would be following. Selkirk had ordered boats to be made in England and taken with the Miles Macdonell party but because of human frailty these were not delivered. In the final confusion which was typical when ships were discharging cargo, an argument developed between the captain of the *Edward and Ann* and the individual in charge of the small boat used for ferrying freight from ship to shore. Various articles, including the boats intended for the river, were not unloaded; instead, they were returned with the ship to London. But as Macdonell mentioned to Lord Selkirk, it was not much of a loss because they were not good boats to begin with — too short, too deep and too light for Rupert's Land currents. In giving this opinion, Macdonell was echoing the sentiment expressed forcefully by William Auld, with whom nobody in the North argued any more than with a polar bear. Plans were made for the construction of new boats during the winter.

Among Macdonell's men was a boat builder, chosen expressly for his skills. He was instructed to remain at York Factory to ensure a good supply of the kind of modified canoes which would be needed by the coming settlers. The Earl asked to be notified about progress in building the riverboats because the supply could become a factor in determining the number of settlers to be allowed to come on successive trips.

There being no good trees of sufficient size for boat lumber, the builder and his assistants were cautioned to recover all driftwood combining soundness and sufficient size for whipsawing.

Auld, whose loyalty to Macdonell was dissolving, warned about the dangers of inexperienced men conducting these canoe-like vessels on the turbulent Rupert's Land rivers. Macdonell, however, professing some knowledge of canoeing from his years beside the St. Lawrence, refused to be worried. He did not minimize the value of experience on any stream with fast and tricky water; it was important indeed to have the benefit of local knowledge and for that reason he was accepting Auld's offer of one experienced man for each boat. But Macdonell doubted if the waters falling into Hudson Bay would test a paddler any more than some to be encountered on the eastern canoe routes. All the bold and able rivermen were not in the North, he seemed to be saying. If he was making a case for the hardiness and endurance of the North West Company's voyageur servants, he was perfectly right in so doing. "I am persuaded," he said, "that Canadian voyageurs would not shrink from these [northern rapids] and I suppose that many parts of the route the traders follow from Canada to the North-West must be equally difficult."[2] Nevertheless, Macdonell would be grateful for the experienced man to be placed in each canoe and proposed that for boats carrying women and children in succeeding parties, the allotment should be two such men for each boat.

And so, the long-anticipated river and lake journey to the "Land of Promise" was about to begin on the Hayes River, even before the last trace of floating ice had disappeared. The commanding William Auld was present to bestow in loud and eloquent phrases a final bit of advice which he knew these green immigrants would need. He was an able trader and his advice was generally sound but too often his boisterous manner in delivering it was offensive. He possessed muscle and stamina and had but slight patience with many of the young fellows, "softies," coming into the service. He did not like the changes taking place in the fur trade; he hated the North West Company and its men for their "rapacity" in the Athabasca which was doing great injury to his source of furs at Churchill River. He probably disliked the idea of a settlement at Red River as much as men of the other Company hated it but he managed to keep it to himself. And he was critical of fur trade policy which ignored conservation principles and allowed the beaver population to fall almost to the point of extinction in some regions. Auld could be helpful and he was helpful to Macdonell. In his wisdom, he prophesied a scarcity of pemmican at Assiniboine and Red River posts because the influence of the Nor'Westers would cause the Indians and Métis to drive the buffalo herds far away. With the needs of the settlers in mind, he sent word to Company posts on the Red and Assiniboine rivers to conserve pemmican and save all available potatoes for seed.

Also present to bid farewell to Macdonell and his party was the unconventional priest, Father Charles Bourke, to whom Macdonell had just given permission to return to Ireland. Macdonell, himself a Catholic, had never shown much enthusiasm for this man, contending to the end that he was "a disappointment and an encumberance. Religion is turned to ridicule."

But Macdonell should have acknowledged some of the priest's good offices, such as writing voluntarily to the *Inverness Journal* to counteract the influence of "Highlander's" letters written to dissuade those who were considering Lord Selkirk's 1811 invitation to become settlers. Macdonell should have admitted, also, a personal interest in Bourke's collection of "precious rocks" gathered at York Factory and Nelson Encampment. He thought sufficient of the "discoveries" of what the priest believed to include rubies, golddust and diamonds, that he was sending samples to Selkirk for verification and analysis, writing: "Should they be found valuable, immediate advantage ought to be taken. Your Lordship might obtain a grant of the Nelson with a mile on each side. . . . I have enjoined secrecy on Mr. Bourke."[3]

The priest deserved full credit for his curiosity and initiative in searching nearby areas for valuable deposits but his faith exceeded his geological judgments and nothing came of his "discoveries," except some choice sarcasm from Lord Selkirk who reported them as common rocks.

Macdonell, who had seen the North West Company's canoe brigades leaving Lachine on the St. Lawrence, tried to produce an equivalent scene. If he had thought of it before leaving Stornoway, he would have provided himself with a British flag for display at this moment but one was now on order to come later with a copy of Arrowsmith's Map of North America, a couple of 3-pounder brass field pieces, a quern for grinding grain, a set of the Encyclopedia Britannica and a quart of appleseed, all of which Lord Selkirk was being asked to forward with the least possible delay.[4]

Each of the boats making ready to depart carried four or five men and up to a ton and one-half of freight and supplies. The signal to be going was given, but there was no French Canadian paddling song or chanson, and as most of the paddlers were clumsy novices, the scene bore only the faintest resemblance to one of the lively departures on the St. Lawrence.

It would be approximately 750 water and portage miles from York to that spot called Pelican Ripple on Red River. If the brigade were to travel at an average of twenty-five miles per day, the distance would be covered in one month. But Auld warned against such optimism. If the men averaged only thirteen miles a day, the trip would last for two months. As it turned out, the average was about thirteen miles and on some days when going against fast water and over multiple portages, they knew they were lucky if they did six miles. But gradually the men — about two-thirds of them from Scotland

and one-third from Ireland — were growing accustomed to river travel and gaining effectiveness. After about three weeks of paddling, portaging and tracking, always with the force of currents working against them, they arrived at the first Hudson's Bay post on the route, Oxford House, perched on a grassy rise of ground close to the river. There they relaxed briefly, noting to their satisfaction that they had now covered one-third of the total distance to Red River. Macdonell marked the occasion with an issue of spirits and the assurance that they would soon come to the big lake and most of the difficult water would be behind them.

At Oxford House there was a surprise in the shape of two young cattle, both yearlings, a heifer and a bull. William Auld knew they were there — or said he did — and in writing to Lord Selkirk tried to take credit for the wonderful foresight he had shown by having the animals taken part way in the previous year. "I had anticipated your designs," he wrote, "by sending last summer two calves from here but on reaching Oxford House, 240 miles from here, I durst not allow them to proceed further in fear of accident in consequence of the men at Brandon House being in a state of insubordination. . . ."[5]

It is very doubtful if Auld did "anticipate" the Earl's "design" in the previous year because there was no land grant until June, 1811, and nobody at faraway York Factory would have any chance of hearing about it until September or October. But it did not matter how the two cattle came to be there; Macdonell was pleasantly surprised to find them, especially after the unhappy necessity of leaving Stornoway almost a year earlier without the eight cattle intended for the settlement. To leave the little herd behind was a difficult decision but it was made after full realization of the amount of valuable space the necessary feed and fresh water would take, to say nothing of the space eight cattle would require. But here at Oxford House was partial compensation and Macdonell and his men seized eagerly upon the bovine pair, with or without consultation, and loaded the uncooperative critters in one of the canoes. The cattle were christened Adam and Eve, with the hope that they would prove fruitful and multiply "and replenish the earth." Quickly they accepted the necessity of stepping in and out of the canoe at the correct times and being on good behavior most of the time.

Before leaving Oxford House, Macdonell hired three more "experienced men," thus bringing his crew back to the total number he had contemplated. During the last days at York Factory he had made many changes in the list of workers, rejecting those who had been troublemakers in the winter and drawing new men from the autumn importation. He thought he had a total of twenty-two but three of these developed cases of fear at the last minute and refused to go. Along with a young Indian, Tipatem, who joined as a volunteer, his leaving party numbered twenty. Now, with the Oxford House additions, he had twenty-three in his party.

By August 11, the little flotilla was at Playgreen Lake, soon to reach Lake Winnipeg. By this time the travelers could rejoice in the realization that the worst of their transportation problems were behind them. Adam and Eve were becoming willing travelers and Macdonell figured that his remaining supply of oatmeal and fat, along with what fish his men would catch while en route, should match the needs of his men until they were at Red River.

Floating southward in a state of comparative peace on Lake Winnipeg, while his men paddled, Macdonell found time to ponder the Earl's instructions touching on most every conceivable point in laying the foundation for a settlement. They were sufficient to make the Captain marvel at the mind which anticipated the numerous and varied problems likely to arise on the frontier, and found plausible answers for them. They were sufficient, also, to worry him; it was all very well for the Earl, sitting in the House of Lords and bored with the dull proceedings of the day, to scribble notes of instructions on matters with which he had no chance of being familiar. For the person on location, where decisions had to be instantaneous and practical, it would be better to be without the burden of a lot of instructions. But like any well-disciplined army officer, Macdonell would not intentionally disregard the instructions from a higher command. He knew the Earl's judgment had an unerring quality about it and he was wise enough to try to make a mental list of all that he was expected to do.

"On your arrival at Red River," Lord Selkirk had instructed, "the first and most important point will be the choice of a situation for the settlement. For the sake of health, a dry and airy situation is essential . . . near the edge of the woods, and the plain should be of fertile soil and of sufficient extent to allow a number of settlers to be spread out on separate lots, each enjoying the advantage of wood, water and open lands fit for immediate cultivation. . . ."[6]

The author of these lines, still a stranger to the country, continued to write with the understanding of a professional agriculturist and the confidence of a long-time resident. He regretted that he could not have accompanied either the vanguard group or the settlers of 1812, as he had done for the settlers to Prince Edward Island in 1803.

As it was, Selkirk had to rely upon Macdonell to carry out the plan as closely as practical to the guidelines delivered at Stornoway. And with more than a year to elapse before he would see Red River, Macdonell had plenty of time to meditate on the tasks before him.

"It may be necessary to make a halt at the first tolerable situation that you find, and set the men to work with their spades,to turn up some ground for winter wheat, while you go with a small party to explore. Perhaps the best spot for this halt will be that marked in P. Fidler's survey by the name of Pelican Ripple [St. Andrew's Rapids on later maps] which he describes as the first plain in going up . . . from the lake."

The Earl's concern about "a dry and airy situation" was inspired, no doubt, by his unfortunate experience at Baldoon in Upper Canada. The other items indicated the same good reasoning. A colony placed at the Rapids, he could have explained, would have had the advantage of being moderately far south in a belt of superior soil and still accessible from the North by sailing ships. Sails would have limited use on the fast northern rivers but they might serve on the 300-mile length of Lake Winnipeg and the relatively quiet water at the lower end of the Red. That this was in the Earl's mind is supported by his advice of just a few months later, that he was sending out a set of sails and rigging for a small schooner to be built on Lake "Winnipic."[7]

Hopefully, Macdonell might find the Company's reliable Peter Fidler to be at York Factory and, with the aid of his knowledge of the country, make a decision about a location for the settlement before starting south. Fidler wasn't there. But nobody could say the decision about situation wasn't a good one. When it is realized that the site chosen gave birth to the city of Winnipeg, it becomes easy to speculate how even a minor change in 1812 could have altered the shape of Western Canadian development. While Selkirk was instinctively fascinated by the Red River Valley, he had some second thoughts and wrote to both Auld and Macdonell recommending that some consideration should be given to the possible advantages of a Dauphin River location. Significantly, the Earl was again referring to a belt of particularly choice soil. The Dauphin River area, as he noted, would have an added advantage in being farther from the United States boundary and safer for settlers if the threatening war should become a reality.

Macdonell, of course, would require a variety of supplies, more by far than he could hope to carry from Scotland, and his Lordship was making certain that everything of importance would be obtainable. Directing his message through the Hudson's Bay Company, the Earl instructed Auld to provide those supplies which he could spare for the great migration southward, whether the journey were in the autumn or spring. He was taking further steps to secure the aid of Company posts in the region of the Red and Assiniboine rivers — Brandon House and Pembina in particular. It would be Macdonell's right to request what he needed. At Brandon, the Earl wrote, "they have a particularly large stock of horses which are tolerably domesticated and accustomed to draw carts. The officers of the Company at these posts are instructed to supply as many of these horses as they can spare, and they may have no difficulty in sparing their whole stock if they have sufficient notice so as to purchase others from the Indians." Proper payment would be made to the Hudson's Bay Company. All transactions between Company and Settlement would be based on fair value.

Brandon House, also, the Earl noted in his instructions to Macdonell, would be in a position to supply seed potatoes, also some seed grain. But if Macdonell wanted Indian corn for planting, Selkirk could inform him how to get it: send someone to the Ottawa and Bungie tribesmen. In any event, the Earl, sitting at some desk in Scotland or England, seemed to know what was needed and how to obtain it. He would not presume to tell Macdonell how much land should be cleared and cultivated in the first year but he would go as far as to say that "the first crop should be as large as possible." He hoped the settlers would see the importance of preparing lands for crops with the least possible delay and authorized Macdonell to tell them that if the harvest response measured up to expectations or exceeded them, the workers accompanying Macdonell would be rewarded with "separate allotments of land to be cultivated each for himself, with the promise that as soon as they have raised a sufficient crop to feed a family and build a house to lodge them, their friends from home shall be brought out to them."[8] But, added the practical Earl, from the time that a laborer in Macdonell's crew was set free to work for himself, his wages would cease. If he required tools and provisions for the first year and was unable to pay, he would be supplied and charged as a debtor to the establishment.

The general plan made it essential to have a land survey. Every person becoming a settler would receive an allotment of from 50 to 100 acres. "The price to be put on the first lots is of little consequence except for the sake of the principle." But a description of the land allotted to each individual should be sent home "so that a grant [or deed] in due form may be sent out to be delivered to the settler on payment of his debt."

For the first season, at least, the Earl ruled, building and tilling activities should be concentrated near the fort, this for reasons of security. Indian attack was an ever-present possibility and the danger of war with the United States seemed to be mounting. Without waiting for a request from Miles Macdonell, his Lordship was forwarding to York Factory by the ship *King George,* "seven or eight cases of small arms and two small pieces of brass ordinance which are to be sent to Capt. Macdonell."[9] The message, directed to Auld, added: "By the same vessel you will receive 4 Iron six-pounders with suitable ammunition which in the present state of our roads cannot be conveyed up the country but may prove of use in possible cases of emergency at Y.F...."

By this time, Selkirk was aware of the circumstances making it necessary for Macdonell to remain near York Factory for the first winter and in case such a contingency occurred again, the thoughtful Earl was forwarding to Auld some additional provisions to be kept on hand, chiefly oatmeal and molasses, "the latter . . . a powerful antiscurbutic." Also in the shipment, the Earl was sending two hampers of "medicines" to be at Macdonell's call.

If there were dangers from warlike people, Selkirk had further advice. He was urging caution but advising any reasonable steps which would strengthen home defenses. One of his proposals to Auld was a 400- or 500-man contingent to be brought out "next year," with himself accompanying to impress any who would consider violence against the Colony, meaning North West Company men, natives, United States invaders or any group with evil intentions. "War seems to be impending between G.B. and the United States," he wrote prophetically. "Our situation will thus become very critical." He hoped that in the event of war, good sense would prevail in Rupert's Land and that the North West Company would be ready to cooperate for purposes of defense, and bring all available strength together to be placed under the command of Capt. Miles Macdonell.

But if the bigger danger should prove to be from the Indians the Earl's advice to Macdonell was to concentrate his settlers on small lots of five and ten acres close to the fort, to be held and cultivated temporarily or until "they can safely take possession of their full lots." Perhaps the reinforcements to be sent out in the following year would remove the necessity for such precautions. In any case, the policy toward the Indians, Macdonell was told, should be one of friendship. He was to work to win Indian confidence, making a deal for land where necessary, with presents preferably in the form of annual gifts.[10]

It was ever clearer that Selkirk would spare neither effort nor cost to ensure success for the enterprise so close to his heart. At that point he was placing complete confidence in Macdonell and it may be that his faith exceeded Macdonell's deserving. But he was backing his faith with tangible rewards. Not only was he paying Macdonell the high salary of £300 per year but was promising a grant in the handsome amount of 50,000 acres to "yourself and your heirs," and extending the hope "that you will not quit the colony till it is fairly established and past the dangers to an infant settlement."[11]

Directing the birth of a settlement 5,000 miles away presented grave difficulties, especially in the years when sailing ships offered the only means of transatlantic travel and communication. But if anybody could and would overcome those handicaps, the Earl of Selkirk seemed the most likely to succeed. He was serious, studious and meticulous and if his purpose was pecuniary and selfish with thought of fortune in emigration and settlement, as some people still insisted, he was hiding it skillfully. Macdonell, advancing toward Red River with every stroke of the paddles, was getting to understand the Earl and his purposes better — and his admiration was growing.

Red River, At Last

Leaving long and sometimes rambunctious Lake Winnipeg and entering Red River, the Selkirk workers knew they were only a day or two away from the halt which could be their destination. It was enough to awaken new interest in the surroundings. The river water was not the color of blood as opponents had alleged and killer Indians were not lurking in the shadows. Pelican Ripple or St. Andrew's Rapids, of which warnings had been sounded, was no more than a minor disturbance compared with wild water enountered in the North. The whole countryside, in late-August dress, appeared warm and friendly and lovely. Straggler buffalo cows with fat calves carrying tinges of yellow in their baby hair grazed peacefully on the west side and Nature was in undisputed possession.

The Selkirk instructions to consider a location bordering River Dauphin as a site for settlement had not been overlooked but they ceased to weigh heavily on Miles Macdonell's mind, partly because an examination of that area would have taken additional days of valuable time, partly because the opinions of men who knew the country favored the Red River. William Auld admitted that Dauphin River at the west side of Lake Winnipegosis would present fewer dangers from attack by Indians and forces from the United States but Red River would be closer to buffalo herds and more productive. Auld was right and Macdonell did not argue.

It was on August 30 that the twenty-three tired boatmen arrived where the Assiniboine River joins the Red — fifty-five days of heavy paddling, portaging and tracking from York Factory — and Miles Macdonell made a hurried survey to determine a location for a temporary campsite. On the north side of the mouth of the Assiniboine, partly hidden in trees, was the North West Company's Fort Gibraltar, looking much like other utilitarian trading posts, low and drab and sprawling, with a sturdy stockade constructed to discourage angry Indians. Macdonell directed his men to pull to the opposite side and there unload the much-traveled bull and heifer, and pitch the tents.

Macdonell, in the meantime, chose to cross to the west side to test the North West Company temper with a visit at Gibraltar. He was well aware of the fulminations from Company officials, leaving no doubt about their dislike for the Selkirk plan, but a visit would give the resident partners a chance to declare their enmity or accept a neighbor without prejudice. Besides, he had a brother, John Macdonell, and a cousin, Alexander Macdonell, in the North West Company service, which seemed like the best of reasons for a display of friendly interest. Macdonell was received hospitably and went again the next evening for a few convivial hours, each time returning to sleep in his own tent pitched where St. Boniface Cathedral stood in later years.

But the Gibraltar sincerity was brought into question a couple of days after arrival when a band of mounted Métis, feathered and painted as if for war, visited Macdonell's camp and, between war whoops, blatantly informed him that the valley belonged to the halfbreeds and the fur traders. All others would do well to depart. Settlers, above all, would not be welcomed. It was rather obvious that the visit, like the "Highlander" letter appearing in the *Inverness Journal* in the previous year, was inspired by men of the North West Company.

It wasn't easy to explain to the halfbreed visitors that Lord Selkirk was the new proprietor and his representatives had legal rights and would be staying. It would be still more difficult to convince the North Westers, however friendly they might appear at the outset, and Macdonell was conscious of the need for a public declaration of the Earl's proprietorship and his own authority as the appointed Governor of Assiniboia. Not that he could expect many guests and spectators beyond his own men, but an invitation would be extended to all the residents at Fort Gibraltar. On September 3, Macdonell went riding with Mr. Wills and sixteen others from Gibraltar and after some friendly horse races, he extended the invitation to all to attend on the east side of the river next day at 12 o'clock.

Macdonell was determined to make the ceremony as impressive as possible. He wanted to think that the New World had witnessed nothing like this. Promptly at the hour appointed, the firing of a gun signaled the beginning of the ceremony and a flag was raised. A few freemen and Indians motivated by curiosity were present and "three of the N.W. Co. gentlemen attended but they did not allow their people to cross."

Having had the benefit of some training from their leader, Macdonell's men furnished him with an Officer's Guard of Honor, under arms, colors flying. Then at the proper moment, while the few guests stood in awe, Macdonell advanced and faced Fort Gibraltar to read the patent conveying the land of Assiniboia to Lord Selkirk and then the companion document giving Macdonell the authority to take possession in the Earl's name. In case there were freemen or others whose only language was French, Mr. Heney of the Hudson's Bay Company was present to interpret the message. As Macdonell reported the proceedings to Lord Selkirk, as soon as the reading of the formal instruments was completed, "all our artillery along with Mr. Hillier's consisting of six swivels were discharged" and three cheers given. For whom the cheers is not clear. Finally, to justify the high hopes of the visitors, "the gentlemen met at my tent and a keg of spirits was turned out for the people."[1]

It was like an Official Opening and men who were not inspired by the formalities and sound of gunfire were moved by the tapping of the keg. Even any who might be annoyed by the prospect of settlement were not too angry to take a drink of Hudson's Bay Company rum. Red River was enjoying a transient peace such as it would not experience again for many years.

Now, as Macdonell realized, he had to begin without delay to give body and shape to the new settlement. Whether he was aware of all the implications or not, the decisions demanding his immediate attention would leave their mark most vividly upon the history of a city, a province and a country. And to magnify the urgency of decision, the next wave of immigrants — genuine settlers with families — might be arriving before the onset of winter. The necessity of erecting shelters and finding food for his workmen would have been burden enough but the presence of women and children would multiply the responsibility.

In view of instructions sent by Lord Selkirk and William Auld to Company posts on the Red and Assiniboine, Macdonell had reason to expect some preparations for his party, some shelters and certainly a supply of provisions like pemmican. The harsh fact was, however, that at the beginning of September, there was simply no provision for either food or shelter. Writing to Selkirk he said, with a hint of anger, that "notwithstanding all the orders the Company posts in this quarter might have had to provide for our arrival, there was not one bag of pemmican or any other article of provisions reserved for us."[2]

To further complicate the food situation and add to the danger of famine, the buffalo herds remained far away, thus reducing the chance of obtaining meat from the natives "who never lay up any stock," but live only "from hand to mouth." The river, offering fish, appeared to be the best hope for food but a scarcity of fishhooks was enough to greatly limit the return. It was a bleak outlook and Macdonell knew he had to act decisively.

Seeing no chance of accommodating and feeding his workers and the settlers somewhere en route if they remained at the Forks, his decision was to send most of his men at once to Pembina where they would be close to a Hudson's Bay Company post and nearer the buffalo herds wintering on the grasses of the plains.

The sooner they started to build huts for themselves and the settlers following, the better. And so, on September 6, Macdonell placed most of his workmen under the command of John McLeod and A. Edwards, the surgeon, and sent them south on the sixty-mile journey to Pembina River. Mr. Heney of the Hudson's Bay Company, who was familiar with the country, accompanied. The men remaining at the Forks would attack tasks like cultivating ground for seeding to winter wheat, and recovering hay for the few cattle and horses and any other animals the settlers might bring. As soon as the party left for Pembina, Macdonell and several of the remaining men went downstream by canoe to consider further the selection of the most suitable location for the settlement.

Confident that he would find a satisfactory site, he took along the bull and heifer, the bushel and a half of precious seed wheat carried from Scotland, and such other stores as might be left at the place chosen for permanency. After a tour taking three days, living exclusively on fish, Macdonell returned to the point of land made by a bend in the river, just about a mile north of the Forks, "as the most eligible spot." At this location, fire had destroyed most of the trees and brush, and weeds and the gumbo sod were the only other obstacles to cultivation. It would be known as Point Douglas and the men were set to work at once to clear an expanse of ground for cultivation by the only means at hand, namely spades and hoes. Cultivation would be followed by the planting of the winter wheat by the time-honored broadcast method. A small and rough log structure was built at the spot to accommodate the hand tools and stores which could be left until spring.

"Next day," the 9th of the month, Macdonell wrote, "I set off on horseback for Pembina, with an escort of three men, and reached there the 12th, a day after my people." There, also, he had to make a decision about a building location and in his typical forthright manner, he selected ground on the south side of the Pembina River where it enters the Red, almost against the North West Company fort. At once he assigned his men to the jobs demanding prompt attention, "one man to fish with a bent nail," others to drag logs for the building of shelters. Men who were strangers to an ax one year earlier were now swinging with commendable aim and force, and log huts were soon emerging in disorder as if dropped from the skies.

While building was progressing, Macdonell was negotiating with local freemen and Métis to devote themselves completely to hunting buffalo for the purpose of keeping the expanding colony of newcomers in meat for the winter.

Pembina now had three posts, the Hudson's Bay Company fort, the North West Company fort, and the new complex of shacks and huts being built for the workmen and settlers which Captain Macdonell christened Fort Daer, honoring a Selkirk family name.

Having seen the Pembina building program progressing, Macdonell, on October 1, started back to the Forks, taking two horses and a harrow — also a supply of buffalo meat just received from the plains. In returning north, he could supervise the planting of that bushel and a half of seed wheat, and if his premonition was serving him properly, he would be present to receive the party of settlers whose leader hoped to reach Red River before the lakes and rivers were frozen and winter would be upon him.

With the aid of the two horses and the harrow, the little plot of ground for the wheat received a thorough grooming to present a moderately acceptable seedbed for the grain to be planted with an involuntary Macdonell benediction.

From wheat, attention turned to hay. Although the season was late, too late for good hay, it was obvious enough that poor hay must be better than no hay and the men went back to cutting and gathering and stacking more of the native grasses grown tall and coarse and dry, mainly with the thought that Lord Selkirk might send some sheep with the settlers.

And sure enough, the party of weary men, women and children — seventy-one altogether — led by that cheerful son of Old Ireland, Owen Keveny, arrived on October 27. There had been another slow ocean voyage, a sixty-one-day crossing to York Factory, but all survived; in fact the party did better than survive because it reached York Factory with one more passenger than at the start, Mrs. McLean having given birth to a daughter "two days before we came to dock."

Most of the people were from the Hebrides and western Ireland and while they might have expected more by way of accommodation, they breathed sighs of relief at having arrived without mishap. Owen Keveny, affable fellow, was a good leader, one who could be a disciplinarian without being offensive.

And in keeping with Captain Macdonell's hunch, there came with the party a flock of twenty-one sheep — seventeen ewes and four rams — intended, hopefully, to furnish a foundation for a New World sheep and wool industry. One ewe died on the ship to York Factory but the other members of the pioneer flock arrived at Red River in good order, in spite of William Auld's warning that they would "inevitably die on the road up."

If Macdonell had intended to leave the livestock to winter beside the hay at the Forks, the very superior character and value of these twenty-one sheep and the special supervision and protection they merited, caused him to change his mind. He was not one to waver in making decisions and when he heard about the importance Lord Selkirk attached to these sheep, he ordered that cattle and sheep as well as settlers be directed to Pembina with the least possible delay.

Instead of taking ordinary sheep like the lowly Scottish Blackface breed which could have been bought cheaply at any point in Western Scotland, the Earl resolved to begin with the best wool sheep available anywhere. His reasoning was that wool of the highest quality could become a valuable article for export from Assiniboia and he determined to provide the best in breeding stock. The sheep chosen were the golden-fleeced Merinos from Spain, the producers of the world's finest wool. Moreover, these members of Selkirk's little band were hand-picked to ensure even the best of their strain.

Having been caught up with the idea of his settlers finding sheep's wool to be a practical and profitable item for export, Selkirk was most enthusiastic about the basic flock. He admitted to visions of high quality wool being pressed into ninety-pound bales — the way farmers of a later period baled hay. Because the wool would have a high value in relation to weight, it would be found practical to transport it by canoe to York Factory and from there to the British woolen mills by sailing ships.

"They are a valuable breed," the Earl wrote about his Spanish sheep, "selected with great care and if they are lost it will not be easy to replace them."[3] He saw the effort as an important experiment and his approach to it was that of the scientist. Had the sheep survived, they might well have furnished the beginning of an important trade and industry. In furnishing instructions to Miles Macdonell, he mentioned that each of the sheep bore an identifying mark; clipped notches in the ears would signify identifying numbers from 1 to 22. Many breeders of pedigreed sheep were still using this marking technique over a hundred years later. All lambs in the Red River flock were to be identified in the same way to relate to their breeding and in due course every fleece from these sheep would be properly ticketed to show individual identity and shipped to England or Scotland for expert appraisal. In this way, the settlers would find a proper basis upon which to cull and select breeding stock for purposes of breed improvement. There was nothing wrong with the plan. Had the sheep survived, the Earl's sheep scheme might have produced notable results and even a new Canadian breed.[4]

The blue-blood sheep managed to reach Red River safely and were under the experienced care of John Maclean. But there was trouble ahead. Between an insufficiency of feed and depredation by dogs and hungry natives, the flock grew smaller rather than bigger. Indians who were seen seeking safety from these strange new animals by clinging to branches in trees, soon discovered a fancy for the taste of mutton. One ewe and two rams died during the first winter and in the spring all the lambs except one were lost. Before very long the valuable Merino sheep were completely extinct at Red River.

Fortunately, the winter was not severe but the snow was deep and with complete dependence upon the buffalo herds which remained deep on the plains, famine seemed to be never more than a few days away. Macdonell had arranged with Jean Baptiste Lagimodière and two other seasoned hunters to keep up a supply of buffalo meat and the arrangement was working satisfactorily until the snow became so deep that delivery at Fort Daer was almost impossible. One young man, Magnus Isbister, perished while trying to reach the hunters' stockpile of supplies.

With the coming of spring, the settlers returned to Point Douglas to start building what they hoped would be their permanent homes and to enlarge their plots of cultivation. It was a great moment when they began to live on the land which was to be their own and one settler thought sufficient of it to give himself a new birthday date.

Adam and Eve and the sheep survivors returned also, to graze on ground which would someday be part of Winnipeg's Main Street. Later in the spring they were joined by three more cattle: a bull, a cow and a heifer calf, which the obstinate but useful Peter Fidler bought at the North West Company's post on Souris River, for the high price of £100. With the birth of a bull calf to Eve, the total cattle population of the area marked by present-day Western Canada, appears to have stood at six — two bulls, two cows and two calves, all grazing at Red River.

The bushel and one-half of winter wheat planted in the previous autumn failed to survive the winter and the small quantities of spring wheat, barley and peas obtained from Brandon House did not do much better. Grubs were said to have destroyed the Indian corn and Macdonell was appealing to Lord Selkirk for more seed for the 1814 planting season. Obviously, the state of cultivation was not adequate for most crops and only the potatoes made a good showing. Macdonell knew what was wrong; he was not blaming the soil or the climate and was confident that with better seed and better cultivation, the reward would be good. He emphasized the need for more cattle, making it clear to Lord Selkirk that the settlement should have at least twelve or sixteen yearling heifers from which to build a herd.

In the absence of more cattle, he would pursue the Earl's instructions to catch buffalo calves and try to domesticate them. Catching the calves was not difficult and several were brought to the Daer encampment but "they died for want of milk," all except one heifer which became so tame that she was a nuisance and she remained around Point Douglas for years, sometimes hitched to a Red River cart, sometimes to a plow. And while the Red River men were catching buffalo calves, Lord Selkirk was proposing an experimental attempt to domesticate the caribou in the North and a test with "musk buffalo" or muskoxen to be brought to Red River. Macdonell was showing no enthusiasm for the proposed caribou and muskox proposals but promised to capture more buffalo calves.[5]

Meanwhile, the little herd of domestic cattle was encountering trouble, especially the two wayward males. First, the bull which Peter Fidler bought from the rival Company at Fort Souris, became unmanageable and dangerous, inviting the observation that he brought with him the mean disposition of the North West Company people. Since Adam was still active and well, the second bull was not needed anyway and in the interest of safety it was decided to slaughter the fractious one. Granted, the small herd did not need more than one bull but at some point during the ensuing winter, Adam felt the urge to wander and, exercising a bull's prerogative, disappeared. A search for the all-important herd sire proved futile and Adam was not seen again until spring when his dead body was observed floating down the river on a piece of ice. Presumably he had gone for a drink at a water-hole and fallen in and drowned. Now there was no mature bull in the Colony, a condition that did not bid well for herd expansion, but fortunately, Adam left behind a young son, the bull calf born to Eve, now the only surviving male of his race on half a continent.

When Capt. Matthey became the Earl's agent at Red River some years later, he mentioned "poor wounded Adam and Eve" as being the most dependable draft animals in service at the time. This is not a contradiction of the story of Adam's drowning but has reference to the original Eve who would be a seven-year-old cow and her son who apparently inherited his father's name and survived a wounding by gunshot to serve as both herd sire and draft animal in the community.[6]

The same Peter Fidler who had enriched the settlement's cattle numbers came down at the end of May, 1813, to survey the farm lots in the area of Point Douglas, so that settlers would know exactly where their land started and ended. Each 100-acre lot, long and narrow, fronted on the river, thereby giving all settlers an equal advantage in access to the water highway and allowing homes to be built close to neighbors. On a farm 220 yards wide and two miles long, the house and other buildings would be situated close to the river's high-water mark; then there would be the cultivated land and back of all the pasture and hayland.

Notwithstanding the failure of almost all crops except potatoes in that first year, people were optimistic and cheerful, sufficiently confident that they were pressing Miles Macdonell to obtain a windmill for use in grinding the grain they were yet to grow. As they came to a better understanding of the country, they were sure they would make fewer mistakes. Already they had demonstrated that buffalo meat in winter and pemmican and fish in summer could sustain them until crops became more reliable. There was nothing wrong with the area, as Captain Macdonell assured the Earl. "The country," he said, speaking like the President of the Chamber of Commerce, "exceeds any idea I had formed of its goodness. I am only astonished it has lain so long unsettled."[7]

He knew the questions Selkirk would be raising and hastened to report. Respecting the Indians, he was still uncertain if a treaty should be made. "Those here do not call themselves owners of the soil although long in possession. It belonged originally to the Crees whom the Assiniboines — a branch of the Sioux — drove off. A small annual present will satisfy the Indians here," he reported.[8]

It was noteworthy that in that first year in the country, the Selkirk people encountered no Indian hostility. A bigger worry appeared to be the possibility of invasion from the United States because of the War of 1812 still gripping the boundary area farther to the east. Some modest precautions were taken but there was no invasion.

Captain Miles Macdonell might have experienced more longing to get into that war than to escape from it. He might have wished he were free to return to his regiment in the East, especially after receiving letters from his brother, John Macdonell, a partner in the North West Company. Brother John expressed his regret that Miles had accepted a position in Lord Selkirk's scheme, prophesying that the Colony would not last long. He was sorry, also, that Miles, because of his obligation to Selkirk, was not in a position to take his place in the armed services where he would, no doubt, qualify for his commission as major "in the Glengarries."[9]

Adding to the danger of the moment for the Selkirk people was the fact that their winter quarters occupied in two seasons at Pembina — whether it was known or not — were actually on the American side of the 49th parallel. But Pembina and Red River were far from the scenes of active dispute and combat, and the war was over before it might have reached the West.

The settlers hoped they could remain at Point Douglas, to be their home base, for the winter of 1813-14, but Miles Madonell ruled that they must go again to Pembina. It was still a matter of food supplies. Crops, except for potatoes, had been disappointing and there was the next group of settlers — the people from Sutherlandshire who were somewhere en route — to be considered. Miles Macdonell, leaving Point Douglas on July 18, traveled to York Factory to meet the newcomers and escort them to Red River but found to his disappointment and anger that a dogmatic ship's captain had discharged the human cargo at the Fort at the mouth of the Churchill River where the people would be obliged to spend the winter. But nothing could be done about it and Macdonell rushed back south with all the speed he could get out of a canoe to see his people there becoming settled in winter cabins at Pembina and reconciled to another six months on a buffalo meat diet.

Surprisingly, the Pembina atmosphere was very much more pleasant in that second winter, mainly because the traders of both the Hudson's Bay Company and the North West Company had deserted their posts. Apparently it was the presence of the settlers and the increased competition for food supplies that drove the traders away. It meant, however, that the settlers had the place almost to themselves and Miles Macdonell had nobody except his own people with whom to quarrel.

CHAPTER NINE

The High Cost of Macdonell Arrogance

If Lord Selkirk had doubts about Miles Macdonell being the best man for the role of Governor of Assiniboia, he mercifully kept them to himself. But others connected with the Colony — and unconnected — had grave doubts and did not hesitate to declare them, making the Glengarry Scot's sojourn at Red River both short and distressful.

Macdonell had much to commend him for the high position. He had muscle and a fine physique; he lacked nothing in courage and carried himself with a proud and soldierly bearing, looking in all respects like a person born to be a Governor or the Chieftain of a wild Highland Clan. It was not surprising that he was a "marked man" in Lord Selkirk's books from the day of their first meeting beside the St. Lawrence River seven years before the Red River Colony was more than a dream. Selkirk corresponded with this commanding fellow and had him in England, ready to take charge of a settlement even before consummation of the big land grant of 1811, upon which the very idea of the Colony depended.

But Macdonell was arrogant and sadly short on diplomacy. As Governor of the Colony, he made needless trouble for himself and costly trouble for the Earl and settlers. He might have considered the tactful approach to be a waste of valuable time in a frontier land or he might have been so much the uncompromising army officer that he found it difficult. In either case, he annoyed his own people and taunted the Montreal men needlessly, making them hate him and adding fuel to the flames of discord already burning brightly.

Many of those in the North West Company were rough-hewn fellows, unrefined and hardhitting, but they were not without honor and most of them could be accepted and respected by Montreal society and retain reputations as good citizens. The reader of history is entitled to draw his or her own conclusions about how much of the trouble at early Red River would have been avoided if Macdonell had been more tactful and less domineering, especially in his dealings with the North West Company. Was it not possible that by the exercise of patience and diplomacy, Macdonell could have perpetuated the initial neighborliness with the nearby North Westers and cultivated an understanding with the Métis, sufficient to have prevented the bloody clashes at the Settlement? Was it not possible that the conflicts reaching a tragic climax in the Battle of Seven Oaks in June, 1816, really began in some of Macdonell's fits of pique and obstinacy?

Although men of that rival Company had vowed to fight the proposed settlement on one of their river lifelines, the local representatives received Macdonell on his arrival at the Forks and at Pembina in the most friendly manner. But he was inclined to mistrust people around him and his suspicions bred antagonisms among those who might have been his friends and a source of lasting strength.

The offending flaws in Macdonell's manner were recognized from the first winter in the country, spent at Nelson Encampment. After annoying his workmen and losing control over them, he had an insurrection on his hands. It didn't escape the sharp eyes of the vindictive William Auld or the notice of others within the Hudson's Bay Company service and they began turning against him. He was in too much hurry to exercise and display his authority, Auld said. He was clever, but not smart enough to see the trouble starting in many of his own actions and he wrote to William Hillier of the Company, complaining of a conspiracy of Hudson's Bay men against him.

Auld would not be an easy person with whom to work but Macdonell was in a position to win and hold that trader's good will and benefit greatly from his support. Instead of cooperating, the two men became enemies and Selkirk, with loyalty to his official agent, accused Auld of throwing "the apple of discord" between Macdonell and certain others in the service and instructed Auld to write no more letters to him.

There was difference of opinion about who threw the "apples of discord" but in any event, the spirit of ill will spread in all directions and although Auld was far from blameless, most Hudson's Bay Company workers and servants were on his side in the disputes. Auld would be a tough and vengeful opponent and it was probably more than coincidence that after Lord Selkirk denied him the privilege of writing directly to him, mail addressed to Macdonell at Red River remained at York Factory at Auld's pleasure. And a letter addressed to Macdonell and marked with instructions for its return to Lord Selkirk in the event of the Governor's death was indeed returned. Auld chose to conclude that Macdonell's usefulness was for all practical purposes dead, and sent the letter back before trying to deliver it. Auld's enmity mounted when copies of certain of Macdonell's outgoing letters to Selkirk fell into his hands; thereafter, more letters going to Macdonell were opened before reaching him.[1]

Selkirk, in the meantime, wrote to Macdonell and enclosed copies of letters of complaint, written by various Red River people, John Howse to object to Macdonell's offensive manner; John McKay, a boat builder at York Factory, reporting maltreatment of settlers and going to the length of taking away their supplies and even repossessing certain plots of land the Governor wanted for himself.[2] As Auld explained it, Macdonell quarreled with Hugh Heney "about trifles", quarreled with Owen Keveny the very day the latter arrived, then with Kenneth McRae, the storekeeper, and with A. Edwards, the surgeon, "all of whom are as worthy and well behaved officers as I ever saw."[3] The surgeon's complaint was of offensive remarks and a refusal to allow the doctor a ration of wine for his patients.

Almost everybody who could write, it seemed, was communicating complaints about the Governor, with Auld — never known for timidity — becoming the most abusive, saying that "if Lord Selkirk had advertised for a fool of the first magnitude, he never could have better succeeded than he has done with the present man. He disgusted every one of the settlers and servants of his own. . . . He has encouraged the Canadian traders to treat him with contempt by his childish partiality."

Auld explained that he had attempted to keep on good terms with Macdonell, constantly trying to correct the mistakes of this "Prince of Fools," only for the sake of the Company. "He has not had sense enough to burn his copies of his scandalous libels which now lay before me."[4]

It was sad to think of an able man doing so little to prevent criticism and enmity. He must have been aware of a certain degree of failure when he confessed to Lord Selkirk that he was encountering mistrust on all sides, Indians, Hudson's Bay Company, North West Company and freemen.[5]

Selkirk did not say that he believed all the charges made against his official representative but he saw fit to advise Macdonell that his method of management was "defective." But those personal differences — many of them petty — touching people with whom he should have been working in cooperation, were of small consequence compared with the quarrels with men of the North West Company.

It was a pleasant surprise for Miles Macdonell in going to Pembina in that autumn of 1812 to discover that the man in charge of the North West Company post at that point was Alexander Macdonell, his cousin and brother-in-law. The Macdonell kinsmen greeted each other joyfully. Why not? Conversation about relatives and old friends came easily and, following the impulse of the moment, Miles Macdonell built his winter home alongside that of the other Macdonell. Having a cousin next door should help to relieve the monotony of a long winter. It was like a declaration of intent to remain friendly, as cousins should remain. And so it was through the early part of the winter; the two men visited back and forth daily and other individuals on the Colony side, like Owen Keveny, storekeeper McRae and surgeon Edwards found occasion to spend much of their spare time, too, visiting with new friends in the North West Company service.

This fraternization continued until Miles Macdonell, in rather typical manner, presumed a conspiracy of his own men against him and found reasons for dispersing the suspects; McRae was sent to the plains to hasten the delivery of buffalo meat, whether he was capable of doing anything about it or not; Keveny went to Brandon House on some equally weak pretext, and Edwards because of his position was acknowledged to be indispensable in the community.

The cordial gestures between the cousins survived a little longer, looking like a complete denial of the bitter feeling which was supposed to exist between the Companies. Even the settlers were surprised and wondered in whispers if their Governor had changed his loyalty. They speculated, also, about Alexander Macdonell having a subtle purpose in cultivating his cousin's friendship. But if there was reason for suspicion, the Governor, on his record, would have been the first to find it and whether he had adequate cause or not, he brought the friendly relationship to an abrupt halt and created in its place a feeling of bitterness and anger.

It took just one short letter to change the diplomatic climate from warmth to frigidity. Writing on April 18, 1813, Miles Macdonell addressed his cousin with chilly formality:

> "Sir — Your insidious and treacherous conduct during the winter in endeavoring to swerve my people from their duty is fully known to me; as well as that of your colleague, Mr. Dugal Cameron. I therefore trust that you will not attempt to intrude your visits here where you can no longer be received as a friend, by
>
> > Your once sincere,
> > Miles Macdonell."[6]

The reply was written and delivered the same day:

> "Sir — Your abusive and absurd note I just now received and since you, without the smallest shadow of reason, run away with such ideas, I shall not therefore convince you to the contrary. My visits shall be no burden to you. At the same time accept my sincere thanks for the attention shown me in the beginning of my illness. Your remark about my colleague, Mr. Dugal Cameron, is to me most astonishing. A person who after a little acquaintance with you wished well of your cause, and spoke of yourself always in the most respectful manner, it is therefore most unfair to say his conduct towards you has been insidious and treacherous. Had it been so, you would have known the result. . . .
>
> > Your very obedient servant,
> > A. Macdonell."[7]

More correspondence with the same bitter tone followed. Alexander Macdonell wrote to say he was returning certain borrowed articles: "2 quarts of gun powder, 12 gun flints, 2 quarts of high wines."

A short time later, Miles Macdonell carried his complaint by letter to the North West Company partners assembled in annual meeting at Fort William:

> "Gentlemen — It is with feelings of regret that I am under the necessity of stating to you the very improper conduct of the N.W.Co. clerks, Messrs. Alex. Macdonell and Dugal Cameron. The former was my neighbor last winter at Pembina and, while the most friendly intercourse subsisted between us, [he] was attempting in the most insidious and artful manner to corrupt my people and seduce them from the service of their employer to join that of the N.W.Co. Towards the end of February, Mr. Dugal Cameron came on a visit

to Mr. Macdonell and adopted the like dishonest proceedings which the accompanying documents taken under oath can fully substantiate. . . . The Indians have been tampered with to induce them to destroy or drive the settlers out."[8]

The letter received the full attention of the Montreal men meeting at Fort William, and Miles Macdonell received a reply signed by William McGillivray, A. N. McLeod and Alexander Mackenzie, saying in part:

"You require us to remove Mr. Alex. Macdonell and Mr. Dugal Cameron from the stations which they held last winter. We are at a loss to devine the grounds on which this requisition is founded. . . . We never can admit the right of any man not interested to interfere in our arrangements."[9]

Selkirk, without knowledge of the recent unfriendly exchanges, was writing to warn his agent that the North West Company will try "to catch at any flaw that could bring us into discredit with the public." The Earl's advice was to "keep clear of any unnecessary collisions" with men of that rival group.

But in spite of warnings, the "collisions" occurred with increasing intensity. The next one had its origin in pemmican, that meaty food staple which was the recognized "staff of life" in buffalo country. Made from dried buffalo meat, buffalo fat and saskatoon berries and packed in bags or sacks of ninety pounds each, it possessed excellent keeping qualities and offered the only practical means by which the all-important buffalo meat could be carried over into seasons when the herds might be far away. It was the invention of prairie Indians but traders, trappers and travelers came to rely upon it. It was a reconized essential in provisioning the voyageurs providing the paddle-power for the fur brigades; most of the supplies upon which both the Hudson's Bay Company and the North West Company depended came from the good buffalo ranges far up the Assiniboine River. The Selkirk Settlers accepted it when there was no alternative and when their growing numbers placed pressures upon supplies and raised fresh fears of famine.

Miles Macdonell was well aware of the dangers and of his responsibilities in relieving them. It was the prospect of more reliable supplies of fresh meat and pemmican that led him to send the settlers to Pembina for their first winter and to return there for the second winter. After the disagreements of the first winter, Macdonell was, of course, relieved to find that the competition for food supplies created by his people at Pembina had induced the traders of both old companies to abandon the Pembina posts, allowing the settlers to have the place to themselves. It made for a more pleasant winter for all who remained. The 1812 necessity of including dog meat in winter rations did not return.

But of the crops planted at Red River in 1813, only the potatoes and turnips gave a fair return, "500 or 600 kegs" of potatoes being the principal harvest. But fresh meat and pemmican were no easier to obtain in that second winter and Macdonell could not overlook the new danger of food shortage when the next contingent of settlers — the Sutherlandshire people

— arrived. This latest group was expected in the autumn but there was delay at Churchill River and the people would not now arrive until the spring of 1814. But regardless of when they came, they would bring many big appetites to be added to those already at Red River. Wisely, Macdonell was considering the possible necessity of conserving all food resources.

The famous Pemmican Order which followed was sound in principle. The method of serving it and enforcing it was not as good unless it was the intention to thoroughly infuriate the North West Company which drew its essential pemmican supplies from the region of the Assiniboine and its tributaries.

After assuring himself that this was now Lord Selkirk's exclusive property and that his Lordship's settlers should have first claim to all food supplies grown thereon, he drafted the Proclamation on January 8, 1814, and issued it over the name of John Spencer, Secretary and Sheriff. After defining the borders of Assiniboia, the Proclamation declared that the food needs of the settlers made it "a necessary and indispensable part of our duty to provide for their support."

"Wherefore," the Proclamation declared, "it is hereby ordered that no person trading in furs or provisions within the territory for the Hon'ble H.B.Co., the N.W.Co., or any individual or unconnected Traders or persons whatever shall take out any Provisions, either flesh, fish or vegetables procured or raised within the said Territory, by water or land carriage for one twelvemonth from the date hereof, save and except what may be judged necessary for the trading parties at the present time within the Territory to carry them to their respective destinations, and who may on due application to me obtain a license for the same. The provisions procured and raised as above shall be taken for the use of the Colony and that no loss may occur to the parties concerned, they will be paid for by British bills at the customary rates.

"And be it hereby further made known that whosoever shall be detected in attempting to convey . . . shall be taken into custody and prosecuted as the law in such cases directs."[10]

The same order provided for the seizure of the provisions being illegally transported, also seizure of the crafts, carriages and cattle involved in the movement.

Macdonell took immediate steps to bring the Proclamation to the attention of the people most concerned in both Companies, sending two of his men — Sinclair and Stitt — to carry it in person to each fort in the area. The intention was to post copies on the gates of all trading places but to do this, there was the annoying necessity of obtaining permission from the traders in charge. The Hudson's Bay Company traders, who disliked the order as much as their rivals, reluctantly allowed the orders to be posted but the North Westers resisted. A copy was duly tacked to the gate at Brandon House where William Hillier carried the responsibility, but at Fort Souris, John Wills declined permission because he refused to acknowledge an authority for such a proclamation. Wills sent copies of the order to neighboring partners for their opinions but his resistance stiffened and Peter Fidler could swear to hearing Wills proclaim that before he would agree to the command, he would assemble the Indians to help him in fighting such an injustice. Miles Macdonell followed by informing Mr. Wills that to guard against acts of resistance, "armed parties are stationed on Ossiniboia River to support the sheriff and his constables."

Macdonell by this time had a better stock of guns and seemed to invite a chance to use them. A supply, including five brass pieces with carriages, had been sent out for his use in the previous September and he lacked only the men who knew how to use them or give instructions for infantry and cavalry service because, said he, "there is no country so suitable for light cavalry as our own extensive plains."

The Governor seemed ready to test the guns, saying boastfully to Auld: "I have sufficient force to crush all the North Westers in this river, should they be so hardy as to resist openly my authority. . . . We are well armed."[11] Such an arrogance and an attitude, to be sure, caused the people on the side of Wills to make ready with their guns too.

It was an uneasy spring at Red River. The North West Company needed all the Assiniboine River pemmican it possessed to provision its big brigades of North canoes moving eastward with cargoes of furs early in the season and westward with trade goods later. The Hudson's Bay Company had exactly the same needs for its York boat crews going to and returning from York Factory. The only difference was that the North West Company servants could afford to be more bellicose and offer more resistance.

The Governor, having declared a primary claim to all the pemmican originating in Assiniboia, was determined to enforce his order. With the coming of more settlers, known to be on the way, there would not be enough of that essential food for all who wanted it and the prevailing topic of conversation up and down the river was the wisdom or folly of the Macdonell action in issuing an order which carried so many possibilities of trouble. Most people agreed that food supplies might be insufficient for all needs but that the North West Company deserved some consideration. Wouldn't consultation before the issuance of the declaration have lessened the risk of violence? The sometimes treachous William Auld told Macdonell it would have been preferable to give a year's notice of the intention to "claim the provisions in this country," but having expressed his opinion on the matter, Auld added that Macdonell must now remain firmly by his decision. Auld promised generously that the plan would now have his support.[12]

The first displays of muscle came in May. A boatload of North West Company pemmican was reported on the 19th of the month to be coming down the Assiniboine, intended, no doubt, for fur brigades moving eastward on the Saskatchewan River. This would be in defiance of the Proclamation and Macdonell swore in four special constables to watch.

These men allegedly saw North Westers patrolling with guns and Macdonell reacted by bringing out and setting up his brass artillery.

John Wills, fearing à seizure of his provisions, ordered that they be temporarily concealed. Macdonell's men, on May 27, discovered the hiding place and took possession of ninety-six bags of the supplies. To the credit of Wills, he came right to Macdonell for a face-to-face discussion about a situation threatening to cripple the North West Company's seasonal activities. Macdonell, satisfied with the demonstration in having taken the pemmican, now offered to return part of it to Wills but it was not enough to satisfy the latter and he ignored it.

Then came the big seizure at Fort Souris, repercussions from which were heard as far as Montreal for the next ten years. Nobody could explain the events better than John Pritchard who was still a servant of the North West Company and stationed at Fort Souris. As he told William McGillivray at Fort William a short time later, Macdonell's Sheriff, John Spencer, knocked at the fort gates and "commanded me to open them in the King's name." Pritchard replied that the order was illegal and he would not open. "You will find no entrance to this fort except a forcible one which must be at your peril."

The Sheriff delivered two blows with an ax and called his men to cut through the pickets. The Sheriff then entered through the breach, followed by Mr. Howes and three other men. Then, after forcing the door to the storehouse, they seized 479 bags of pemmican, 93 kegs of grease and 865 pounds of meat.

Having effected the seizure, the Sheriff arrested Pritchard on a charge of resisting an order for entry but he was released soon after on an order from Captain Macdonell. Both Sheriff Spencer and Howse would get their turns to be arrested later, on charges of stealing provisions.

This was like a declaration of war and the traders saw their very occupations being threatened. At this season of the year there was not much time for debate. Brandon House, property of the Hudson's Bay Company, on June 3 surrendered 190 bags of pemmican to Macdonell at Fort Douglas and probably cursed him at the same time. But the North West Company simply had none to spare and John Wills, on July 9, rather than invite an immediate clash with possible loss of both time and pemmican, asked Macdonell for permission to remove the Swan River pemmican from Souris to Gibraltar, it being understood. of course, that Swan River was outside the boundary of Assiniboia and therefore beyond the embrace of Macdonell's Proclamation. It was a reasonable request but Macdonell was not in a pliant mood and the North West Company men from Swan River and Fort Dauphin were taken prisoners. Wills and Cameron wrote to protest these further indignities, adding: "Your having taken up arms will not intimidate us." The writers could add what Macdonell probably knew, that "Mr. Howse is detained at this place and will be taken to Montreal on a charge of burglary." A few days later, Howse wrote directly to Macdonell, asking that his imprisonment be negotiated and offering the information that food shortage on North West Company tables was really serious, a number of men at "this fort" had no food for several days.

Giving the impression that he could no longer be bothered by complaints or had no time for them, Macdonell wrote to the North West Company men, asking them to desist from further communications to him.

At the same time, two other North West Company partners, Duncan Cameron and John McDonald of Garth, came in person to reason with Macdonell, asking that the Company pemmican be allowed to pass unmolested. Macdonell, apparently enjoying this recognition of an exalted authority, refused, but the North West men were wise enough to remain cool and cordial. Again, on June 17, John McDonald of Garth was with Macdonell, pleading a case of serious food shortage at Fort William, a situation attributed to the United States war and the difficulty of making the customary importations of corn. He seemed most reasonable in the proposition he presented: if Macdonell would let the North West Company have its pemmican from the Assiniboine now when the need was so urgent, he would promise on behalf of his Company to return 175 bags of pemmican for use by the colonists in the next winter. More than that, he offered ten North West Company canoes to be sent at once to York Factory for oatmeal for the Colony. Macdonell accepted this offer, as indeed he should have, and on the next day the pemmican arriving from the Souris River seizure, was turned over to the other Company at Fort Gibraltar. When the balance of the Fort Souris provisions arrived on July 15, Macdonell kept 100 bags and sent 176 to Gibraltar. Sheriff Spencer who carried out the raid and seizure was greatly irritated by what he saw as a loss of his efforts, and resigned from his office.

Macdonell seemed slightly more tractable. Peace, even though very temporary, returned to the river community and Macdonell and McDonald dined amiably together. In writing to confirm what had been decided when he sat in conference with the North Westers, Macdonell expressed a hope for more willingness on the part of both sides to make reasonable sacrifices. As for the offer of the North West Company men to send ten canoes to York Factory for oatmeal, Macdonell set it to record that he would "deliver a bag of pemmican in exchange for every bag of oatmeal or piece of 90 lbs. weight that you may bring."[13]

The proposed deal for York Factory oatmeal was a good and sensible gesture but unfortunately it could not be carried out. Before Macdonell finished writing the letter, he received a report that forced a complete change of plans and he added a postscript: "By the boats just arrived I have learnt that there is no oatmeal or other provisions to be spared from Y.F. which renders it unnecessary to send down canoes to the coast."

There may have been indications of a momentary peace at Red River but when the accounts of Macdonell's Pemmican Order and a partial acceptance of it by the local traders reached the Company partners in summer session at Fort William, the official North West Company anger burned as never before. The wrath was due in part to Macdonell's contemptuous order and in part to those North West Company servants who had yielded even slightly to it. Between the Colony and its Governor, the menace appeared bigger than ever and something would have to be done about it, something decisive. The Lords of the Fur Trade sitting in annual court at Fort William devised a plan for the complete liquidation of that menace and hoped it would work.

CHAPTER TEN

The Sutherland Settlers

As the long-suffering Sutherland settlers finally approached Point Douglas in the summer of 1814, their young and personable leader, Archibald MacDonald, stood erect in his canoe, and half a hundred heads bowed with him to breathe a Presbyterian prayer of thanksgiving. The year and two months since leaving their Highland homes would be remembered for hardship and sorrow. How could they forget their friends who had died en route and how could they forget the bitter disappointment of being stranded helplessly to spend a long and depressing winter in the sub-Arctic north? The tests were severe but the Kildonan and Clyne people never abandoned hope and good cheer. They represented the best possible seed-stock for a new land.

Lord Selkirk, as one who admired thrift and vigor and resourcefulness, had an especially warm spot in his heart for these people who were mainly from two parishes in Sutherlandshire. They caught his attention in 1812 when "in the Parishes of Clyne and Kildonan, one big sheep farm led this year to the dispossession of more than 100 families." In being evicted from the lands on which they had lived so long that they thought of them as their own, their only crime was in being tenants on farms likely to return bigger landlord dividends as sheep runs.

Appeals to government failed to identify any reasonable alternative upon which honest and hard-working rural people could build for the future, and they were returning in a rebellious mood when Selkirk intercepted them and presented proposals for mass migration. The Highlanders were quick to embrace the idea and Selkirk, in turn, was quick to embrace them as the settler stock he wanted. His first proposal was to send 100 or 200 of the men as soldiers to defend the Colony in case of attack from the south, with families to go later. That, however, was not acceptable and "they determined to emigrate all in a body," the Earl wrote to Miles Macdonell. "They were at a loss how to proceed when I stopped in and they have with joy accepted my proposal of settling them in Red River. The numbers who are anxious to go greatly exceeded that which I could have ventured to send this year but as they have still an outgoing crop on which they can maintain themselves till next year's embarkation, I have persuaded them to remain in their old habitations till next spring. . . . I have promised that the provisions requisite for the support of these people for a year after their arrival shall be supplied on credit. . . . You will lay out land for them. . . . Tho they are working for themselves and on their own bottoms, I feel quite as much interest in their success as if they were in my immediate employment. . . . The Sutherland men seem to be in person and in moral character a fine race. . . . I have promised that they shall have the option of purchasing at 5/-per acre cash or 10/-partly on credit, or a perpetual lease of half a bushel of grain per acre annually. . . . But the amount of money to be received from the people is a matter of secondary importance in comparison with their being well satisfied with their treatment. . . . The Sutherland men are rigid Presbyterians."[1]

The cost of transportation from Scotland to Red River would be ten pounds per person but 700 wanted to go. For practical reasons the number had to be reduced to about a hundred and Stromness in the Orkneys was named as the point of embarkation. After a series of all-too-familiar delays blamed conveniently on North West Company obstruction, the good ship *Prince of Wales*, with Captain Turner in command, departed on June 28, 1813. Lord Selkirk was there in person to wave farewell and convey his good wishes.

The sea journey was relatively short in time and long in trouble, the latter being explained by an outbreak of fever — probably the dreaded typhus or "jail fever" known to be highly contagious, especially where unsanitary conditions existed. Seven people, including two or three members of the ship's crew, died at sea. Nearly all the passengers were ill and to make matters worse, the first victim of the disease was the good doctor and leader, P. Laserre. There was nobody to take his place as guardian of the public health, and he would be sorely missed. For the role of leader, fortunately, there was a second-in-command, the young and able Highlander, Archibald MacDonald, and for what consolation it would offer, he was supposed to have some knowledge of medicine. He had worked for over a year for Lord Selkirk, helping to prepare for this exodus of Highlanders, and he was a favorite with both the Earl and Lady Selkirk. He was personable and energetic; he had everything a leader needed except experience, but he assumed responsibility unhesitatingly and held the confidence of the people around him. It meant that Red River would have yet another official bearing the imprint of the same Highland Clan, another with the typical fiber but, fortunately, with a slightly different spelling of the name.

At a moment when the immigrants needed solace, the ship's captain seemed to become impatient and merciless. Having grown tired of sick people, his main concern was to unload and be rid of the ailing cargo. Instead of considering their accommodation and sailing for York Factory as planned, he sought the fastest means of terminating the voyage and steered for the mouth of the Churchill River, site of the mighty Fort Prince of Wales. But the Churchill site offered no practical approach to either Red

River or York Factory. And the great stone fort, strongest in the entire Hudson's Bay Company system, lacked accommodation for a large body of immigrants.

The captain must have understood. He must have realized that some preparation had been made for the temporary accommodation of the settler group at York. And Miles Macdonell, having left his friend, John MacLean, in charge of the settlement, departed Point Douglas on July 18, expressly to be present at York Factory when the Gaelic-speaking men and women from Sutherlandshire arrived. With William Auld, he was standing by, ready to extend a welcome. But it would have made no difference to Captain Turner who was tired of the whines and odors of sick people, and the Sutherland contingent, with twenty-two men and women still suffering from the fever, were dumped unmercifully at the shore. Unable to prevail upon the skipper, Archibald MacDonald, on August 24 — six days after arrival — wrote to Miles Macdonell at York Factory, reporting his distressing predicament.

Miles Macdonell received the message and fumed helplessly. Captain Turner alone, he told Lord Selkirk by letter, was to blame for putting into Churchill, "contrary to the advice and opinion of every officer and gentleman in the ship. I hope he shall be made to smart severely for his brutal stubbornness. Had he come first to this place, the sick should have had immediate relief in fresh provisions and all the passengers should have got to the settlement to winter."[2] As it was, no hope remained of the people going through to Red River until the following spring or summer.

As soon as Captain Turner's determination to dock at Churchill was known at York, that man of loud and many words and ready action, William Auld, embarked in an open boat in the night to go to the more northerly port, intending to use his authority to force Turner to bring the settlers to York or "suspend him from the command altogether." One can only imagine the heat of argument when those two obstinate fellows came face to face. One or the other had to yield and Turner appeared to give in to a degree — perhaps just enough to escape from the threatened suspension — and agreed to reload the passengers and cargo and steer toward York Factory; but before the ship was clear of the loading zone, it grounded on a gravel bar, making it necessary to unload again. The circumstances invited suspicion and a question: Was the grounding of the ship a deliberate act? Nobody except Turner could be sure.

Captain Turner now had his way and was turning his ship toward London, leaving the sick and unhappy people stranded where they would have no choice but to spend the winter in the bleak and isolated and frigid vicinity. As the captain guided the *Prince of Wales* across the Bay, Auld was returning to York Factory by water, cursing Turner and criticizing the immigrants as "the laziest, dirtiest devils you ever saw."

To make matters worse for the settlers, it looked like a winter without tea because of the loss of five chests of the stuff in the harbor when it was being unloaded. The man entrusted with the unloading had chosen an inappropriate time to indulge in drinking rum and an accident occurred. If he had had to face the Sutherland women in a winter without tea, he would have had many occasions to regret the error of his alcoholic ways.

It was now too late in the season to entertain thoughts of a trek from Churchill to Nelson with hope of reaching Red River before freeze-up. The outlook was bleak, any way one viewed it. Adequate shelter was one consideration; provisions were another. In trying to live through the winter without proper food, Auld could see nothing but disaster. He wondered, even, if he should have sent the settlers back to Scotland for the winter but recognized the danger of more sickness and more deaths en route and concluded that the decision to let them stay was the best the circumstances would have allowed.

There was no room for the Sutherland people at the stone fort and the logical alternative was to move about fifteen miles upstream on the river to the mouth of Churchill Creek or Colony Creek where there was fishing and where "tolerable wood" could be obtained for shelter and building materials for log huts. More than that, the area was believed to offer reliable supplies of wild meat, particularly rabbits and birds described as partridges but probably ptarmigan.

Within the period of four weeks from the time of arrival, six more of the immigrants died from the insidious fever said to be transmitted mainly by body parasites. Others were still weak but the disease was running its course and only a few of the newcomers had to be carried for the fifteen miles to winter location. Attention turned now to the construction of a winter village of huts and shacks and every able-bodied adult took to the recovery of suitable logs, either from driftwood or from the forest of dwarfed trees. The log shelters lacked windows and anything better than dirt floors. The spaces between the logs were chinked with mud and the pole roofs were overlaid with muskeg moss.

There was enough dead wood nearby for fuel, and Auld was right about the sufficiency of fish in the creek and partridges or ptarmigan in the brush, so that the squatters were not to be hungry. At a midpoint in the winter it was estimated that 8,000 of the birds had been taken for provisions and Auld figured that the food hunters would take as many more before spring. There was still the danger of nutritional deficiency and scurvy threatened until the discovery of the Indian remedy, spruce tea.

Being active people, they were in danger of suffering from boredom. They might have frequented Fort Prince of Wales, fifteen miles away, had it not been for an incident when a few of the men visited there in November and remained to spend the night in one of the houses. Probably there was gaiety and the flames in the fireplace were allowed to burn too high and the result was a serious fire with loss of considerable personal property. It was human nature to try to place the blame and the visitors were accused of carelessness. Auld happened to be present at the time and with his special aptitude for finding fault, the fort welcome vanished.

At the first sign of spring, the settler people were becoming restless, eager to be moving. The weak ones could not walk through the deep snow to York Factory and the stronger ones could not wait. The only solution was to travel in two parties and on April 6, the very next day after one of Auld's men came to serve as a guide, fifty-one of the most robust people — thirty-one men and twenty women — started on foot. Winter's snow was still deep and the traveling party started single file. As Archibald MacDonald told it, the guide took the foremost position, followed by the men hauling sleds loaded with provisions, tents and blankets, then the women on snowshoes, and at the rear, one of the sturdiest young men, ready to help if anybody ahead of him needed it. And that very important personage, the piper, took his place at the exact center of the line where the strength-giving strains would reach everybody.

The first day was cold and trying, MacDonald wrote, and three of his followers complained of cramps. Nightfall found the party making camp "in the first wood directly opposite Churchill Factory," suggesting a location close to the site of the big terminal elevator which is modern Churchill's most conspicuous landmark. Then, rather apologetically, MacDonald said they "did not leave our first night's encampment till 4 in the morning which was an hour too late at least."[3] One of the cramp victims, Andrew McBeath, was unable to move a limb but another man volunteered to haul the McBeath luggage. There was still the problem of making the unfortunate McBeath mobile and useful. It was a time of home remedies and the treatment administered in the northern snow is worth noting. First there was the bleeding, the extraction from the sick man's arm of twelve to fourteen ounces of venous blood, and then a sponging with a hot "decoction of spruce." If MacDonald's account is accepted, McBeath needed only the assistance of his wife's arm to be up and moving with the party, which speaks well for the treatment or the McBeath brand of physical resilience. The only concession to the sick man was help from MacDonald and "the strongest of the females" in taking turns to haul his sleigh until the evening camping hour of five o'clock.

After the first day, the rising "signal in the morning was never later than three oclock."

Auld's men had placed caches of food at strategic places along the way. When the original supply of ptarmigan was nearing depletion, the travelers came upon a stack of 202 birds of the same species left for them. Auld had his shortcomings and could be most annoying but now and then when the need was great, he rose to the role of friend and filled it well. The weary travelers breathed a blessing upon him again when they were intercepted on the trail by one of Auld's men who furnished "570 partridges, 62 lbs. of oatmeal, 40 lbs. pemmican, 11 pieces of pork and 20 lbs. biscuits."[4]

A little farther along, they met two Indians from York Factory who were present on instructions to deliver 35 pieces of pork and 100 pounds of oatmeal. What the travelers did not realize at the time was that Auld's York Factory was at that moment short of provisions, especially of meats.

The painful malady of cramps returned and there were more delays but on April 18 — twelve days and 150 exhausting miles through the snow from their winter homes — the tired travelers reached the Hayes River and found that the thoughtful ruler of York Factory had tents erected and ready for them. What a happy relief to be this far along and feel the security of the tough William Auld's authority, even though York appeared as a damp and drab place. One disappointment was the absence of cows because MacDonald had been led by Lord Selkirk to expect a "few cows" which he might be able to take along to Red River. The explanation was to be found in a meat shortage in the previous winter when the cows were all slaughtered.

Notwithstanding their hurry to reach York Factory, members of the immigrant party were obliged to wait for more than a month in order to have ice-free water. Only on May 23 were they able to start but from the benefit of Auld's experienced river guides and the Sutherland stamina brought to the paddles, the party was able to make particularly good progress and reached Red River on June 21, the longest day of the year.

It was too late in the season to be planting most crops but these people wanted nothing more than to be self-supporting and independent and soon planted forty-two kegs of potatoes for themselves and their Sutherland friends who would be following.[5]

Although it was late for planting, it was otherwise a favorable time for arrival, affording ample opportunity to build and prepare for the next winter. Miles Macdonell, knowing of Selkirk's feeling of admiration for these Sutherlandshire people, did all in his power to help them and land allotments were made at once, 100-acre lots on the west side of the Red River, downward from Fort Douglas. Macdonell encouraged the newcomers to "build their houses in knots of 5 or 6 families together for mutual security," in the manner of the first Selkirk settlers in Prince Edward Island, but these new people, with an extra measure of independence and self-reliance, had no will to be needlessly close to neighbors and Macdonell did not insist. He, too, was probably vulnerable to the spell of the Gaelic tongue and he was distributing twelve horses, promising to deliver them as soon as they were needed. He was undertaking, also, to reserve eight or ten "heiffers" for the "best behaved men", to be turned over as soon as the cattle were available.

For Lord Selkirk, separated by the broad Atlantic Ocean and beset with numerous rumors about ill will and dissension in his Red River Colony, it would be most refreshing to have Archibald MacDonald's first report after completing the long journey: "It is with the greatest pleasure," he wrote, "that I can report to your Lordship that they [the Sutherlandshire people] never were happier and more contented in Kildonan than they are here already."[6] As if it might reinforce his contention, he told the Earl of John

Matheson Auldbraichie and Barbara Sutherland being married "the other day."

Archibald MacDonald did not overlook some of the more unpleasant aspects of Red River as he found them, the "Pemmican business," for example, and with undisguised criticism of Miles Macdonell's policies, he used uncomplimentary terms like "absurd" and "mismanagement." He recognized the unfortunate jealousy between Macdonell and Auld and saw the settlers turning more and more to Auld. Far worse than that, some of the settlers were turning to men like Duncan Cameron in the North West Company and it meant trouble.

Planned Destruction

As the Sutherland people saw Red River in the summer of 1814, new log huts and small plots of cultivation scattered along the Point Douglas shoreline gave the first tangible indications of permanency — little enough for two years of effort. There was more proof of the goodness of nature in furnishing "fish, flesh, salt, sugar and fruit." It was an encouraging sign when men like James Bird, Thomas Thomas and John Pritchard, old hands in the fur trade, were quietly inquiring about the purchase of land with the idea of building homes and retiring there.

And Lord Selkirk, instead of being discouraged, was inspired anew by his admiration for those most recent settlers and ready with more ambitious proposals for the Colony. He was instructing Captain Macdonell to be prepared with supplies of hay for the possibility of cattle and sheep being driven from his Baldoon Settlement by trail through the areas of Detroit and Chicago. But before the letter reached Macdonell, the United States and British soldiers engaged in the War of 1812-14 discovered the delicious quality of mutton and the Baldoon flock was decimated. There was still the hope of delivering cattle. "The Yankees have made an end to my sheep," he wrote later, "but I believe it possible that the requisite supply of cattle may be obtained." He would inquire about obtaining 100 cattle at Prairie du Chien, in Wisconsin.[1]

Exercising his customary imagination, Selkirk was sending rye and parsnip seed for planting, hoping always to find a new crop which would be a great success. Going forward to Red River, also, were plans for the erection of a windmill, and a horsepower mill to serve when the wind failed. He was telling Macdonell to look for rocks of millstone texture and density on the east side of Lake "Winnipic." The Colony should be made more self-sufficing, he reasoned, and to that end, why not use wood resin or spruce gum instead of imported pitch? Why not local salt from nearby salt springs? Why not homemade soap, and sugar from Manitoba maple trees, and wood pegs instead of imported nails, as the Norwegians used? Macdonell was told to consider the ultimate construction of a distillery to utilize surplus grains. He should be planning a winter road to York Factory and thinking about new products for export, perhaps salted buffalo tongues, buffalo hair, tallow, hemp, flax, tobacco or madder. And another thing: Selkirk's agent should be setting an example of thriftiness and industry, with fewer requisitions for luxury items like wines, cheese, butter, biscuits, coffee and chocolate.[2]

But these recent arrivals saw more than signs of progress; they saw the Red River community torn by ill will and Captain Macdonell being blamed for much of it. Almost as conspicuous as the proof of nature's bounty were the signs of human defects, mistrust from within the Colony and fear of retaliation from without. The fears were amply justified because Phase Two of the Pemmican War was just starting.

With an immediate advantage in manpower, Captain Macdonell had played the part of a bully and enforced his will within the Settlement and against the North West Company. For his actions, he could not escape criticism and was feeling the loss of respect and prestige. According to William Auld, Macdonell confessed months earlier that he was completely tired of the Colony and wished he had never known it.[3]

The sharpest rebukes reached him from the very person he hoped most to satisfy, Lord Selkirk. Sensing an inadequacy, Macdonell wrote to the Earl on July 24, begging "that your Lordship be not prevented by any delicacy to send a suitable person to take my situation, as I find myself unequal to the task of reconciling so many different interests."[4]

Selkirk's letter of reprimand was for ignoring instructions to avoid acts which would endanger the peace. Referring to what he called "the Pemmican business," the Earl cautioned Macdonell to keep within the bounds of his legal authority. "I am surprised," he said, "that you should have thought the measures consistent with my instructions, particularly as Mr. Hillier pointed out to you a passage in my letter directly cautioning you against any act of such a tendency."[5]

Even the settlers whose food needs led to the controversial Pemmican Order of January 8 disapproved of the dictatorial manner in which their Governor had issued and tried to enforce it. Macdonell was feeling the increasingly hostile climate both within and beyond the Colony.

Arrogant as he was, he was not beyond discouragement and he grew more irritable. Appointing the faithful Peter Fidler and the youthful newcomer, Archibald MacDonald, to take charge of the Colony, the Governor's canoe carried him northward soon after the Sutherland people were assigned to their farms. The misguided fellow could not be blamed for wanting a change of scenery and he would escort settler arrivals of the current year back to Red River. But absence from the troubled Colony, which should have brought relaxation, made him more tense, and at York Factory he came to the verge of nervous collapse, so near that those people who were with him felt it necessary to take his guns away.

Poor Macdonell! His trip to the North was a bad experience. All his mistakes and follies and worries returned to haunt him. His chief critic,

William Auld, was still at York, although soon to be relieved of his post, and his presence would do nothing to cure the Governor's depression.

Dr. A. Edwards, who was at York Factory at the time, did not describe the trouble as a "hangover," but it had some of the symptoms. Regardless of the diagnosis, the man needed sympathy, something about as scarce as fresh eggs at York Factory.

As the doctor made comment, "Macdonell appeared dejected this afternoon."⁶ The patient was worried about the existence of certain embarrassing letters and documents, including those concerning the alleged theft of a silver spoon involving his friends, the MacLeans. Auld and Edwards agreed to burn the papers in question and Macdonell seemed relieved but still unhappy.

After a sleepless night he sent for the doctor who found him in deeper depression than ever, saying "he had ruined Lord Selkirk as well as the Colony, that nothing but death could relieve him, that it was entirely his own fault ... called himself a villain, said that the Colony was ruined entirely by his mismanagement, explained that he was a wretch, and knew not what he had done, that he was too bad to live and too great a coward to die, and that he could not look up even to the Almighty."

As the doctor explained further, the depressed man took a drink, saying he "wished it was poison." At this point, his companions removed his gun and saber and left him alone for four hours, after which he felt better.

Days later, having largely recovered from the depression, Macdonell expressed a wish for an assistant who would relieve him of some of the Red River pressure. Then, on September 9, while still at York, he wrote remorsefully to Selkirk, admitting that he was distressed and miserable at "the backward state" of the Settlement. Feeling the justice and weight of his Lordship's reproaches, Macdonell wished "to Heaven that I had not put myself in a position to deserve them." The expenses at the Settlement, he confessed, were enormous "and most unsatisfactory to Your Lordship." He hoped Lord Selkirk would come out to Red River in the next year.

As soon as he heard of Macdonell's emotional state, the Earl wrote to the brother, John Macdonell of the North West Company, suggesting that he travel to Red River in the hope of bringing help and encouragement to the Governor. Had the brother gone, his influence might have changed the course of events very greatly.

As it was, the Red River situation was deteriorating rather than improving. The forceful North Westers had no thought of accepting the insults of the Pemmican Order and the seizures without a fight. They had disliked the idea of an agricultural settlement from the beginning and when it was planted in an area which they had long regarded as their trading ground and on a river which was one of their important canoe highways, their anger mounted. Now, the presence of huts was giving the Selkirk scheme the aura of permanency, reminding the Montreal men that any steps to halt the development would have to be taken quickly. The hated order to restrict the movement of their own pemmican seemed to give them a more ample justification to remove the entire Colony menace, even though force were needed.

William McGillivray and other leaders in the North West Company were at Fort William for the summer meetings which brought together the partners and servants from both east and west. The site was the pivot point at which the East met the West, where the pemmican-eating voyageurs from as far as Athabasca exchanged their cargoes with the eaters of pickled pork and corn meal from Montreal, exchanged bales of western furs for bales of eastern trade goods and started on long return journeys. It was where the powerful Company partners met to chart plans for capturing a bigger share of the western furs for another year. For a few weeks each summer, the Fort William halls rang with gaiety and boasting and scheming. To men of the older Hudson's Bay Company, it was a place of mystery.

In this year of 1814, the reports delivered at the great annual meetings were both good and bad. The Company's trading tactics had again paid off with a dominant share of the back-country furs. The distressing news was from the Assiniboine and Red rivers where the Governor of the Selkirk Colony was resorting to provocation by confiscating pemmican supplies which represented the essential food energy to keep the Company's canoes in motion. The colossal nerve of this man, Miles Macdonell! Highland anger came to white heat in men with names like McGillivray, Fraser, McLeod and Mackenzie. And that was not all; no less disturbing was the allegation that some North West Company men in the region had yielded to the iniquitous order, allowing themselves to "compromise with our honour at Red River." It was made to sound positively shocking, like kidnaping or robbing graves. John Pritchard was accused of failing to put up a fight when the Colony's Sheriff called to seize the pemmican, and John McDonald of Garth had acted like a coward in accepting a pemmican compromise worked out with Miles Macdonell. These and other North Westers who condescended to negotiate for the pemmican which was really their own were severely rebuked. It was William McGillivray who said it was not the value of the pemmican that annoyed him as much as the insult offered to his Company.

Having reprimanded their people for giving in to Miles Macdonell, members of the council, meeting behind closed doors, agreed that the Colony on the Red River was really part of an ill-disguised plot to destroy the North West Company. The Montreal men had to be ready to strike back with more force, they agreed, to remove the settlement or destroy it by any means. How was it to be done?

A subtle, double-barreled plan was proposed and strangely enough, its implementation was assigned to two of those North Westers, Duncan Cameron and Alexander Macdonell, whose names had been connected with laxness in dealings with Miles Macdonell. There is no evidence that either was guilty of weakness and both would have resented the suggestion. But they were ready to take on the new and subtle tasks. For Alex Macdonell, the job was to indoctrinate the Métis people to make them see the settlers as enemies whose Colony must be destroyed.[7] For Cameron, the undertaking was even more sneaky, to convince the settlers that there was no future for them and no escape from trouble at Red River, then persuade them with a promise of free transportation by Company canoes to Upper Canada, to quit the Colony. It was agreed, too, that Miles Macdonell should be arrested on charges of theft, and removed to Montreal for trial.

W. B. Coltman, who was called later to investigate the Red River trouble, quoted from a communication written by Alexander Macdonell following the Fort William meeting, in which he referred to the tasks assigned to Cameron and himself. "Much," he said, "is expected of us. . . . One thing certain, that we will do our best to defend what we consider our rights in the Interior." And then there was a confession: "Something serious will undoubtedly take place. Nothing but the complete downfall of the Colony will satisfy some by fair or foul means. A most desirable object if it can be accomplished, so here is at them with all my heart and energy."[8]

This, Coltman identified as the first act of the conspiracy to destroy the Colony, as conceived at Fort William.[9] Other evidence obtained by Coltman revealed warrants issued for the arrest of Miles Macdonell and others, also authority issued to the partners wintering at Red River to offer the settlers free passage to Upper Canada and provisions for the journey. When the Colony was weakened by depletion of population, the natives, by raiding it, would surely knock it out, terminating forever Selkirk's much-vaunted scheme for agriculture in the fur country.

As for Miles Macdonell, he would be brought out in chains, his cousin promised. This would teach him a lesson about the error of trying to stifle the movement of pemmican and making the awful blunder of trying to prohibit the running of the buffalo by means of horses — with a penalty of three months' imprisonment for the first offence and three months plus forfeiture of the guilty man's horse for the second offense.

The Settlement's population in the autumn of 1814 stood at about 200. Captain Macdonell believed that by restraining the outward movement of pemmican, he could take and feed another 250 people but space on Company ships in that year proved to be a limiting factor and only fourteen newcomers were brought to join the settlement. Macdonell hoped that the emigrants of that year would include some cats. The entire country was overrun by mice, he reported to Selkirk, and "half a dozen cats will be necessary to form part of next year's emigration."[10]

In his relations with the North West Company people, Macdonell was being no less belligerent. On his return from York Factory, still ignorant of the plot hatched at Fort William, he issued an order to vacate the nearby Fort Gibraltar, directing it to Duncan Cameron:

"Take notice that by the authority and on behalf of your landlord, The Right Honourable Thomas, Earl of Selkirk, I do hereby warn you and all your associates of the North West Company to quit the post and premises you now occupy at the Forks of the Red River within six calendar months from this date . . . 21st day of Oct., 1814

Miles Macdonell."

There is doubt if Macdonell really expected the order to be carried out or if he issued it merely as a formality by which he hoped to perpetuate the Earl's land claim. A similar order was sent to other North West Company posts within the Selkirk land grant, but whatever the intent, it was one more irritation and inspired the North Westers to fresh determination.

Eager to redeem the good name of the North West Company men accused by friends and colleagues of compromising with the Governor of Assiniboia, Duncan Cameron and Alexander Macdonell lost no time in embarking actively upon the double plot. It was now or never. Simon McGillivray's failure to block the Settlement plan at its source in Scotland and England meant that it had to be stopped at Red River. If more than general principles were needed, hadn't the Governor's Pemmican Order followed by seizures of provisions provided it? This was no time for a half-hearted effort and others in the North West Company would be watching to see how their two colleagues were succeeding. The smoldering unrest among the Natives would have to be blown into flame and the hard and dangerous lot of the settlers would have to be magnified to make them seem unbearable.

Alex Macdonell was not considered to be particularly clever but he could be treacherous and he stood well with the halfbreeds. Cameron, who returned from Fort William parading the uniform of a Captain of the Voyageurs' Corps — now defunct — had a pleasant manner and a good command of Gaelic, all that was needed to win Highland hearts. Moreover, in returning from Fort William, Cameron carried warrants for the arrest of both Miles Macdonell and Sheriff Spencer on charges related to the pemmican affair. Spencer was arrested first, while settlers gazed in astonishment. With a more daring leader, they might have rallied to release their Sheriff by force but Miles Macdonell was at that moment on his way back from York Factory with the fourteen immigrants from the ships of that season; Archibald MacDonald was young and Peter Fidler was not a fighter. Spencer was led away, protesting.

As winter set in, Cameron presided at Fort Gibraltar, becoming more amiable in the presence of the settlers. His door was ever open and the Selkirk people soon discovered that the Gibraltar welcome was much warmer than that at Fort Douglas. When they called, Cameron displayed the best of Highland hospitality, offering food and the more beguiling refreshments, and talked about free land and peaceful living in Upper Canada.

"He's a gude man," settlers leaving Gibraltar were saying of Cameron, without finding corresponding compliments for Miles Macdonell.

By late winter there was much conversation about Cameron's offer to furnish transportation and rations for as many families as wished to move to Upper Canada where living would be easier and human life safer. Interest in Cameron's offer was growing and a few people were already deserting the Colony. James Smyth who had remained at Fort Daer did not want to be excluded and wrote to Cameron: "I understand your honor have proposed to relieve a poor distressed people by taking them to Montreal next spring. I hoap you will count myself and family in the number, as I assure you it is well known that I was still against the taking of the pimiken."[11]

Toward spring there were rumors of halfbreed attack and as Cameron told it with an assumed air of sadness, there was nothing he could do to prevent it. Taking no pains to be either consistent or logical, he was trying, at the same time, to convince those settlers who were placing their trust in him, that the Colony's cannons should not be allowed to remain with the unstable Miles Macdonell. It was for their own safety, he said, that the field pieces should be removed to Fort Gibraltar.

On April 3, 1815, he addressed a note to Archibald MacDonald, saying:

> "As your field pieces have already been employed to disturb the peace of His Majesty's loyal subjects in this quarter, and even to stop up the King's highway, I have authorized the settlers to take possession of them, and to bring them over here, not with a view to make any hostile use of them, but merely to put them out of harm's way. Therefore I expect that you will not be so wanting to yourselves as to attempt any useless resistance, as no one wishes you, or any of your people, any harm.
>
> I am, Sir,
Your very obedient servant,
(Signed) D. Cameron,
Captain, Voyageur Corps,
Commanding Officer, R.R."[12]

The letter was entrusted to George Campbell, one of the Selkirk deserters who, in the company of several like himself, proceeded to Archibald MacDonald's house to read the letter to him. The plan for the seizure was well drawn; while Campbell and his cohorts were engaging MacDonald's attention and preventing him from leaving his quarters, a horse-drawn sleigh stopped at the Colony storehouse where one of the men broke the door to make way for the removal and loading of the field pieces, a swivel gun, a small howitzer and the cannons — nine pieces of artillery in all. As soon as these guns were loaded and on their way to Fort Gibraltar for "safe keeping," a musket was discharged as a signal to Cameron that the task had been completed. But the sly Cameron was a spectator in hiding throughout and needed no signal. He emerged and gaily joined the party converging upon the big fort where he would offer congratulations and refreshments. The guns were delivered as planned, a skillful stroke on Cameron's part to prevent serious resistance to the rest of his plans.

More settlers deserted, taking with them muskets issued by Miles Macdonell and these also were welcomed at Fort Gibraltar. Archibald MacDonald arrested one of his laborers who had assisted in breaking into the storehouse sheltering the field pieces and saw immediate reprisals from the Gibraltar side; George Campbell, leading a party of armed men including some of the North West Company clerks and Cuthbert Grant — the halfbreed leader — broke into the Governor's house and released the prisoner. This, too, was believed to be on orders from Cameron.[13]

On Miles Macdonell's return, after the seizure of the field pieces, he wrote a warrant for the search of the missing weapons and sent a party of twenty men to execute it. But Cameron would allow only four to enter the stockade gate and with his own men standing by with drawn muskets and fixed bayonets, refused to allow the search, making it clear that he considered it his duty to prevent cannons from falling into irresponsible hands.

Cameron, at the same time, was holding the warrant signed by Norman McLeod, senior partner in the North West Company and magistrate for Indian Territory, for the arrest of Miles Macdonell. The charge was breach of the peace and theft of pemmican. Macdonell, however, disputed the jurisdiction and refused to be arrested. After all, he too had the status of a magistrate.

Macdonell's proposal to Selkirk was for a military government for the Settlement, but the Earl believed it unnecessary, pointing out that by the H.B.Co. Charter, the Governor of any of the Company's establishments, with members of his council, could try both civil and criminal cases, "according to the law of England. You have therefore authority to act as a Judge but to do this correctly, it is necessary that you have a Council. . . ."[14]

There remained unresolved a great question about jurisdiction. Did the Canada Jurisdiction Act, passed by the Imperial Parliament in 1803 to give the legal responsibility for Indian Territory to the courts of Upper and Lower Canada, allow a Canadian magistrate like McLeod to exercise authority in Lord Selkirk's Assiniboia? Lord Selkirk and men of the Hudson's Bay Company answered with a resounding "No," while those of the North West Company said "Yes." The question remained unresolved, leaving Cameron convinced that it was his right to arrest Macdonell, and leaving the latter believing Cameron's warrants carried no weight within the bounds of Selkirk's grant, or in any part of Rupert's Land. Cameron became bold to the point of issuing orders for individual settlers to surrender "their muskets in the King's name."

Late in May, Alexander Macdonell came down from Qu'Appelle, bringing with him a group of ten or twelve Cree Indians, presumably to furnish psychological backing for Cameron's warning of an Indian attack upon the Settlement. While these natives were there to participate — perhaps unwillingly — in the Cameron war of nerves, a dozen horses belonging to the settlers were shot with arrows during night-time raids. It suggested Indian attacks but the Indian spokesman admitted that his people had no quarrel with the settlers. The shooting was then believed to be the work of the Métis or of Cameron's own servants.

These Indians did not seem to know why they had been brought to Red River but after some days, allegedly kept in a state of drunkenness, they departed. Other Indians from a southeastern section, according to one of the Saulteaux chiefs, were invited to attack the Settlement but declined. Obviously, the state of belligerency was becoming more explosive.

During early June there was intermittent shooting between North West Company servants and Métis on one hand and settlers on the other. In one exchange, four settlers were wounded and one died from the injuries. The well-known John MacLean was "badly wounded in the hand."

Cameron was still determined to capture Miles Macdonell, dead or alive, but let it be known that if the Governor would surrender peaceably or if the settlers would undertake to deliver him at Fort Gibraltar, the aggressions against the Settlement would cease. Macdonell was reluctant but worried settlers, thinking that Cameron would be as good as his word, prevailed upon him to give himself up. He surrendered and soon discovered that he would be taken to Montreal to face trial. If he had any illusions about his surrender saving the Colony, they were quickly dispelled and in a letter to Selkirk he admitted the fear that "it is to crush the Colony they have made a point of getting me."

His last act before surrender was to ask Archibald MacDonald and Peter Fidler to supervise the affairs of the Colony for the summer.

Cameron had played his part well; he was now in possession of the principal portion of the armaments belonging to the Settlement and in charge of the Governor. It was easy to sense the complete collapse of the Colony and the wild welcome he would receive at Fort William when he arrived there with the good news. A few days later, June 20, when the canoes were being made ready for the trip to Fort William, 134 men, women and children from the Settlement lined up to accept the Cameron offer of a free ride and victuals to Upper Canada. The number represented about two-thirds of the settlers, leaving only about fifty behind. For those leaving and those remaining, it was a sad separation, comparable in intensity to the joy it brought to the North Westers. The canoe to which Macdonell was assigned carried also Alexander Mackenzie and Simon Fraser of fame in earlier exploration, traveling to the Fort William meetings. Cameron, the Master Mind in the current drama, was sharing the same company.

Alexander Macdonell would have charge of Fort Gibraltar during Cameron's absence and as soon as the brigade had departed, the climactic part of the North West Company plot became brutally plain. Mounted Métis made raids by night, firing their guns recklessly, setting fire to buildings, tramping down crops and gardens. Cattle were driven away to Frog Plain and horses were seized. The only bull upon which all hope for herd expansion depended, was slaughtered and quartered for consumption at the Fort. Alex Macdonell remained in the background but there could be no mistake about his guidance as he provided the ammunition, boarded the halfbreeds and their families, and sheltered them in his fort "guarded by our artillery," as John Pritchard noted.

After a series of harrowing attacks and more burning of houses "over our heads," the settlers notified Alex Macdonell that they would quit the settlement and be ready to leave in a couple of days. Saulteaux Chief Peguis and forty warriors, sympathetic and friendly toward the settlers, visited Gibraltar asking that the settlers be left to live in peace but finding no willingness to end the aggressions, they visited the settlers offering to escort them down the Red River to the lake. The offer was accepted and the friendly Indians did their part, leaving the fugitives to make their own way across the lake to the Hudson's Bay Company post known as Jack River House. The Settlement was now completely depopulated except for the defiant John McLeod and three of his friends who refused to yield to the North West Company's harassment. Finding a cannon Cameron's friends had overlooked, the determined fellows barricaded themselves in a blacksmith shop and with links cut from a heavy chain for cannonballs, they were able to keep the attackers at a distance. Their self-assigned task was to try to protect the little plots of crop in case the settlers should return.

Settlers having departed, the Métis friends of the North West Company could hardly wait to indulge in the plundering of homes which was to be part of their reward. They raided the Settlement's stores and finally set enough fires to brighten the night skies for miles.

On the eve of departure from the Settlement, James Whyte the surgeon, Archibald MacDonald the young leader, Peter Fidler the man of many parts, and James Sutherland the Chief Factor signed a hastily drawn letter to Lord Selkirk, explaining their reasons for leaving. Without reviewing "past sufferings," they told of the North West Company's guilt in alienating settlers and even converting some to become enemies of the Colony, also about the "40 Halfbreeds who have already pillaged your property, burnt almost all the houses in the settlement, and who are daily continuing such lawless conduct and threatening to involve us in further misfortunes unless we quietly leave the River. ... the Halfbreeds who are without a doubt spurred on by the N.W.Co. will stick at nothing to exterminate the settlement."[15]

Next day, June 25, as settlers embarked by canoe for Jack River, Cuthbert Grant, Bostonois Pangman, William Shaw and Nicholas "Bonhomme" Montour, signing on behalf of the Métis, passed a note of agreement to Sutherland and Whyte, confirming what had been decided, mainly: "All settlers to retire immmediately from this river and no appearance of a Colony to remain."[16]

Even with the stubborn John McLeod clinging to residence in the blacksmith shop, it looked like the end of the Settlement and men of the

North West Company chuckled with satisfaction. Duncan Cameron who was personally escorting the prisoner, Miles Macdonell, and the departing settlers on their way to Upper Canada, was received at Fort William near the end of July like a conquering hero. Although humiliated by a charge of moral softness one year earlier, he was now being showered with praise, especially for his maneuvers in gaining possession of Selkirk field pieces and muskets. Reward for Cameron and Alex Macdonell was reappointment to the same stations they had occupied in the previous year. And for individuals who deserted the Settlement to help Cameron's cause by delivering settlement chattels like guns, tools and horses, there was proper recognition in the form of trading credits. The man who turned in five new guns — even though stolen — received a credit of £10. Men who cooperated generously with Cameron received gratuities ranging from £3 to £20. Surpassing all others in this category of recipients was George Campbell, honored by being seated higher than the Company clerks at the Fort William banquet table and presented with a gift of £100. "Campbell," said Cameron, "is a very decent man, and a great partisan who exposed his life for the North West Company."[17] For Campbell, at least, being a deserter from the Settlement — an enthusiastic one — paid well.

For Fort William, it was a year of rejoicing. For the settlers who fled to Jack River at the far north end of Lake Winnipeg, not sure if they would ever return, it was their most distressing year. And there was no promise that their next year might not be even worse. If they had known how bad it could be and would be, they would never have returned. Moreover, it was difficult to recognize even a ray of hope for an agricultural identity in this hostile land.

CHAPTER TWELVE

Robertson to the Rescue

"I am happy to inform you that the Colony has been all knocked on the head by the N.W.Co.," Simon McGillivray wrote at the beginning of July, 1815.[1] In view of what had just happened at Red River, the downfall of the Settlement seemed like a logical conclusion. Events leading to the destruction were almost exactly as Duncan Cameron and Alexander Macdonell had planned, and colleagues were proclaiming them excellent tacticians.

Miles Macdonell, a prisoner in transit to Montreal where he was to stand trial, was eleven days on his way when news reached the brigade telling of the attack followed by flight of the remaining settlers. He hated his captors more than ever but was powerless. He succeeded in writing a note to Lord Selkirk, in which he concluded sadly that his surrender had not, contrary to promise, saved the Colony. The settlement had been overrun and plundered; buildings were reduced to ashes and cattle driven away, the report explained. The safe departure of the people, Macdonell understood, was due to the good offices of a body of Indians, voluntarily assembled to escort "our people" with their personal belongings "safely out of the river."[2]

Nursing reasons for being both angry and sad, the Governor sat in silence contemplating his probable fate. He knew the warrant for his arrest was born in animosity and it accused him of disturbing the peace; but before he left Fort William, his accusers had Archibald Norman McLeod write a new one, this time charging him with "assisting, counselling and abetting one, John Spencer, on or about the 7th day of June, 1814, at Riviere La Sourie, in the Indian Territory, aforesaid, in breaking open a house or store belonging to a Company of Merchants, trading under the name of the North West Company, and then and there feloniously taking and carrying away a quantity of provisions, viz about 479 bags of pemmican, 93 kegs of grease, 875 lbs. of dried meat. . . ."[3]

The canoe journey, day after day, with nothing to do, was monotonous, especially to an active man. The natural scenery was beautiful but there was nothing else to see — except for that unexpected westbound canoe brigade seen on Lake of the Woods. Inasmuch as Macdonell was the unwilling passenger with the North West Company's brigade, and the passing canoes comprised a Hudson's Bay Company outfit, both steersmen kept their distance without the slightest inclination to exchange greetings. Neither side wanted peering eyes but both sensed something mysterious. It was unusual to see Hudson's Bay Company canoes on this route at any time, and especially unusual to see them westbound in July. And it was no less unusual for North West Company canoes to be moving eastward with women and children as well as men for passengers. But brigade officers on both sides would live with unsatisfied curiosity rather than stop to expose their own passengers.

The North West Company brigade was, of course, the one carrying 134 men, women and children from the settlement, also Miles Macdonell, moving at a uniform rate of forty paddle strokes per minute away from Red River — for most of them, forever. And in the Hudson's Bay Company brigade, westbound, were Colin Robertson and John Clarke and 100 men recruited in Montreal for service in the Athabasca region where the old English Company had suffered repeated intimidation from the trading opposition, and lost out in the business. The 100 men, mainly French Canadians, had been chosen for fighting qualities more than handsome faces. Robertson, the author of the idea, believed that nothing but muscle and force would make an impression.

Soon to be recognized as The Man of the Hour, Colin Robertson — now thirty-six years of age — had worked long enough with the North West Company to understand their tactics thoroughly. His connection with that Company had ended six years earlier when he was dismissed by John McDonald of Garth, but not because he was not well regarded. In joining the Hudson's Bay Company, he brought strong views about the importance of securing a share of Athabasca trade and now he was doing something about it, bringing punching power to the far region.

The Athabasca was regarded as the choicest fur country left on the continent and the North Westers chose to believe they held it by right of discovery. Peter Pond, pronounced the "wildest man" in the fur trade and one who was a pioneer in the North West Company, was the first white man to penetrate to that part for trading. This Connecticut Yankee, in 1778 — three years after pooling his trade goods and sharing his pemmican with Benjamin Frobisher and Alexander Henry to establish the birth of a new and powerful trading Company — went over the Methye Portage, down the Clearwater and into the Athabasca River to build a post about forty miles from the Lake. He was accused of one murder and suspected of another, but deserved to be remembered for some better performances like planting a garden beside his river in 1779, the first in what became Alberta. But it was Pond's harvest of furs, beyond belief in both quantity and quality, that drew the eyes of other Montreal-based traders and brought them to the region. The volume of prime furs in Pond's first winter was so great that he was unable to get all out in the spring.

Naturally, Pond's friends wanted to claim the Athabasca as their own. Why not? Hadn't the Hudson's Bay Company used the Royal Charter granted in 1670 to uphold a perennial claim to trade monopoly in all of Rupert's Land, interpreted as the entire country whose waters drained to Hudson Bay? The North West Company partners and proprietors refused to acknowledge the validity of that Charter and scoffed at the monopoly which its claimant had never been able to enforce. Nevertheless, it did not escape their attention that the Athabasca drainage was to the Arctic — not Hudson Bay — and was not by any stretch of imagination a part of Rupert's Land. If the English Company would try to cling to monopoly trading rights in one area where the validity of a Charter was open to question, why shouldn't the North Westers try to establish and enforce a discoverer's monopoly in Athabasca? It was worth trying and the Montreal men resolved to keep the others out. The English Company, feeling depression resulting from declining fur harvests and rugged competition, needed a share of the good Athabasca trade and was determined to have it.

It was planned that the 100 men in Colin Robertson's expedition would stock up with needed supplies at Jack River, the very place to which the hard-pressed settlers from Red River had gone for refuge. But Robertson, after seeing men, women and children in the eastbound canoe brigade on Lake of the Woods, entertained grave suspicions and was eager to see for himself the state of affairs in the Red River Colony.

At the mouth of the Winnipeg River, Robertson, with twenty of his men, veered southward and up the Red River to Point Douglas, there to discover the awful truth, little left but ruins where innocent people had been trying to make homes. From the indomitable John McLeod and his three-man garrison — Archibald Currie, James McIntosh and Hugh McLean — Robertson was able to obtain the whole shocking story. McLeod and his friends announced in the presence of the attackers that they would represent the Hudson's Bay Company and were not leaving. From their blacksmith shop fortress adorned with a small cannon, they defied the attackers but saw the burning, the theft of horses and the deliberate damage to crops. Robertson listened to the account of Miles Macdonell's arrest, and the other violence leading to evacuation of the Colony. He was horrified but on learning that one-third of the former residents were at Jack River, he recognized a new and clear responsibility. Instead of accompanying the recruited men, he would leave them to John Clarke; as soon as he could communicate his decision to them, they were on their way to Athabasca without him, on their way to face the wrath of Archibald Norman McLeod and his treacherous workers. Robertson would now direct his full attention to the needs of the ejected Colonists.

He was well aware that another group of settlers was already on the way from northern Scotland and something would have to be done for their accommodation, somewhere. It should be at Red River and he had John

McLeod's concurrence that the refugees at Jack River should now return, to try again.

As Robertson anticipated, to persuade the refugees to return to the source of their unhappy memories was not easy. They were fearful of further attacks and some favored going back to their homeland, however they might accomplish it. But Robertson was persuasive and succeeded in convincing them to come back with him.

John McLeod and his trio of friends were elated to see the settlers arriving at Point Douglas on August 19 and had words of encouragement. Demonstrating faith as well as courage, McLeod was already rebuilding what he hoped would be the Governor's house or Fort Douglas, a log structure 40 feet long, 20 feet wide and 16 feet high. Indeed, McLeod and his friends had not been idle; they could point to the growing potatoes from 100 kegs of plantings, all hoed and healthy. And the wheat and barley in the little fields had recovered from the June attempts to destroy them. Soon new huts were arising from the ashes of former ones, some of the men making log homes for the third time.

Exactly one week after Robertson led the remnant of settlers back to Red River, the next contingent of Selkirk people landed at York Factory, eighty-four men, women and children, almost all from the parish of Kildonan in Sutherlandshire. Among them were stalwarts who would be needed urgently, the like of the distinguished leader, Robert Semple, John Matheson who was a school teacher, an expert Scottish miller carrying millstones, and James Sutherland, an elder in the Church of Scotland and who, in the absence of an ordained minister, was authorized by the Presbytery of Ross-shire to marry, baptize, bury the dead, and conduct meetings with much reading of scriptures and long prayers. Semple was coming with a dual appointment, to be Governor of Selkirk's Assiniboia, and Governor-In-Chief of Rupert's Land. He was forty-nine years old, an Englishman born in Boston and likely to be much more popular than the unfortunate Miles Macdonell who was by this time in Montreal. "No person could be better fitted for the situation," said John Halkett. "He was a mild, steady, just and honourable character."[4] In a letter to Colin Robertson, written before leaving York Factory, Semple declared himself for "a due mixture of conciliating measures and of firmness."[5] In the same letter, he thanked Robertson most graciously for the leadership and encouragement he brought to despondent settlers as he found them at Jack River.

The newcomers would have the benefit of Peter Fidler's experience and guidance in making the journey from York to Red River but would not reach their destination until early November. Actually it was November 3, and in the meantime John McLeod's good crop was harvested, 1,500 bushels of wheat and lots of barley and potatoes. That was encouraging but otherwise, sad to say, bitterness and intrigue were again raising their ugly heads in the community, which reached as far as Fort Gibraltar and Qu'Appelle.

Duncan Cameron, disappointed at seeing the Colony's resurrection from its ashes, began again to molest the settlers. Robertson, whose suspicions were ever in tune to the conduct of people with whom he once worked, was watching closely, and when he was informed of an attack upon the Hudson's Bay Company post at Qu'Appelle, of which John Richard MacKay was in charge, he reacted in anger. This had to be the work of Alexander Macdonell and Duncan Cameron, and with no regard for his position of weakness because of the small number of men around him at the time, he resolved to strike. As Cameron, sporting his fine uniform, strolled for health and pleasure beyond the security of his fort, Robertson and his aides sallied forth and arrested him, then moved on to take possession of the fort. In so doing, the assailant recovered two field guns and thirty muskets taken months earlier from Fort Douglas stores.

Cameron was submissive and after giving a promise to leave the settlers alone, he was released and given the return of his fort. The bold act, it was hoped, would serve several purposes: it should remind Cameron that Robertson, as a former North Wester, could be a match in rough tactics. But more important, the forthright action followed by release would serve to demonstrate to the Métis people and freemen that the egotistical Cameron, parading in an officer's uniform as the highest authority on Red River, could be humbled too.

But Robertson was smart enough to know that another storm created by a conflict of interests was brewing. He received reports that Alex Macdonell at Qu'Appelle was up to his old tactics, trying to incite the halfbreeds and Indians by the fear that the settlers were coming to deprive them of their lands. It was an effective ploy: these agriculturally minded immigrants were dangerous people. Cameron added for the benefit of the freemen: "They will prevent you from hunting. They will starve your families."[6] Both Macdonell and Cameron seemed to be saying, too, that the attacks upon the settlement in the previous June proved inconclusive; the next onslaught must be complete and final.

Sensing the growing danger, Robertson wanted to communicate the Colony's need for better protection to Lord Selkirk who was expected in Montreal by the end of autumn. But how was a message to be delivered at such distance under winter conditions? No ships would be moving from York Factory at this season and all direct water connections with Montreal would be frozen. The only means of delivery would be by a reliable messenger on foot. It would be an extremely difficult assignment and Robertson expected trouble in finding a man to take it. To his surprise, he had a volunteer almost immediately: the robust and versatile Jean Baptiste Lagimodière, calling himself a freeman.

This young man was well known to residents, having been engaged to hunt buffalo to sustain the immigrants in the first two winters in the country. He was born in the French Canadian community of Maskinonge, close to the St. Lawrence. In his boyhood he could outrun, outpaddle and outfight any other of his size and age, and when he was old enough he rode away to the far West in a North West Company freight canoe. After four years, he returned to Maskinonge and married his sweetheart of boyhood years and when he wanted to go west again, she insisted, to his horror, that she would go too. It was a land in which no white woman had ever set foot, he insisted, and she should not go. But her will prevailed and the brigade of 1807 carried husband and wife to the new and uncertain Red River area. In successive years she produced the first legitimate white baby in what became the province of Manitoba, the first in Saskatchewan and the first in Alberta. Marie Anne and Jean Baptiste were both making history and when they heard about settlers coming in 1812, they hurried back to Red River to be spectators. Now Jean Baptiste was saying farewell to his wife and children and setting out with nothing more than snowshoes, gun and blankets to carry Colin Robertson's message to Selkirk in Montreal. In sending him on his way, Robertson knew that if anybody could get through to Selkirk, Jean Baptiste Lagimodière was the one.

The colonists had sufficient winter food for a change. Some of Semple's recent arrivals were sent to Pembina to utilize the log huts there but wherever they were, they found comfort in the knowledge that there was wheat in store, potatoes in cellars, fish under the ice and buffalo nearer than usual. But the fear of more violence in the spring was ever present. Cameron seemed subdued for much of the winter but not Alex Macdonell. Rumor had it that the latter was again mustering halfbreeds for a knockout thrust at Point Douglas in the spring.

Governor Semple, although still a stranger in the country, made a trip up that way in December and called on Alex Macdonell. The reception lacked cordiality. Semple took the opportunity to request the return of certain guns stolen from Fort Douglas and was refused. This man was still the major source of dissension and clever at disseminating it. After a winter visit to Qu'Appelle by Cameron, Robertson noticed a difference in his attitude — not for the better. It was presumed to be due to the Macdonell influence. To test him on the promise he had made to leave the settlers alone, Robertson sent one of his people to Fort Gibraltar to act the part of a disgruntled settler. Cameron, sure enough, reacted with an offer to transport the man and his family to Upper Canada. When this came to Robertson's ears, he concluded that Cameron had forfeited his right to freedom. It is just possible that Robertson was over-eager in looking for an excuse for the employment of his expanded manpower.

Anyway, on March 19, Robertson descended upon Fort Gibraltar, seized the post for the second time in half a year and made Cameron a prisoner. This action so corresponded with the wish expressed in a letter Lord Selkirk was writing to him on March 30 that it looked as if the westerner was reading the Earl's mind. The letter would be the first written after receiving Robertson's communication at the hand of Lagimodière and it was to give assurance that: "I shall lose no time in coming to your support." The Earl's main plea was to try to "secure the persons of D. Cameron and Alex. Macdonell," and a few others, Seraphin Lamar, Cuthbert Grant, and William Shaw. "These persons I wish to have kept in safe custody till Mr. Semple's arrival and my own." The trouble was that Robertson would not receive his Lordship's letters for months.[7]

While arresting Cameron, Robertson did not fail to gather up some open letters on the Fort Gibraltar table. In one of these, Cameron was asking friends at Fond du Lac to send Indians for the spring campaign against the Settlement. This was so revealing that Robertson seized all the mail in sight and obtained more proof of the North Westers' plans to crush the Colony, once and for all.

Semple, returning to Red River, approved of Robertson's aggressions and then took the opportunity to draft a list of seven complaints or charges against Cameron and to read them to him while he was a most uncomfortable and captive audience:

1) You are accused of seducing His Majesty's subjects settled on Red River and the servants of the Earl of Selkirk to desert and defraud their masters and one to whom the former were largely indebted.

2) Of collecting, harbouring and encouraging Halfbreeds and vagabonds with the avowed purpose of destroying an Infant British Colony.

3) Through the means of these men thus collected, of firing upon, wounding and causing the death of His Majesty's subjects defending their property in their own houses.

4) Through the means of these men headed by your clerks or the clerks of the N.W.Co., such as Cuthbert Grant, Charles Hesse, Bostonois Pangman, William Shaw and others of burning a fort, a mill, sundry houses, carts, ploughs and instruments of agriculture belonging to the said infant Colony.

5) Of wantonly destroying English cattle brought here at an immense expense and of carrying off horses, dogs, and other property to a large amount.

6) Of encouraging Indian tribes to make war upon British subjects attempting to colonize, representing to them according to their ideas that cattlemen would spoil their lands and make them miserable, and expressing your hope they would never allow it.

7) Without unnecessarily multiplying charges it appears now by your own letters that you were making every preparation to renew the same atrocities this year, if possible on a more extensive scale, collecting the Halfbreeds from points still more distant than before. . . .

Such are the principal charges you will be called upon to answer. It would be easy but at present unnecessary to swell the catalogue. . . .[8]

Robertson's successful seizure at the Forks inspired his inexperienced friends at Fort Daer to take the neighboring North West Company post and in so doing, take the well-known Métis, Bostonois Pangman, as a prisoner. But this only vexed the halfbreeds generally, actually helping the Macdonell-Cameron cause more than hurting it. Robertson was annoyed because it damaged a relationship with certain influential halfbreeds he was trying to cultivate in friendship.

Now, what was to be done with the prisoner, Cameron? Robertson feared that holding him would invite Macdonell's halfbreeds to attack for reasons of rescue and favored sending him away quickly to York Factory and on to England for trial. But Semple was vacillating and Robertson was becoming annoyed at the Governor's indecision. It was a Semple weakness becoming clear.

At this point, a letter came to Cameron from Alex Macdonell, and Robertson, to be sure, opened it. Telling Cameron that "the storm" would soon break, it was a clear revelation of intention. With supreme confidence, the writer said: ". . . A storm is gathering in the North ready to burst on the rascals who deserve it; little do they know their situation. Last year was but a joke. . . ."[9]

Acts of violence were being reported more commonly from the west. A Hudson's Bay Company brigade of six boats carrying pemmican came under Métis attack and was robbed of its provisions for use in the Red River campaign which was expected to start soon. Next, about forty-eight halfbreeds broke into Brandon House and indulged in joyful plunder while the residents were prevented from leaving. In due course, the attackers left but, after nightfall, thinking they had overlooked some gunpowder and spirits the first time, returned for a second search. As Peter Fidler told it, their threats to burn the fort led some of the Hudson's Bay Company servants to sleep out with the "Crees and Stones" that night. "Better company," he added.

Colin Robertson, upon hearing of these trespasses, wanted to pursue and try to force recovery of the lost goods, perhaps head off a more serious attack. But Semple, the more temperate and cautious person, was not inclined to immediate action. He preferred to wait for the insurgents to carry the fight to him. Unable to endure inaction any longer, Robertson announced that he was taking his prisoner and going to York Factory. His last word of advice, however, was about the folly of an order to pull down Fort Gibraltar and use the logs to reinforce Fort Douglas. This more than anything, he was sure, would infuriate Alex Macdonell and the Métis and drive them to an all-out offensive. But this time, Semple acted with determination and about as soon as Robertson was on his way, he and thirty men began to dismantle the neighboring post and float the logs down to complete the house and fort which John McLeod had started during the previous summer. Similar action was directed at the North Wester's fort at Pembina, with anything of use or value being floated down to the Settlement.

By this time, Robertson and Cameron were well on their way but as it turned out, the trip was a mistake because they arrived at York Factory after the ships had left for the season and Cameron had to be held there for almost a year. It was all a mistake because in England the charges against Cameron were dropped and he returned to Canada with a case against those responsible for his arrest and detention and succeeded in gaining a damage award of about £3,000. The only good thing about the enforced absence from Assiniboia was that both he and Robertson missed the awful clash of June 19.

CHAPTER THIRTEEN

The Awful Day of Seven Oaks

June 19, 1816, was the awful day, casting a pall of deathly gloom over the riverside Colony. Surviving men were crazed by frustration; women and children could not curb their tears as the dead from the brief but conclusive battle were counted, and all responsible adults were obliged to consider their next move forthwith. Of the twenty-two dead, twenty-one including the Governor were from the side of the Colony; one was from the other side. Almost a score of the cabin homes along the river were suddenly without husbands and fathers.

"Will Miles Macdonell's Pemmican War never end?" some were asking in anguish. "Does it have to be a war of extermination?"

To the latter question, certain individuals in the fur trade were, by their actions, answering "Yes," contending that there was not room in this land for both fur interests and farming — and furs deserved the priority. The native people could still hear, ringing in their ears, the speech said to have been made by Duncan Cameron as he faced a group of freeman and halfbreeds: "The purpose of our sending for you at this time is that you should engage with us [in] destroying or dispersing the colonists on the river for which you shall be supplied with all the necessaries for your equipment, such as horses, arms, ammunition and clothing. If they should disregard this warning, you are then to destroy and exterminate them by every means in your power, and you shall be rewarded with all the plunder and property which you may find in the Colony belonging to it. . . . If the colonists are allowed to increase, the consequence will be that they will make you slaves, put hoes and spades in your hands and oblige you to till the ground for them."[1]

The complainants could have been pardoned for failure to penetrate the future, even 150 years, to see an annual production of 500,000,000 bushels of wheat and other grains and animal products in similar proportion coming from the same fur country, but here was a battle being fought primarily to prevent an experimental search for something more beneficial and more enduring than furs.

That the clash of the day was so completely one-sided made it the more shocking and suggested massacre. But was it massacre or just an unfortunate battle with rashness on both sides? The debate was to continue for years and, as is common in human nature, each side blamed the other. Governor Semple could hardly be called the aggressor and yet he was leading a party with arms toward the mounted Métis. And the halfbreed leader, Cuthbert Grant, could insist, in his own self-defense, that he had a clear and legitimate purpose in riding to the river to reach it at a point a couple of miles north of the Forks. He was quite obviously veering away from Fort Douglas, possibly to avoid an immediate confrontation with Semple's people.

But the credibility of Grant's story of his alleged desire to avoid being offensive was weakened by promises of violence from his scheming sponsor, Alexander Macdonell at Qu'Appelle. Displaying regret that the attacks upon the Colony in the previous year had been inconclusive, having failed to effect permanent riddance of the settler menace, he promised that the 1816 effort would be different and make that of the previous year seem like a "trifle." Less than ninety days before the 19th of June, while he was making every attempt to recruit halfbreeds for his evil design, a letter intercepted by Colin Robertson assured that one of the leaders, William Shaw, was "collecting all the Halfbreeds in the surrounding Departments and has ordered his friends in this quarter to prepare for the field. . . . God only knows the result."[2]

Nobody except the Deity might comprehend all, but the evil and cheerful designer at Qu'Appelle could promise a brilliant show, as his words made clear: "Notwithstanding all that is to be done, you will see some sport in Red River before the Month of June is over. . . ." It would thus be difficult to hold this man and his side blameless for the terrible disaster that came close, indeed, to extinguishing the Colony, permanently.

Certainly there was provocation on both sides and Alexander Macdonell could think very properly of directing a force to rescue his friend and colleague, Duncan Cameron, from the clutches of Colin Robertson. And to all loyal servants with the North West Company, the supreme act of arrogance came following the second seizure of Fort Gibraltar when Governor Semple, on June 10, ordered the dismantling of the post. In the succeeding days, all useful parts were floated downstream to be incorporated in Fort Douglas and what remained, including one bastion, was destroyed by burning. Governor Semple had to assume full responsibility because even Colin Robertson had disapproved and had left the Colony while the demolition was under way. More than anything that happened in the early part of that year, the complete destruction of Fort Gibraltar looked like an Act of War and made Cuthbert Grant and his Métis followers firm in their conviction that they were embarking upon a righteous cause. W. B. Coltman, who was appointed a Commissioner to investigate the trouble, believed that Semple, by this particular act, "put an end to all probable prospect of an amicable settlement," and left him depending solely on "physical force for the protection of the Colony."

Whatever his errors and weaknesses, Semple appeared to be confident. Those who brought warnings about the growing dangers found him cheerful and unworried. Robertson was not one to be frightened easily but he was a practical fellow and Semple's easy-going way drove him to the decision to leave on June 11. He left in anger. When he relented and sent back a message to tell the Governor of his willingness to return if wanted, the offer was declined.

Perhaps the Semple self-assurance was acquired in part from other people around him. Commissioner W. B. Coltman drew from Francis Delorme, an interpreter in Semple's service, an observation that the fighting strength of the halfbreeds was being underestimated. In the course of conversation with the Governor and John Pritchard a few days before the battle, Delorme offered some advice about the best strategy in the event of conflict and warned that the colonists would not have much chance of success in an engagement against the Métis on the plains, although they would have substantial strength when fighting within the protection of their own fort. Pritchard scoffed, saying that "50 Englishmen were equal to 200 Half-breeds," to which the interpreter felt constrained to add that "50 Halfbreeds on the plains would kill 200 Englishmen."[3]

On the 17th, two days before the battle, a friendly halfbreed, Moustouche Boutino, who recalled a debt from once having a wound treated by the Colony doctor, came to Fort Douglas to warn that Alexander Macdonell and Cuthbert Grant and a party of halfbreeds, apparently prepared for war, had reached Portage la Prairie and could be at Red River, probably to attack, within two days. His information was that the intention was to capture Fort Douglas and take the Governor as a prisoner in retaliation for the arrest of Duncan Cameron. If there was resistance or an armed threat, the Métis would open fire.

Nor was the friendly halfbreed alone in trying to be helpful. In the course of the same day, two Saulteaux chiefs and about ten of their followers came to offer active aid in case of attack. The Governor, still unworried, thanked the chiefs for their generous intentions but said he did not look with fear upon the prospect of attack and thought the Indians should keep out of the quarrels that non-Indians were having among themselves.

The friendly halfbreed was right about the mounted troop at Portage la Prairie, riding toward the Forks. The explanation given to the investigating Commissoner was that sixty to seventy men under the skillful command of Cuthbert Grant were riding to furnish escort for two cartloads of pemmican — twenty bags of the stuff — to be delivered at a certain point on the Red River to meet the need of canoemen in a brigade expected from Fort William.[4]

The Qu'Appelle troop of this year was ahead of that of the previous year in organization and training. Alexander Macdonell saw to that. Michael Bourassa and Antoine Houle were captains of the group which included four Indians, six Canadians and the balance halfbreeds. Most of them had been servants of the North West Company, many of the halfbreeds and Canadians having served as Company clerks and interpreters and others had been canoemen in Company brigades. One thing they had in common, regardless of pedigree, was a wild, free spirit that would rebel against restraint or more than a modicum of civilization. They followed their captain-general, Cuthbert Grant, with complete trust.

Grant was one-quarter Indian and three-quarters white. His father, Cuthbert Grant, senior, was a Scot, and his mother a native woman of mixed blood. The boy was born at the post his father operated on the upper Assiniboine River, in 1793. After the father's death in 1798, the boy, with William McGillivray as guardian, and with money from the estate, went to school in the East and in Scotland. On his return to his native land, there was, quite naturally, a position as clerk with the North West Company awaiting him.

For just such a young man, the Company would find many uses — and here was one. While working in various parts of the Company's trading area, he met and impressed many of the leaders in the trade, including John Pritchard in whom a lasting respect developed. By his position and capability and personality, he was able to exercise wide influence. And through marriage, his influence was extended still more. One sister was the wife of John Wills who was stationed at Fort Gibraltar for a time, and Elizabeth MacKay to whom Grant was married, was a sister of John Richard MacKay of the Hudson's Bay Company at Brandon House.

But while he was a hero to the Métis, Cuthbert Grant was soon to be the most feared and hated man of the country to the settlers, at least for a few years. In the course of time, with the help of the Hudson's Bay Company, he won the respect of almost everybody along the two rivers. But as of this moment, he was entering the lives of the Red River residents like an evil monster.

It was a calm evening when the June days were long and the hours of darkness short that a young man in the watchtower at Fort Douglas dropped his spyglass and raised the alarm: "The Halfbreeds are coming."

The Governor and several other men nearby — including John Pritchard to whom Canadians are most indebted for an eyewitness account of all that happened that day — stepped forward to peer through the glass. The young fellow at the lookout was right; armed men on horses were approaching along the river road. They didn't seem to be in much hurry but there was an immediate stir of excitement in the fort. Governor Semple and a few of the men conferred briefly and then the Governor announced: "We must go at once to meet these people. Let twenty men follow me."[5]

By Pritchard's estimate, there were between sixty and seventy men at the Fort at the time and twenty-six including himself, stepped forward, reached for their guns and stood ready to accompany. Whatever faults Semple may have had, lack of loyalty to his own people was not one of them and all present were prepared to follow his instructions. But he made it clear that he did not want any more to go with him.

By this time, the horsemen were seen to change their course and move northeasterly to bypass Fort Douglas. It made no difference to the Governor; he was going to meet them or intercept them anyway. He started boldly, with his men filing after him, to go north on the trail skirting the river at sufficient distance from the water to leave most of the homes between the road and the stream. As the twenty-seven brave fellows advanced, they met many settlers fleeing to the fort, making no effort to hide their fear.

After having traveled about a mile, an opening in the trees gave Semple a clear view of the horsemen against the evening sun, now appearing more numerous than originally estimated. With this realization, he called a brief halt and instructed John Burke, the storekeeper, to return to the fort for "a piece of cannon" which the Governor had declined to take in the first place. But the Governor felt they should not wait for the three-pounder field piece — which never did arrive at the scene of the conflict — and pressed forward.

Almost at once they found themselves facing the mounted horsemen, frightening to see. Although the majority were Métis, many were feathered and painted like Indians advancing on the warpath. In view of this and the disparity in numbers, a sudden sense of danger came over the Fort Douglas men. Pritchard told that "by common impulse," they began to retreat, "walking backwards, at the same time extending their line."

The horsemen changed courses again, advanced toward the Governor's party at a gallop and "surrounded them in the form of a half moon." At such close range, any rash act could start a war. One of the so-called Canadians, Boucher, identified the Governor and rode up to him, making wild gesticulations and shouting: "What do you want?"

The Governor replied: "What do you want?"

"We want our fort," Boucher answered.

"Then go to your fort," the Governor replied, knowing, of course, that the fort for which the man inquired was Gibraltar, now dismantled and destroyed.

The two men were now very close and the Governor, perhaps unwisely, reached forward and took hold of Boucher's gun. The testimony given to Commissioner Coltman by Michael Heyden differed only slightly. Boucher, according to this witness, addressed the Governor, saying: "Why did you destroy our fort, you damned rascal," to which Semple replied by grabbing the bridle of Boucher's horse and shouting: "Scoundrel, do you tell me so!", then calling on his men to take the man prisoner.[6]

The act of seizing either the gun or the bridle would, in the heat of the moment, foment another act and almost immediately, according to Pritchard, "a general discharge of firearms took place." But Pritchard, with a reputation for honesty, was ready to admit that he could not be certain about the side from which the first shots came. In any case, the outcome was sure and fast. "In a few minutes almost all the Governor's party were either killed or wounded." Still the survivors were shown no mercy; Captain John Rogers, "having fallen, rose up again . . . ran toward the enemy . . . raising up his hands and in English and broken French, called out for mercy." The answer was a shot through the head. Near him, dead, were James White, the Colony doctor; Alexander MacLean, a leading farmer, and J. P. Wilkinson, the private secretary to the Governor.

Semple, as Cuthbert Grant explained the circumstances to John Pritchard, was wounded by a shot from the gun of the Métis chief himself, but totally conscious. Lying on the ground with his hip shattered, Semple spoke, asking his assailant if he were Mr. Grant. Being answered in the affirmative, he said: "I am not mortally wounded and if you could get me conveyed to the Fort, I think I should live."[7] Grant indicated willingness to accommodate the request and left the wounded man in the care of one of his followers, only to have an Indian ride in quickly and shoot him in the breast.

John Pritchard, who was to leave the best and most reliable account of everything, was one of the few Semple men to escape death that day. About the only others to survive were the ones who fled at the outset of shooting. Pritchard owed his escape to the fact that he was well known to many of those riding with Grant. After being a clerk in North West Company service for thirteen years — for nine of them in the Assiniboine Valley and two of them as master of the fort at Qu'Appelle—he should have friends among the Métis people, and did. He was in charge of Fort Souris on that day in 1814 when Sheriff Spencer and his men forced their way in and seized a large quantity of pemmican on Miles Macdonell's orders. But thinking of quitting the rough-and-tumble of fur trading, he could think of no place more attractive for retirement than the Red River Settlement. Miles Macdonell and Lord Selkirk gave their approval. Obtaining the blessing of William McGillivray at Fort William in 1814 was not as easy, because the North West Company chief was hoping to depopulate rather than populate the Red River district. McGillivray offered to find an attractive alternative homesite at York in Upper Canada, but Pritchard's heart was set on Red River where he had many acquaintances. But with McGillivray's opposition, he knew he would have difficulty getting back to Red River and his plan was to travel to Montreal and then on a 4,000-mile roundabout journey via Hudson Bay and York Factory, all to allow retirement at Red River.

So it was on that day of battle, Pritchard went through without a scratch but it pained him to see the awful loss and the grief created, twenty-one of his Red River neighbors dead and one dead and one wounded among Cuthbert Grant's sixty-two followers. It was fortunate that as a prisoner of the victorious side, Pritchard could talk with Grant and do something to ease the distress of the colonists. Grant told him, candidly, that what he was doing was on behalf of the North West Company "and not for any other cause." He said, also, that he did not expect to be fighting the colonists that day but when the Governor led his troop in arms to intercept the Métis, a battle was almost inevitable. Grant had expected the conflict would take another form on another day, probably an "ambush," with the halfbreeds, taking instructions from Alex Macdonell, seeking to starve the residents into surrender and abandonment of the riverside. The destruction of the Colony would then follow.

As a prisoner, Pritchard was taken to the Métis camp at nearby Frog Plain where Grant told him that an attack would be made on Fort Douglas that night and if the occupants fired a single shot, bloodshed would follow. At this point Pritchard pleaded for the lives of women, children and men at the fort and asked what Grant would demand to assure against more violence and loss of lives.

If the colonists would surrender all their property, they would be allowed to leave in peace, Grant replied. He would even provide them with an escort until they had safely passed the North West Company's trading area around the river and lake. This he believed necessary because of two other parties of halfbreeds in the river area, one under the command of William Shaw, son of Angus Shaw, and the other under Simon McGillivray, son of the Honorable William McGillivray. Clearly, Grant's real objective was the abandonment of the settlement.

Pritchard asked if he might be permitted to convey Grant's terms to the Sheriff at the fort, with a promise to return to resume the role of prisoner in Grant's hands. The Métis chief considered and then agreed that Pritchard might go, but warned him to be careful how he acted and to realize that he could not escape and death would be the price for trying.

Pritchard went out into the night and found Fort Douglas a place of intense grief and mourning, "women, children and relatives of the slain being in perfect agony . . . and despairing for the lives of those who yet survive." Although it was late at night when Pritchard left Grant's camp the first time, he made three trips back and forth before obtaining a clear understanding between Sheriff Alexander MacDonell and the Métis chief.

It was Grant's order that the settlers would have to be away in two days. In the meantime, he authorized an inventory of all the goods and equipment being left behind, with one copy of the list going to Sheriff MacDonell and one kept for the North West Company.

Suddenly, Grant called for a delay in leaving. It was difficult to understand but then it became known that the master intriguer, Alexander Macdonell had sent word that he was coming and wished to be present to see the settlers leave. It was known that he accompanied Grant's troop from Qu'Appelle to Portage la Prairie and he may not have been very far away at any time. The settlers did not want to see him, the women particularly. They did not trust him. Pritchard communicated this fear to Grant who seemed to understand and offered to personally take up a guard duty and sleep in the fort for the next couple of nights, a safeguard against prowlers.

Once ready to go, the settlers were anxious to be leaving the scenes of so many unhappy memories, and Pritchard again interceded with Grant, inquiring why they should be waiting for Macdonell who would want only to steal some of the glory of the Colony's collapse, steal it away from Grant as Pritchard took pains to suggest. Grant was impressed and ordered the canoes to leave as soon as the Declaration he prepared was signed. The Declaration read: "All hostilities to cease on both sides. All prisoners to be immediately released. The Hudson's Bay traders to be respected and private property of the whole settlers, officers and servants to be protected until out of the N.W.Co. tract in Lake Winipic. A sufficiency of provisions to be given the whole until they reach York Factory and all the boats and vessels sufficient to bring the whole settlers, officers, servants and baggage.... Upon the foresaid conditions I promise to embark on the river here in the course of the day on 25th. Forks of Red River, 20th June, 1816."[8]

The Proclamation carried Cuthbert Grant's signature and all the residents along the river were expected to sign.

John Pritchard may have thought he was going to Jack River with the settlers — as he had done in the previous year, but he was wrong. On the second day of travel, the boats were intercepted on the lake by a North West Company brigade carrying a party of senior officials and partners, Archibald Norman McLeod, Sir Alexander Mackenzie, Simon Fraser and so on. McLeod asked if Robert Semple were in the party and was told that he was dead. He then inquired for John Pritchard and when that worthy was pointed out, McLeod ordered him and certain other selected individuals, listed for arrest on McLeod's warrants, to be transferred to the eastbound canoes, to be conveyed under guard to Fort William and then to Montreal for trial. The charges were not explained.

Here were more sorrowful separations. Was there nothing left in this land except grief? men and women were asking. Just to think: the soil was so good and generous and the human reception so despicable! For some of those being paddled away, it was like entering the unknown. For some, too, it was the second such sad retreat in a year from homes they were growing to love. It seemed most unlikely that they would ever return after the second eviction. They hoped to go to Jack River and possibly on to York Factory and back to the homeland where they would never be rich but had a good chance of being safe. Red River would be a bad memory. How cruel were the ways of humans!

If only they could tell their troubles to Lord Selkirk!

CHAPTER FOURTEEN

Selkirk on the Way

News traveled no faster than the speed of a birchbark canoe on a summer stream or a man with snowshoes in winter. More than four months passed before Lord Selkirk heard about the 1815 destruction of his river Colony. It was a shocking revelation with which to be greeted as he and Lady Selkirk arrived at New York, en route to Montreal; and yet it might not have been a total surprise because a strong premonition of danger to the colonists began to grip him a short time before sailing from Liverpool on September 8.

Conscious of his own uncertain health, the Earl was bringing his new family physician, Dr. John Allan, a young man not yet out of his twenties and only recently discharged from the Imperial Navy. The plan was to take a house in Montreal for the winter where Jean Selkirk might remain when the Earl traveled west to see his Colony on the Red. How he longed to cast his eyes upon the setting which was familiar to him only in his imagination.

The report about the attacks upon the Colony was most disturbing. He wanted more information but details were distressingly difficult to obtain. He hastened to Montreal, expecting he would learn everything about the invasion. He heard only that 134 of the colonists had deserted to accept the North West Company offer of transportation to Upper Canada and that the remainder had taken flight to the north end of Lake Winnipeg. Beyond that Montreal seemed to maintain a stony silence.

The Earl should have realized, of course, that Montreal was North West Company territory, with the senior partners dominating the city's social and business life. They had the most money and the most influence. William McGillivray might have been voted the Leading Citizen. He maintained one of the most expensive homes and had been named recently to the high office of Legislative Councilor, partly in recognition of the help his North West Company voyageurs played in the capture of Michilimackinac during the War of 1812, partly because of his standing in the community. Now he was the Honorable William McGillivray. All this was understandable but Montreal's aloofness to Lord and Lady Selkirk on their arrival was more difficult to explain. There should have been something in the nature of a public greeting. It smacked of prejudice on the part of a community taking sides in a conflict raging far to the west.

In departing London, Lord Selkirk was supplied with Hudson's Bay Company authorization for an approach to the Montreal Company on that thorny question of bringing order to the trade. Although never an admirer of North West Company practices, he was hopeful for a negotiated arrangement which would remove the cruel and costly competition from the industry, either by partitioning the trading area or cooperating in some manner. The letter from Governor Joseph Berens, Jun., to Selkirk just before the Earl's departure from Britain indicated willingness to explore for a possible solution, provided there was full acceptance of one very basic and almost sacred principle, namely the validity of the Hudson's Bay Company Charter. "In any compromise with the N.W. Co.," Berens wrote, "the main object to be attended to is the preservation of the chartered rights of the H.B. Co. . . . If the N.W. Co. acknowledge these rights by relenquishing to us all their posts within these limits [meaning Rupert's Land] and agree not to occupy any new ones without our permission, we will agree to debar ourselves from trading in Athabasca to the north of our territories, or in Canada to the south of the height of land."[1]

Indeed, the English Company officials would be willing to consider a further concession if it would bring a certain end to the violence: to allow the North West Company, under specified conditions, to use Hudson Bay water for shipping. Altogether, it meant that the Earl was in a favorable position for bargaining, but those wickedly inspired aggressions against his Colony in recent months robbed him of his enthusiasm. He would have trouble in maintaining a poise of good will and forgiveness in the presence of William McGillivray or A. N. McLeod long enough to conduct a discussion. Nevertheless, he did talk with John Richardson, mainly to explore possible boundaries if a division of territory were favored. And, of course, a substantial part of the western trading ground was the Earl's private property and he did not hesitate to make the point very clear. Not even the directors of the Hudson's Bay Company could make any contract with that land which, he said, "is my separate and independent property." In any case, the climate for negotiation was not favorable. The Earl could not hide that animosity and distrust which he revealed to Joseph Berens before leaving England — also before hearing of the latest indignities at Red River.

"However respectable many members of the North West Company may be," he wrote, "we know that among their partners are individuals who have hardly a better notion of law or justice than the Indians themselves; men with uncultivated minds and impetuous passions." Under the circumstances, the necessity of affording protection to ensure the safety of the colonists, "should be apparent, especially to Governments."

Joseph Berens, on behalf of the Company, communicated Selkirk's concern to Lord Bathurst, Colonial Minister, asking that a small military force be directed to Red River. The Colonial Secretary, in turn, wrote to Sir Gordon Drummond, Governor General in Canada, asking for his views about Selkirk's wish. Just why the Colonial Secretary would turn to Sir Gordon is not clear; in the first place, the gentleman probably knew nothing more concerning the Red River situation than was being told in Montreal street conversation, and secondly, he had no jurisdiction whatever in the remote district of Red River.

In making the request for information and guidance, the Colonial Secretary cautioned Sir Gordon against any act or expression of an opinion "which may tend to affect the question in dispute between the Hudson's Bay and the North West Companies."[3]

Notwithstanding the warning to avoid any act which might tend to affect the question in dispute, "the Governor General turned to the most unlikely persons for advice," to William McGillivray, the senior official in the Montreal Company. The letter marked "Confidential" and signed by the Governor General's secretary, recognized that "some of the servants of the North West Company are suspected of being concerned in this diabolical plot." But, the letter added, Sir Gordon had such high respect for the "heads of that most repectable body that he has not hesitated to ask them for the information which they possess and which His Excellency is equally assured they are too honorable and conscientious to withhold."[4]

McGillivray had indeed gained a high degree of favor with the governing officers. His Montreal image was one which others might well covet and, naturally, he would wish to safeguard it. His reply to the letter was written at almost the exact time the Métis and servants of McGillivray's Company were mounting their attack on the settlement. The letter was a denial in the most solemn terms of "allegations whereon this shameful accusation is founded." Instead of doing the settlers an injury, he explained, his Company fed them during their first winter in the country when, otherwise, they would have starved while waiting for Lord Selkirk to fulfill his promises. If there were quarrels at Red River, they would arise, no doubt, from the "arrogant and violent conduct of Lord Selkirk's agents."[5]

McGillivray's suave reply was, by John Harvey's admission, sufficient to completely remove "from His Excellency's mind all traces of an impression unfavourable to the honourable character and liberal principles of the heads of the North West Company, had any such impression existed." Sir Gordon concluded that "if lives and property of the Earl of Selkirk's settlers are or may hereafter be endangered, that danger will arise principally from the conduct of Mr. Miles Macdonell, His Lordship's agent, who appears to His Excellency to be actuated by anything but a spirit of moderation and conciliation in his language and demeanour towards the servants of the North West Company."[6]

By this time, still unknown to the people in the East, Miles Macdonell was a prisoner, soon to be delivered to law officers in Montreal, and the Colony was in a state of destruction from having been brutally broken up by Métis attacks instigated by partners and servants of the North West Company. But enough had been said and done to ruin Lord Selkirk's chance of obtaining a military force for the protection of the much-exposed colonists, presuming, of course, that those driven out would return and those expected as newcomers in late 1815 would arrive. It was suggested by officials searching for reasons for refusing requests for soldiers that sending a military unit to Red River might be the means of starting an Indian war. Why run the risk of starting a more serious conflict when guilt for the existing one was so difficult to apportion? No military force would be provided.

By October, the 134 settlers who accepted North West Company transportation to the East, were in Upper Canada, many of them subsisting on rations issued on the authority of the Governor General. Miles Macdonell was in Montreal, unlikely to be brought to trial. For anybody who wanted it, more information about the attacks which wrecked the Colony at Red River was now available, but McGillivray still blamed Miles Macdonell and the Colony for what happened; and Selkirk and Macdonell blamed the North Westers for putting the Métis up to it.

It was a long winter for Lord Selkirk as he waited for word concerning the forty or fifty of the settler people who fled the Settlement in June. Finally, Colin Robertson's report carried by the robust Jean Baptiste Lagimodière over almost 2,000 miles of winter's snow, was delivered on March 10. It confirmed that the destruction of the Settlement was almost complete, but there was some good news also, that those settlers who had fled northward had halted at Jack River and had finally been persuaded by Colin Robertson to return. They had come back to find their crops recovering from the June beating and were rebuilding when the messenger was sent away. The fourth contingent of settlers, headed by Robert Semple who would be the new Governor, had not arrived but was expected at any time. The main part of Robertson's message was a call for help. He needed and would need mén and guns.

What about it? Should the Earl carry out his plan to go west? The few friends who constituted his advisers — mainly Dr. John Allan who was his physician, and Samuel Gale, a junior law partner with James Stuart, believed he should not go. The risks were too great. Something approaching a state of war existed and the Earl would be a marked man. Actual threats against his life had been sounded, but he was undeterred. He did not abandon hope of securing a small military force to accompany. With more settlers arriving so soon after the recent collapse of the Colony, something in the way of protection was needed more than ever. He would renew his request, try again to obtain a government force.

But official policy was unchanged. Sir Gordon Drummond reported to Lord Bathurst that military protection for the Colony was, in his opinion, "decidedly impractical." Even the Earl's plea for ten artillerymen was denied and he was told by officials trying desperately to justify their actions or lack of action that the North West Company had made a similar request for a military guard to protect their interests against Hudson's Bay

Company and Selkirk Settlement aggressors. It was proably a clever ploy on the part of the North Westers who had demonstrated an unusual ability to look after themselves. But they succeeded in impressing the Governor General with the point that "they are as much entitled as any other class of His Majesty's subjects."[7]

Then to make the official point more convincing, the Earl was reminded that the decisions with respect to soldiers were being made for his security; a military escort as requested might have an unexpected effect and end in "your destruction and annihilation of the escort."

Both the Imperial and Colonial leaders, in their wisdom, reached the conclusion that the entire Selkirk scheme was ill-advised. Why an agricultural colony out there in the fur country anyway? Wouldn't it be better to have a fur industry with proven antecedents and guarantee of a future than a struggling agriculture plagued by harsh climate and cold soil?

One of John Halkett's letters to Selkirk reported an interview with Lord Bathurst, confirming beyond doubt the Ministry's poor opinion of the whole program. The noble Lord could see some merit in sending a military force to the far West to protect the Indians, but as for the non-Indians, if they were so reckless as to go into that remote part, they could fight it out among themselves and settle their own differences. Halkett sensed outright opposition and heard Bathurst say "he regretted you [Selkirk] had embarked in the scheme," an undertaking he considered "wild and unpromising."[8]

Officialdom chose to believe it was discharging its duty by simply calling publicly for an end to the outrages being perpetrated by both Companies. If either side or any individual persisted, there would be punishment. But apparently the people needing the warning were not listening to the proclamation and the worst outrage of all was just ahead.

Nevertheless, the Earl's determination to make the trip to Red River brought the Governor General to agree to a minor concession: while denying a force of even moderate size, he would and did grant Lord Selkirk leave to take a small and strictly private bodyguard, "solely for the purpose of your personal protection." This was followed by the issuance of a commission making him a Justice of the Peace in Indian Territory.

As the order for a guard was given, "His Excellency, the Major General Commanding, is pleased to approve a party consisting of a non-commissioned officer and six privates being detached from the Company of the 37th Regiment stationed at Drummond's Island, Lake Huron, as an escort for the personal protection of the Earl of Selkirk during his intended journey through the Indian country. This party is to be composed, provisioned and brought back to their station at His Lordship's expense."[9] Selkirk had no hesitation in accepting the conditions. Not only would he be willing to pay the cost of a personal guard, but he indicated readiness to finance the bigger military group if it were authorized. But approval for the bigger and more important body of men being refused, he turned to the idea of a group of discharged soldiers which for official purposes would be a party of prospective settlers for the Red River Colony, but unofficially, the Earl's private army. As it happened a battalion of foreign soldiers, mainly Swiss mercenaries who served during the War of 1812-14, was being disbanded. Selkirk hired eighty privates and four officers of these so-called de Meurons, named for a former Commanding Officer. Other ex-soldiers were employed to bring the total to about 100. These men would accompany the Earl to Red River as paid servants rather than as soldiers but keep their guns handy at all times. They would have the privilege of becoming settlers on Red River land the Earl would make available if they so desired. Colonial officials might not endorse this expedition with more than a slight military character but they were obliged to admit that what Selkirk was doing was not illegal, and he prepared to travel.

Making ready to move was like placing an invading army in the field. Near spring, the Earl drove by horse and sleigh from Montreal to York — later Toronto — to advance his plans and engage some specialized helpers like Alexander Wood, who was to become his official agent there, and Thomas Clark, who would supervise the ordering and assembling of supplies. Having completed certain arrangements and driven back to Montreal, he could prepare messages for Colin Robertson and place them in the hands of Jean Baptiste Lagimodière who, hopefully, would return to Red River with the same expedition which marked his eastward trip. But Jean Baptiste's return was disappointing; he grew fond of Montreal and was in no hurry to start back and then, when he was on his way, he yielded to temptation in and about York and remained too long. In the course of his celebrations, he talked injudiciously until friends of the North West Company thereabout knew as much concerning Lord Selkirk's plans as Jean Baptiste knew. Because of those indiscretions in speech, the North West Company people knew he was coming and he was captured by Indians acting for the Montreal men and taken as a prisoner to Fort William.

Miles Macdonell, a free man once more, was preparing to return to Red River. He would leave a few days earlier than Lord Selkirk, with a small party. Lord Selkirk believed that the appearance of Macdonell in the river community would have a beneficial effect, "demonstrating how little the boasting threats of the N.W. have realized."[10] The Earl with his personal escort of regulars from Drummond's Island began the journey on June 17, just two days before the awful affair at Seven Oaks. His course of travel would be by Fond du Lac on the west side of Lake Superior, a route less likely to see North West Company travelers.

The journey would be long and tiring but nobody would be hungry if the requisitioned supplies could be delivered as planned. An initial list of food and arms ordered included the following items:

100 barrels of prime pork	@ $28.00
2000 pounds of lard or grease	@ .20
500 gallons of high wines	@ .50
2500 pounds of gunpowder	@ 1.00
100 "musquets" with bayonets	@ 18.00

    4 light six-pounders or smaller
    2 nine-pounders
  300 rounds of shot
   12 boats
      Sails and rigging for same[11]

Then there was a supplementary list of supplies to be forwarded to Sault Ste. Marie, including another 500 gallons of wine, 4,000 pounds of tobacco, 20 barrels of gunpowder, 50 muskets, 2 brass guns weighing about 500 pounds each, and by special request from the Earl, 2,000 pounds of beef, "slightly corned" as a change from pork. And to create a minimum of suspicion when traveling through North West Company country, the guns were to be packed, "like ordinary heavy goods."

Miles Macdonell, having started about as soon as he could be certain of open water and favorable traveling conditions, was making good time. His return seemed like a triumph. He knew he was going back to a very different community. Most of the faces he knew so well would be absent, new ones would be present and he, instead of occupying the highest command, would be serving under the new Governor-in-Chief, Robert Semple. He expected to see Colin Robertson and John MacLean and Peter Fidler in whom he had confidence, and he would probably catch a glimpse of Duncan Cameron and his cousin Alexander Macdonell in whom he did not have confidence. But there was much that Miles Macdonell did not know — until within half a day of paddling from the mouth of Winnipeg River when he was informed of the awful truth, the tragedy of Seven Oaks, the death of Governor Semple and twenty of his brave men, and the flight of the colonists, for the second time in a year.

What was Miles Macdonell to do? If nobody among the colonists was left at Fort Douglas, there was no purpose in continuing in that direction. If he did continue on, the crazed men who wrecked the Colony would probably take him prisoner again, perhaps murder him. But regardless of the consequences of going on, he saw it as his duty to communicate the terrible account of another bloody onslaught to Lord Selkirk. He wasted no time, ordered the canoes reversed to begin the return, hoping to reach the Earl's party before it entered Lake Michigan. He knew that in starting on this unplanned part of the journey, he and his men faced food problems. At one stage all food supplies had been consumed and starvation was a threat, until good fortune threw them in contact with Indians from whom he was able to buy fish and wild rice.

He had more good fortune in catching up with Lord Selkirk's party at Sault Ste. Marie on July 24. The Earl received the latest report from Red

River in shocked silence. It might have occurred to him that Bathurst was right in describing this as a "wild and unpromising" venture. But he knew he had an immediate decision to make. Which way should he turn? Should he go back toward Montreal or was there a reasonable alternative? His friends said: "Turn back." Miles Macdonell, uncertain that he would find the Earl, penned a note before reaching him and dispatched it with friendly Indians, explaining what he knew about the casualties and the destruction of "all our stores and buildings, and the abandonment of the river by all the survivors of our people." His advice was then presented in earnest terms: turn back to Montreal, at least until a bigger and stronger force can be assembled. Concluding, he said in pleading tones: "If we lose you, My Lord, all is lost."[12]

At the same time, the Earl's personal doctor, John Allan, was warning of the increasing dangers, saying: "Let me implore you to remember that your life is utterly indispensable for the success of the Colony."[13] The doctor's advice was: "Turn back."

But Selkirk's inclination was to pursue and confront the people he believed to be responsible for these crimes, the proprietors of the North West Company. After considering thoughtfully, he saw his course clearly and he was not to be dissuaded. Instead of continuing on the course initially set or returning to Montreal, he ordered an advance to Fort William, the summer headquarters of the North West Company. The concern's full strength would be there at this season and he might not have enough manpower to deal appropriately with these evil schemers. But this disregard for law and property had gone far enough. There were risks but he would take them. Prof. Arthur Silver Morton of Saskatchewan said that Selkirk tried to persuade John Askin, a Drummond's Island Justice of the Peace, and Charles Oakes Ermatinger, a Sault Ste. Marie Justice of the Peace, to accompany him to effect the appropriate arrests but they declined. He was sorry to be deprived of the support of their offices, but in their absence, he would do what had to be done, himself.

Moving against Fort William as he did was a bold and courageous act; it might also have been an act of folly.

CHAPTER FIFTEEN

Flimflam at Fort William

Fort William — that massive emporium in logs at the mouth of the Kaministikwia River, overlooking Lake Superior — was the scene of the great summer meetings of North West Company proprietors and servants when the new storm broke. Men with the best known names in the fur trade were present, William McGillivray, Archibald Norman McLeod, Alexander Mackenzie, who was known as "the Emperor," Simon Fraser, who gave his name to a mighty river, and others with fierce Highland pride and Gaelic accents. The Wintering Partners were in a cheerful mood, knowing that once again they had triumphed over their trading opponents and obtained the bigger share of furs in the back country. It had been like a tèst year in the rich Athabasca region; the English Company fared badly, not only in collecting furs but in finding enough food for the needs of its people. By Peter Fidler's accounting, the Hudson's Bay Company had taken only thirty-seven packs of furs out of the Athabasca and the food situation, owing to the "vigorous measures adopted by the N.W. Co. in that quarter" was so serious that "14 men and one woman and one child perished by hunger," while others in the service yielded to deliver all their goods to the North West Company in order "to obtain a bare supply of provisions."[1]

If more were needed to bring joy to the hearts of the North Westers planning and plotting and celebrating at Fort William, the news of the recent death-blow to Lord Selkirk's settlement at Red River would furnish it. Sure enough, it was destruction for the second successive year but this time, with the death of the Governor and some of his leading men, it looked conclusive.

With so many Company successes, the Fort William celebrations were more boisterous than usual, at least until a mid-afternoon hour on August 12, when a loaded bateau, and then eleven more of the same, entered the river and passed the fort. Company officials gazed curiously, then turned to count their own men, more than 200 able-bodied fellows, all seasoned fighters.

Could this be a threat to the sovereign might of Fort William? It was indeed a threat. Red River would have rated so recently as the focal point of British North American trouble which reached a climax in what became known as the Massacre of Seven Oaks. Now, less than two months later, Fort Douglas had a ghostly quietness about it and Fort William was about to seize the distinction of being the very epicenter of conflict.

The first of the boats entering the river carried Lord Selkirk and the seven men from the 37th Regiment who joined the expedition at Drummond's Island — one sergeant and six privates — to become Lord Selkirk's personal bodyguard. Upstream, about a mile from the fort, the boats pulled to the opposite shore and men prepared to make camp. And following closely was the bigger brigade conveying the ex-soldiers from disbanded regiments, restless for something to do and secretly glad to be pitching tents within quarreling distance of the North West Company, whose men they, too, were learning to dislike.

What happened from this point in time forward was well documented because of the multiplicity of sworn statements by men on both sides in the argument which was to occupy the Canadian courts for several years.

From the moment of arrival, Selkirk was in no mood to waste time. He had come to look upon North Westers as criminals and he was in a hurry to bring their leaders to justice. Not even waiting for the other boats to come up, he wrote a letter to William McGillivray, the senior agent in the other Company, demanding to know why John Pritchard, Peter Pambrun, Louis Nolin and some others from Red River were being held as prisoners. Capt. D'Orsonnens was instructed to deliver the hostile letter to the fort. If William McGillivray was puzzled about boats entering the river, his curiosity was quickly dispelled and he realized that an angry British Earl had become his neighbor. But displaying no emotion and making no offense, the Nor'Wester chief, instead of writing a long denial about holding the men as prisoners, simply sent Pritchard and Pambrun back with the captain to demonstrate by their presence that they were not prisoners.

Certainly, these men were taken from Red River immediately after the Seven Oaks affair although the prison type of surveillance probably diminished until the men were moving about with a fair degree of freedom. Pritchard, as a former clerk with the North West Company, might have come to feel quite at home with these people, many of whom he knew very well from other years. But now, having Pritchard and others in his tent, Selkirk seized the opportunity of taking testimony and evidence from them to support his next step, whatever that might be.

The next day was the 13th and for the Fort William residents, a very unlucky date. Early in the morning, Lord Selkirk called John McNabb, a member of his party, and revealed his intention to proceed with the execution of a warrant for the arrest of William McGillivray, charging treason and conspiracy and being a party to murder. It was for McNabb and Donald McPherson to serve the warrant later in the same day. As McNabb told it, "In the afternoon, we proceeded to the execution of our office in a Bateau with nine men who had arms concealed in the vessel."[2] Bringing the boat to a stop close to the fort, McNabb and McPherson proceeded inside, brushing boldly past surprised men standing in the gateway. The nine others from the boat followed, unarmed, to take up positions at the gate. Lacking nothing in nerve, McNabb and McPherson called aloud for William McGillivray who was, sure enough, within hearing distance. The fact was that practically all the North Westers were there.

McGillivray's name was extremely well known, better known than his face, and neither McNabb nor McPherson would have recognized him. But instead of trying to hide his identity or feign absence, he acknowledged the call and invited the two visitors into his apartment where the warrant for arrest was served instantly. The great trader, as McNabb noted, "acted like a gentleman." He read the warrant without a sign of bitterness and then prepared to answer the summons by going to the Earl's tent. He took time to consult two of his colleagues, Kenneth Mackenzie and John McLoughlin, about accompanying him to the Earl's tent and being prepared to become bail for him.

McGillivray, displaying perfect composure, halted to complete a letter he was writing when interrupted, and then accompanied the visitors, but electing to travel in his own canoe. On McGillivray's appearance in the Selkirk tent, the Earl caught the idea of extending the arrests and immediately ordered his men to arrest Mackenzie and McLoughlin also. Still not satisfied, Selkirk made it known that he wanted the arrest of all the North West Company partners at the post and as soon as warrants were made ready, McNabb and McPherson were going again to the Fort. If what happened at Red River on June 19 was instigated by the North West Company leaders — and he believed it was — then all the partners were criminals and deserved to be treated as such, the Earl reasoned.

But as McNabb and McPherson knew very well, this would be a bigger and more dangerous assignment and they would take a bigger force for support. Capt. D'Orsonnens, Lieut. G. A. Fauché and about twenty-five men, all formerly of the de Meuron Regiment, were called to go. Armed with warrants for arrest as well as with guns, the party landed as before and proceeded to enter at the gate. But it was different this time; the assembled North Westers — proprietors, servants and a number of Indians — looked more defiant. Undeterred, McNabb served warrants on "two of the gentlemen," and met resistance with the third, John McDonald of Garth, who announced in angry terms that they would tolerate no more arrests until Mr. McGillivray was released and returned. At this moment an attempt was made to close the gate and shut out the two visitors. But McNabb knew he could have strong support the moment he called for it. He gave the cue; a bugle sounded and Capt. D'Orsonnens and his constables bounded forward "with much alacrity" and blocked the closure of the gate. The captain called upon his men to seize the protesting McDonald and then to place the struggling and shouting fellow on one of the boats to be taken before Lord Selkirk.

The invaders moved quickly. With the two officers and their men remaining nearby, McNabb and McPherson advanced into the fort without further obstruction. Two small cannons were seized and placed where the North Westers could not use them. The constables moved inside and stationed themselves through the fort and the two men with the papers proceeded to carry out what remained of their duties "by the arrest of the other gentlemen named in the warrant."

The bugle call which sounded at the first resistance at the gate brought Capt. Frederick Matthey and the rest of the Selkirk men from the encampment and these, also, were soon inside the stockade. In rather short order, all the prominent proprietors of the North West Company were being conveyed in two boats to stand before Lord Selkirk in his capacity as magistrate and justice of the peace. Capt. D'Orsonnens and Dr. Allan remained at the fort to carry out another duty which Selkirk, acting like an experienced military commander, had not overlooked; warrants were written to cover the search for and sealing of papers belonging to the arrested men, also the securing of "all arms and warlike stores which may be found within the said fort." It would not do to allow guns and ammunition to fall into the hands of people who would use them in some rebellious way.

The prosperous propietors arraigned before Lord Selkirk as he sat solemnly in judgment in his tent made an imposing picture. This was a new and hateful experience for them, especially when the person presiding was the one they knew only as a rival and an enemy. But they acquiesced to his proposal, promised on their honor that they would make no resistance to his authority and take no hostile measures if permitted to return to their fort for the night. They were allowed to go but Lieutenant de Graffenreid and twenty of the Selkirk men remained on sentry duty during the night.

An air of peacefulness seemed to settle over Fort William at nightfall but there was an uneasiness within and, perchance, an overconfidence on the outside. Lord Selkirk, by a masterstroke of strategy, had gained the upper hand and seized the big and crucial depot, but he should have known that the North Westers were too smart to let him enjoy such domination for very long. He found next day that the assurances given were not guarantees against vandalism and recrimination. It was discovered that in spite of guards and sentries, seals protecting personal papers were broken and some papers were burnt in the kitchen fireplace. Likewise with the guns, locks were ruptured and some of the weapons were secreted away upstream during the night. A search warrant issued from the Earl's tent brought discovery of a cache comprising four cases with eight or nine guns in each, hidden under hay in a loft, also forty fowling pieces, all "loaded and primed." Elsewhere, eight barrels of gunpowder which had been taken from the fort were found in a tree-covered situation about half a mile from the fort.

These suspicious maneuvers suggested the possibility of a surprise thrust to push the Selkirk party far back and the Earl, knowing what to expect, dispersed the fort's manpower. The voyageurs who manned the North West Company brigades, muscular fellows, were ordered to remove their tents from inside the fort walls to a location across the river, while Selkirk's own people moved to occupy the ground immediately in front of the fort, or between the fort and the river, where they would be in a favorable position to respond in case of a sudden attack.

His Lordship, after conducting an examination of all the arrested men, concluded that the evidence justified their appearance before the courts in Upper Canada. He resolved to send them to York and on August 17, forwarded copies of all warrants and affidavits taken in the course of his investigation to Governor General Sir John Coape Sherbrooke. To D'Arcy Boulton, Attorney General of Upper Canada, he sent similar documents, also a message, saying: "I send you a cargo of criminals of a larger scale than usual." And knowing there would be an attempt to have these men released on bail, he made a plea that any such application should be denied in order to put down "the most detestable system of villainy to prevail in the British Dominions."[3]

His Lordship asked Lieut. G. A. Fauché, one of the former de Meuron officers, to take charge of the prisoners and convey them to York. Three big canoes loaded with the North West Company proprietors — including William McGillivray but omitting Daniel Mackenzie — left Fort William on August 18 and progress across the lake was satisfactory until the 26th when a fateful storm blew in across Superior and engulfed one canoe and took the lives of nine of the twenty-one people traveling.

Lieut. Fauché, to ward off criticism of his command, explained how the canoes moved much as usual during the morning hours and a noontime stop was called for purposes of lunch, about fifteen miles from Sault Ste. Marie. During this pause, the wind increased but because the travelers were on the leeward side of the island, they did not realize its violence. Nevertheless, before starting again, as Fauché explained events, he consulted William McGillivray who knew the lake from many years of traveling to and from Fort William, asking if it would be dangerous to proceed, to which the pioneer trader was reported to have said it would not be dangerous in the least as long as the guides and voyageurs exercised care. Accordingly, the canoes pushed off and the men soon felt the violence of the gale. With the wind driving from the west, it was at once too late to turn back. The order was given to steer for the "first point of land which lay on our left, in order to save ourselves if possible."[4]

As the canoes neared the island, one of them upset and notwithstanding the help attempted by men in the other two canoes, nine lives were lost. Kenneth Mackenzie, a partner in the North West Company, was among them, also one sergeant, one private and some Indians in the service of the North West Company. After reaching the island with the surviving canoes, the men returned to the scene of the mishap but found no bodies. Later the body of Kenneth Mackenzie was recovered and taken to Sault Ste. Marie for burial.

Lieut. Fauché's party which left Fort William on August 18 arrived at York on September 3 but to the distress of all who were growing weary of travel, it was not the end of the journey. Selkirk, in writing to the Attorney General asking him to receive the eight prisoners "arrested for crimes of the highest atrocities," added that Fauché would look to him for direction in delivering his charges; in other words, to which jail should they be taken? But upon making inquiry for the Attorney General in York, Fauché was informed that the official was in Kingston. He and his party went to Kingston, but by this time, the Attorney General was in Brockville. By the date of arrival at the latter place, the accused men had applied for a writ of *habeas corpus* and the officer was instructed to proceed to Montreal "where we arrived on the 10th of September and where the prisoners were all admitted to bail."[5]

Montreal was receiving the reports of Lord Selkirk's actions with severe criticism. Nothing that the North West Company had ever done produced such public anger. The seizure of Fort William to the citizens of William McGillivray's city sounded like common plunder and then, to deny bail to one of Montreal's leading citizens, was adding insult to injury.

At the departure of the North Westers, Lord Selkirk remained at Fort William, for all practical purposes, the Administrator. Having met with success in carrying out his planned move against the proprietors at that place, he grew more daring and more possessive. Overlooking the chance that Canadian courts would not uphold his charges against McGillivray and his friends, he moved from one bold provocation to another. He drew upon Fort William stores to meet the needs of his own people and detained the outgoing brigades, westward and eastward, and thus had most of the season's inventory of furs which should have been moving to Montreal. His reasoning, it seemed, was that the furs, with a value close to half a million dollars, could be compensation for loss of pemmican from Assiniboia and other losses which had been inflicted upon his Settlement. Carried away by the joy of control over rivals who had tried again and again to ruin his plans, the new urge was to turn his power to good use. Seeing himself in a strong bargaining position, he would work out a plan for settlement of all the injuries and disputes between the Montreal traders on one hand and the Hudson's Bay Company and his Settlement scheme on the other. There being no other responsible representatives of the North West Company remaining behind at Fort William, he tried to involve Daniel Mackenzie and some Company servants in agreements which they had no authority to sign or even discuss.

Selkirk was able to gain the signature of Daniel Mackenzie who, notwithstanding his status as a Company partner, could not commit the parent body. Selkirk seems to have kept Mackenzie in partial confinement and in a state of partial sobriety. In any case, the man's apparent willingness to sell Fort William and sell fort provisions and fort cattle and sheep was something which could not stand legal scrutiny.

When word of the alleged transactions between Lord Selkirk and Daniel Mackenzie reached Montreal, the Earl's solicitor, Samuel Gale, was sufficiently exercised about it to write a warning that the reported agreement with Daniel Mackenzie for the sale of Fort William, "cannot be considered binding because D. Mackenzie was not possessed of authority." Moreover, Mackenzie was being represented as having been pressed to execute a fraudulent sale, having been influenced by fear. Gale warned that it could be damaging to the Earl's reputation.[6] There was Gale's hint, too, that Selkirk should abandon both Fort William and the trip farther west, and return to face the growing problems in the east.

Surely the Earl could not expect to escape being held accountable, regardless of how wicked some of the North West Company policies might have seemed. And naturally, William McGillivray and his colleagues, as soon as they gained their freedom by bail in Montreal, set about to reverse the stream of legal accusations and bring Lord Selkirk to the courts on any or all of various charges, false arrest, theft of a fort, conspiracy, and more to come.

The first attempt to obtain an Upper Canada warrant for the Earl's arrest failed but one was drawn by a Drummond's Island magistrate, Dr. David Mitchell, and sent to Fort William by special constable. The fellow, probably looking shabby and seedy at the end of the long journey, tried to serve the warrant but was unsuccessful. Selkirk's resistance on that occasion might have been his biggest public error and the reasons he offered for refusing to be served were not very convincing. The result was serious criticism and a considerable loss of prestige. In finding reasons for questioning the validity of the warrant, he alluded to a signing magistrate who was said to be rarely sober after midday. The constable, who didn't look like a constable, was without identifying credentials, all of which were points worthy of consideration. It was in the Earl's favor that he wrote at once to the Lieutenant Governor offering his reasons for refusal to be served.

"A few days ago," he wrote, "a canoe arrived here bringing two clerks of the N.W. Co. accompanied by a man who gave himself out as a Constable charged with the arrest of several gentlemen here, myself among the rest. On examining his warrant, I observe it to be in several respects irregular and founded on the recital of an affidavit full of the grossest perjuries. It was signed by Dr. Mitchell of Drummond's Island whose notorious habits of intemperance render it in the highest degree probable that his signature had been obtained surreptitiously. The Constable when asked if he had any letters or credentials of any kind, could produce none, which confirmed the idea of being an imposter."[7]

Some historians presume that the murder of Owen Keveny when under arrest would place Lord Selkirk on his guard, but in any case, he, as one who had been writing warrants for arrest very freely, did not have an acceptable excuse for resisting this one, and his actions brought a flood of denunciation upon him, some of it from sources as far away as Lord Bathurst.

Appearing quite horrified, Bathurst, in writing to Sir John Sherbrooke, said: "By resisting the execution of a warrant issued against him, Lord Selkirk has rendered himself doubly amenable to the laws ... upon a true bill being found against him, you will take the necessary and usual measures in such cases for arresting his Lordship and bringing him before the court from which the process issued. Surrounded as Lord Selkirk appears to be with a military force, which has once already been employed to defeat the execution of legal process, it is almost impossible to hope that he will quietly submit to the execution of any warrant against himself, so long as any opening is left for effectual resistance."[8]

Being far away, Selkirk was probably not aware of the mounting public disapproval, especially in Montreal — and York was not much better. A further indication was directed to him late in October, a notification that His Excellency, the Governor General, had found it necessary to revoke the previous order making the Earl a magistrate and justice of the peace within the Indian Territories. "Your powers and functions," the letter said succinctly, "are at an end."[9]

A few days later, a jury empaneled at Sandwich accepted evidence of the Earl's forceful entry to Fort William and new warrants were issued for his arrest, also a new order to restore the fort to its "lawful proprietors."[10]

All things considered, it was a tragic year and peace in the fur country seemed more remote than ever. Conflict was rife all the way from Athabasca to Montreal and thinking people were asking: "What next?" Samuel Gale in his warning to Selkirk mentioned the possibility of the North West Company directing "a very formidable army at Fort William" next spring, also the possibility of the North West Company being now inspired to attack York Factory, "because they believe that if they could obtain possession of [that post] the whole of the H.B. Co.'s affairs would be thrown into confusion and it would be impossible for the Company concerns in the Interior to recover from the embarrassment and difficulties."[55] Gale went on to point out that the Earl's forcible occupation of Fort William would make it easier for the other Company to justify its action in seizing the like of York Factory.

Poor Selkirk! His mistakes in 1816 threatened to be far more costly than he could have imagined. They were costly. But this was the price he was prepared to pay for a farm Colony away to the west, a Colony in which practically nobody in public life, except himself, could see any future.

CHAPTER SIXTEEN

The Silver Chief at Red River — At Last

Lord Selkirk's unscheduled call at Fort William detained him there for eight and a half months, delayed his visit to Red River by almost a year and created involvement with Canadian courts that lasted for three years. It produced nothing of lasting good and was probably the means of shortening his life.

Naturally, the new turn of events worried him, With more than a hundred men drawing wages from him, he could see the cost of the expedition assuming ruinous proportions, and he must have known that William McGillivray's return to York and Montreal in the humiliating role of prisoner would generate a fresh wave of misunderstanding, and a fresh demand for revenge. But in his zeal to fulfill a purpose at Red River, the belabored Earl could see no alternative to this dangerous course of action.

If the eastern lawmakers, who listened to McGillivray and pictured Selkirk as a person with piratical tendencies, could have reached him, they would have ended his westward tour very suddenly. But forcing submission upon a man at faraway Fort William, especially in the winter season, was not easy and not practical. The warrant for his arrest issued from Drummond's Island and delivered at the beginning of November was rejected — wisely or unwisely — and the next one, prepared with greater care, was too late to reach him before Fort William was effectively isolated by frozen rivers and lakes. And before the bearer of the new warrant could get to Fort William in the spring, the Earl was on his way to Red River, looking more and more like a fugitive trying to stay beyond the reach of justice.

Meanwhile, the eastern authorities, with backing from London, were induced to make an objective assessment of the cause of the disturbances. At last, they would appoint an investigating commission with wide powers. It was not too soon. It was approximately what Lord Selkirk had requested when he heard about the attacks on his Colony in 1815. And it was exactly what Lady Selkirk requested later. Worried about the safety of her husband, she wrote to Sir John Sherbrooke on August 17, the very day on which the Earl was forwarding copies of warrants for the arrest of William McGillivray and his colleagues to the Attorney General of Upper Canada, notifying him of the dispatch for trial of a "cargo of criminals." Her plea was for some official intervention to prevent further violence, saying "Lord Selkirk unaided cannot enforce compliance with the Proclamation." His Excellency replied from Quebec in familiar terms, saying he would find it impossible to take steps likely to change the mood of the offenders. After another few days, Lady Jean displayed a feminine determination by writing again, this time suggesting specifically that "two or more persons possessing your confidence and invested with the authority of Government [be sent] to enquire into the nature and causes of these atrocities."[1]

The delivery of this communication to the Governor General would precede by a few days the arrival in Montreal of Favorite Son William McGillivray, and whether it was his charge of the Earl of Selkirk stealing his best fort, or Lady Selkirk's request for an investigation that prompted action will never be known, but within a few weeks, a commission such as she proposed was being appointed.

While Lord Selkirk, on October 30, was writing to Sir John Sherbrooke, repeating a request for an official inquiry into the death "last month of Mr. Owen Keveny, an officer of the H.B.Co., murdered in cold blood by assassins employed for the purpose by one of the partners of the N.W.Co.," Sir John was writing to Selkirk to announce the appointment of "the Hon. William B. Coltman, Member of the Executive Council of this Province, and John Fletcher, Esq., one of the principal Magistrates of police here, to be Magistrates for the Indian Territory and Commissioners of Special Enquiry with full powers and instructions in each capacity."[2]

Coltman was highly regarded. He was also a friend and political colleague of William McGillivray. Fletcher was not as well known. Having made these appointments, the Governor General moved at once to revoke the commissions of all other magistrates serving in the Indian Territory, so that the Commissioners would be the only ones with such powers. Reporting to Lord Bathurst, Sherbrooke was especially high in his praise of Coltman who, he said, would be paid 150 guineas per month with "a further allowance of 750 guineas as an indemnification for the loss which he must immediately sustain by being so suddenly obliged to abandon his concerns," His associate, Fletcher, would receive 50 guineas per month and a further allowance of 250 guineas "for the preparations necessary for the undertaking."

The Commissioners would not lack authority; in addition to the exercise of the office of magistrates in the far country, they would be empowered to inquire into all the recent offenses, arrest perpetrators and transmit them to Upper Canada for trial. They acted quickly, leaving Montreal to embark upon official duties on November 7, but were obliged to admit soon thereafter that winter conditions would prevent them from traveling to Fort William before spring.

Although unable to reach either Fort William or Red River during the winter months, the Commissioners were active and able to accumulate much evidence of the kind available in Montreal, most of it critical of Lord Selkirk's activities. William McGillivray and friends would see to that. The most startling item of information was the sworn statement from Daniel Mackenzie, the former North West Company partner who, for reasons best known to Lord Selkirk, remained at Fort William after the accused partners were shipped out as prisoners. Later stories about this man's confinement differed substantially but as he vouched for the circumstances, they placed the Earl in a bad light indeed.

Sworn before James Gruet, Notary Public, and D. Mitchell, Justice of the Peace, at Drummond's Island on November 11, 1816, Mackenzie's story had a fantastic ring about it: "I, Daniel Mackenzie, Esq., a retired partner of the firm of the North West Company, having been detained a prisoner at Fort William, by Lord Selkirk's orders from 13th of August to the 11th of October, 1816, during all of which time I was in a state of inebriety and actually deranged of mind, did by the persuasion of Lord Selkirk and his agents, sign certain papers and instruments of writing, purporting to be a sale of goods, packs of furs, vessels on the stocks, an indenture of agreement to leave to arbitration certain disputes and differences between His Lordship and the North West Company, and a letter to the Interior stating that the North West Company was ruined, all which papers were dictated by His Lordship and his servants. Therefore, from the causes above, the dread of a long imprisonment and in hope of obtaining my liberty, I did sign the said papers, although unauthorized so to do. Therefore, I do by these presents, now that I have my liberty, solemnly protest against all acts done by me as aforesaid during the period above stated. In witness thereof I have signed and sealed these presents at Drummond's Island, this 11th of November, 1816."[3]

The North Westers, to be sure, made much of Daniel Mackenzie's story and presented him as a prize exhibit.

After Selkirk's seizure of Fort William, traffic began again to move toward Red River. Of those who were at Fort William when the Earl moved in, Jean Baptiste Lagimodière was the first to start back. He had been absent over a year and his wife, Marie Anne, and friends supposed he was dead. The fact was that on his return from Montreal, he was captured by Indians working for the North West Company, beaten and taken as a prisoner to the fort where he remained until the place was captured by Selkirk's force. He was at once a free man and had a choice: he could start at once for Red River or wait to travel with a party of Selkirk's ex-soldiers. He did not do either; he remained for a while in case Selkirk needed him and then, when the soldiers were almost ready to start west, Jean Baptiste, with longer strides and more stamina than the old soldiers, set out ahead of them, saying: "I'll see you at Red River."

Arriving at the Forks a few weeks before Christmas, Jean Baptiste was part of a joyous reunion. But Red River was not the same. The settlers were missing and the riverside had a deathly stillness. Jean Baptiste nursed a secret, however. He had benefited from a bitter lesson about talking too much in the York area and he was not now telling all he knew, except to whisper to Marie Anne that Selkirk's soldier-settlers or settler-soldiers would be coming soon and Fort Douglas would be wrenched from the North West Company and halfbreed occupants.

Lord Selkirk had accepted the necessity of remaining to hold his gains at Fort William throughout the winter, more to prevent the enemy from recovering a position of strength at Red River than for the mere sake of holding a fort on Lake Superior. Still he was anxious to rescue his Colony and with that in view he was sending Capt. D'Orsonnens with about thirty-five officers and men. They were starting away on September 10, knowing very well that winter would be one of their enemies before long. Miles Macdonell did not start with them but he overtook the party at Rainy Lake and allowed his usual officious ways to become offensive to the officer commanding. Having had some military experience and knowing the area better than D'Orsonnens, the domineering Macdonell elevated himself to a leadership role. Writing later to Andrew Colvile he said of this expedition that it was "planned and executed by me, although the chief merit of it was given afterwards to Capt. D'Orsonnens who from his want of knowledge of the habits of the country and the natives could no more execute it than he could fly. The de Meuron soldiers were well aware of this and refused to advance with him till after I had joined them."[4]

Believing that a state of war existed with the North West Company, Selkirk's men halted to seize the rival post at Rainy Lake, draw upon its stores and enjoy some relaxation. But winter was at hand and the leaders knew they should be trying to gain their objective before the extremely cold weather set in. Already they had ice and snow with which to contend and were resigned to sleighs and snowshoes instead of canoes. And to pull the loaded sleighs, what would be handier than horses and oxen found there at Lac la Pluie? The animals, to be sure, would have an added value; in addition to hauling the freight, the horses and cattle would be most useful to the settlers at the end of the journey. It might have been termed plundering or rustling but it was irresistible and five horses, two cows, one heifer, one bull and two oxen were added to the expedition. When one of the oxen slipped on ice and broke a leg, the animal was slaughtered and the bull was promptly shod and hitched to work for his living.

The course was to be by way of the Winnipeg — or Winnipic — River, the route taken most commonly in the summer season, but according to Miles Macdonell, he advised the more southerly course, to strike the Red River at a point near Pembina. Macdonell's guidance was accepted and the men, on snowshoes and growing tired of winter, reached the Red River on the last day of the year. With numbers now swollen to a total of sixty by the addition of Indians, they had no trouble in taking the Hudson's Bay Company post, Fort Daer, which was being occupied by North Westers; at that point they turned north to follow the straightest possible course to Fort · Douglas, hoping it was still standing.

Traveling conditions grew worse rather than better and about midway between Pembina and Fort Douglas, the weary travelers tramped into a howling January blizzard. Animals as well as men suffered. The light eastern tents were totally inadequate. But being so close to their goal, they pushed on, perhaps too fast because the horses and cattle became exhausted and gave up, all except one of the Rainy Lake cows with the will and stamina to take the lead and break a trail through the drifts.

The storm ended but the cold lingered. Traveling more slowly now, the snowshoe brigade came at nightfall on January 9 to a sheltered spot which Miles Macdonell said was only a couple of marching hours from Fort Douglas. Here, Macdonell's knowledge of the area was recognized, and although he was not popular with the official leader, he was allowed to draw upon his memory and direct the approach.

Making a brief stop during the chilly hours of that last outdoor evening of the journey, the men made light ladders as part of the preparation for the assault. They listened to instructions and then at a late hour made bright by an almost full moon, they advanced upon Fort Douglas. They moved noiselessly, except for the crunch of snowshoes on crisp snow, and with the aid of the ladders, went over the stockade fence without awakening the slumbering occupants and took possession of the fort without a struggle. Archibald McLellan, the North Wester in charge, was held as a prisoner while the other residents were turned out at the early morning hour to find living quarters elsewhere. The Selkirk men, on the other hand, would have the luxury of a roof over their heads for the first time in many days.

Jean Baptiste Lagimodière was the first to greet D'Orsonnens and his followers and report on the events of his own journey back from Fort William. Yes, his wife and children were safe; Saulteaux Indian Chief, Peguis, had taken good care of the family.

Miles Macdonell had seen to it that the Hudson's Bay Company flag was raised over Fort Douglas and wished fervently that he could have communicated the good news to Lord Selkirk. But Macdonell knew and all the men knew that this was not necessarily the end of trouble because hostility prevailed right across the country. The North Westers, after the Selkirk seizure of Fort William, took various Hudson's Bay Company posts, including the important Fort Wedderburn in faraway Athabasca. Rumor from the north warned of a plan for a major attack originating in the Athabasca region for the purpose of taking and removing all the Hudson's Bay Company trading posts on the Saskatchewan River. The will to violence was not dead; it was very much alive, but it might be that the balance of power was changing slightly. Soon after the return to Fort Douglas, William Laidlaw, who was to gain prominence as the manager of Lord Selkirk's first experimental farm, led a small detachment to recover Bas de la Rivière Winnipic, situated just a couple of miles up from the mouth of Winnipeg River. Everybody was doing it.

Word reaching Jack River, whence the settlers had fled in the previous June, telling of the Fort Douglas recapture, brought rejoicing. People who, with horrible memories of Seven Oaks, vowed they would never return, were now listening with interest: "Lord Selkirk's soldiers have gained possession of our fort," they were saying, "and the Earl himself is coming out this year."

Red River appeared in a new light and as soon as traveling conditions were favorable in the spring, men, women and children were preparing to move south to reclaim their land and begin again to build log huts beside the river. For some of them it would be the third attempt at home construction in five years. This time they would be able to begin the log work with the confidence and skill that come with practice.

The crop of 1816 had been a total loss because nobody had been present to take off the harvest and 1817 wouldn't be much better; the return of the settlers would be late for seeding and in addition, there would be a serious shortage of seed except for possible small supplies to be borrowed or bought from Hudson's Bay Company posts like Brandon House. At least, the cropland previously broken and cultivated could be made ready for seed without much difficulty.

Lord Selkirk, leaving part of his body of hired helpers behind to guard Fort William, departed that place on May 1, starting for Red River. Unknown to him, the North Westers were already converging with strength upon the Lake Superior post and about the time he was arriving at the Forks on the Red, June 21 — one day after his forty-sixth birthday, William McGillivray's men were recapturing Fort William.

Setting foot upon Red River soil made for a happy moment for the Earl, also a strange one; it was almost like a homecoming in spite of the fact that he, as owner of seventy million acres of coutryside, was viewing it for the first time, more than six years after acquiring it. His deep feeling of affection for it was something he could not hide. There he stood surveying the riverside scenery, catching a vision of another chain of waterfront houses soon to appear, mainly below the fort and on the same side of the river. The first of the de Meurons, the ones who accompanied Capt. D'Orsonnens and Miles Macdonell, were beginning to build on the land of their choice, on the east side of the river where the city of St. Boniface was built later.

He had a natural fondness for soil and liked what he saw as he kicked his heels into the highly fertile Red River clay, a rich inheritance from the deep silt of a postglacial lake known as Agassiz. He walked southward to the place where Fort Gibraltar stood before its demolition, and northward across the riverlot farms which had been allotted to the Kildonan people, asking questions as he sauntered about wild flowers and birds. Best of all, he was able to talk with the few settlers from Jack River who returned early to do such planting as time and seed supplies would allow. The rest of the settler people were expected shortly. He longed to meet them and late on an evening when the days were still long, the Alexander MacDonell who was the Colony Sheriff rode to Fort Douglas to inform all present that the returning settlers had paddled their way as far as Frog Plain, less than three miles north of the fort, and were camping there for the night.

It was good news and early next morning, the Earl walked in light rain to the campground to be the first to offer a welcome. There he moved among the surprised colonists, chatting amiably, then saw them take to their boats for the last time to paddle a short distance farther to the particular river lots they recognized as their own.

The former courage returned and as the eager people took to building or rehabilitating homes, the Earl mingled with them, offering encouragement or advice. Often as he walked, he would be surrounded by settlers who wanted only to shake his hand or hear his comment, perhaps about agriculture in which he could demonstrate a masterly grasp.

It was on one of those occasions, August 10, when surrounded by his settlers, that he announced Western Canada's first debt adjustment program: for those who had suffered the loss of buildings and improvements through recent invasions, land debts would be canceled. About twenty-four families would have their land free of debt. Then speaking of other matters, he said that part of the lot on which he stood would be reserved for the construction of a church, and a site on the next lot would be kept for "your school."

He went on to confirm the land allotments as based on Peter Fidler's survey of four years earlier, with farm lots measuring 220 yards or 40 rods on the riverside, and 1980 yards or 360 rods in depth. Thus there would be eight farms per mile of river frontage, each one comprising ninety acres with added woodlot allowances farther back or across the river.

He showed a complete understanding of the needs of the people and talked to them in the most practical terms. It was regrettable, he said, that the Merino sheep from Spain did not survive, but the search for a high quality exportable wool was worth pursuing and the experiment should be repeated. Likewise, he regretted the troubles encountered in trying to obtain a good foundation of breeding cattle. He had hoped to drive a herd from Baldoon in Upper Canada to Red River. The American War had prevented that drive but he would see that a substantial herd would be brought in by one means or another.

Oh yes, he tried to obtain an experienced brickmaker and was inquiring about someone with the knowledge and ability to erect a gristmill and a sawmill. He would continue his search for the seeds of new and promising crops which might prove peculiarly suited to this soil and climate. In advancing new and novel ideas, the Earl was always far ahead of others and as he saw Red River with so many frontier problems, he recognized a clear need for an experimental farm and in characteristic Selkirk fashion, set about to determine the most suitable location for one.

Making the first Treaty with Western Indians was one of the Earl's distinctions during the few months he was at Red River. From the very beginning of his newest Colony, he had been most anxious to have the native races treated with justice and had instructed Miles Macdonell against neglect of this matter. Macdonell had replied that he found the tribesmen indifferent about negotiating for anything as sacred as soil, and he did not make much progress. But that did not satisfy the Earl and the chiefs were requested to assemble for talks. First there was the problem of determining which chiefs could and should speak as original proprietors. There had been tribal shifts in occupation. The Cree, it seemed, held the Red River area at one time and then they retired farther westward and the Saulteaux, a western branch of the Ojibway, moved in. Present were five chiefs who, with their signing marks, were as follows:

Oukidoat

Muchiwikoab

Rayagierebmoa

Muchitooukoonace

Peguis

They saw the Earl distributing presents, studied his quiet dignity and listened as he explained what they were asked to do. They admired him and called him the Silver Chief. Then after much speech making, on July 18, they signed the Treaty, making over to King George III for the benefit of Lord Selkirk all the lands fronting on the two rivers for prescribed distances on both sides of the Assiniboine as far up as Muskrat River which entered above Portage la Prairie, and on both sides of the Red from its mouth to the point of Red Lake River. The lands surrendered would extend approximately two miles back from the rivers or "as far as a man can see under the belly of a horse on a clear day." In the vicinity of Fort Douglas and Fort Daer, more depth of land would be required and at each of these places, the area forfeited would be in the shape of a circle with a radius of six miles. Payment for this land concession would be 100 pounds of good tobacco to be turned over to the Saulteaux at the Forks and 100 pounds to the Cree at Portage la Prairie each year at the beginning of October. With the passing of time, Indians changed their views somewhat but for the first twenty years after the Treaty, the native people were quite satisfied.

But the Earl's stay of a few months at Red River was not without its anxiety. His enemies would not leave him alone. The North West Company, although having suffered a temporary setback at Fort William, was as belligerent as ever and more vengeful. One of the easterners in pursuit was William Smith, Deputy Sheriff of the Western District of Upper Canada, who arrived at Red River on June 24, almost before the Earl had time to stretch his spindly legs on the Red River sod. The visitor was giving the impression that he was present to convey the Proclamation of May 1, 1817, issued by the Governor General in the name of the Prince Regent, calling upon all parties to end their hostilities and restore forts and materials seized during the prolonged conflict. It was soon apparent, however, that this man was really in pursuit of Lord Selkirk, to enforce a warrant for arrest.

It was not the first time for Selkirk and Smith to meet; the latter arrived at Fort William before the former's departure and presented a writ for the restitution of that post to the North West Company but the Earl refused obedience, offering reasons why he should not comply. Smith responded with warrants for the arrest of the Earl, Captain Matthey and Dr. John Allan, naming felony in the charge. These also were rejected and on Selkirk's order, Smith was arrested and placed in the fort jail.

After Lord Selkirk left for Red River, the Fort William property was reoccupied by the North West Company on Smith's authority and then the same officious deputy sheriff, who was suspected of working for the North West Company, came on toward Red River, behaving exactly like a North Wester along the way, presumably to make good the Earl's arrest. But on reaching Fort Douglas, he was promptly arrested for the second time and detained.

Then, exactly two weeks after Selkirk came to Red River, Commissioner William B. Coltman made his appearance, bearing the Prince Regent's Proclamation. His more unenviable job, however, was to assess blame for the widespread disorders, arrest guilty parties and generally restore order.

His first interview was with Lord Selkirk and he found the Earl to be friendly. Willingly, the Colony's founder read the Proclamation publicly, calling for an end to all hostility, adding with regard to river travel that: "All the world then is free and may pass as they choose."[5] This effectively nullified the earlier order from Miles Macdonell to use the cannon to fire upon any of the suspected enemies using the river in the vicinity of the fort.

Coming from the East, Coltman could be expected to have a North West Company bias. He admitted to the hope that his presence in the West would restrain both parties but he expected to have more restraining to do on the Selkirk side. That opinion was changing and he was recognizing a continuing treachery on the other side, even to the point of a plan for another attack on Selkirk's Colony, of all things.

Arriving at Lac la Pluie when on his way to Red River, Coltman found "the gentlemen of the North West Company assembled in a state of much irritation and many of them preparing to set out in a body for the Red River, apparently with a disposition by no means favorable to peace."[6] Making the situation more ominous, a large body of Indians and halfbreeds was said to be standing by. Coltman believed his presence served to stall what could have been another destructive blow at the Settlement.

One of the annoyances expressed at Lac la Pluie was the arrest of the Deputy Sheriff of the Western District of Upper Canada who was traveling, according to Coltman, with a "further view to the personal arrest of Lord Selkirk for the imputed escape from Fort William." Naturally, the Commissioner, upon arrival at Red River, had a special interest in this William Smith whose real motives were becoming clear. Although a deputy sheriff should be impartial, Coltman discovered that Smith was among the North Westers guilty of a breach of the peace in a wild display at the recapture of the Lac la Pluie post. It seemed to confirm what Selkirk had suspected about the man, and Coltman, in ordering his release, ordered, also, that the Deputy Sheriff be bound over to keep the peace.

Coltman was not seeing Selkirk as blameless, not by any means, but he was finding proof of the North West Company action in trying in vain to persuade the Indians to move against the Colony, and then in winning the halfbreeds to the plan for Colony destruction. There was no doubt; the Company men had even gone to the length of rewarding the active perpetrators. He was accumulating evidence of a plot or plots to murder Selkirk. Intercepted letters from that evil schemer, Alexander Macdonell, hinted suggestively of "some fine places on the River Winipic." Elsewhere among the letters: "The Halfbreeds will take him whilst he is asleep, early in the morning," and then the suggestion that "they can get Bostonois to shoot him."[7]

Coltman very much regretted his failure in issuing warrants against the said Alexander Macdonell and the other author of mischief, Archibald Norman McLeod. Both were too fast for Coltman. The warrant against Macdonell "could not be executed owing to his unexpected escape into the interior from Bas de la Rivière, where I met him, as I supposed, on his way to Fort William in July last; this flight certainly adds to the suspicions against Macdonell, and combined with other circumstances, calls for the most vigorous measures to bring him to trial. A similar observation appears to me also to apply to the case of Archibald Norman McLeod, against whom I likewise conceived it my duty to issue a warrant, which I sent to Mr. Fletcher at Fort William, but this also failed to be executed, owing to the very short stay he [McLeod] made at that place or at Montreal, from whence he proceeded to England."[8]

The restoration demanded by the Proclamation, unflattering to some of those involved, showed how far the western community was from a realization of peace. Some of the transactions at Red River must have been most trying to Lord Selkirk and discouraging to Coltman. At times the arrogance of the North West Company men appeared to invite violence, as in the case of a small cultivated field adjacent to the site of Fort Gibraltar and claimed formerly by those who occupied that post prior to its disappearance. The field had been planted recently to barley by the Selkirk people. But according to the strict terms of the Proclamation, the field would revert to the Canadian Company, even if Lord Selkirk believed it was part of his land grant of 1811. But what did the North Westers do about it? By Coltman's account, they turned their "cattle" to graze on the barley likely to be needed urgently in a Colony where food shortage had been nigh chronic.

The account raises another question. How would the North West Company happen to have cattle at that place and time? Coltman did not explain fully but there is reason to believe the cattle invited to eat the settlers' barley were the bull, ox and couple of cows that Capt. D'Orsonnens' men took or rescued at Lac la Pluie in their tramp westward eight months earlier. If so, the North West Company could advance a reasonable claim, even though its people would have no use for the animals and would not consider returning them to Lac la Pluie. But nothing could have justified the wicked act of slaughtering these animals while settlers with urgent need for cattle looked on with expressions of disbelief.

Coltman, who must have been disgusted at what he witnessed, did not hide his admiration for the Earl to whom the conduct was infuriating but who "peaceably acquiesced" when Coltman advanced his opinion that under the Proclamation, the Montreal men were within their rights.[9] To remove the chance of dispute, Coltman formally authorized the North West Company to take possession of the Gibraltar field "together with the crop growing thereon . . . notwithstanding claims set forth by the Earl to the said piece of ground as being his rightful property . . . I the said W. B. Coltman did conceive it to be my duty as Civil Magistrate and Special Commissioner to maintain the N.W.Co. in possession of the said piece of land."[10]

Coltman appeared to be an honest man, although certain individuals believed he was more interested in peace than in justice. Selkirk cooperated graciously but objected to so much searching for North West Company chattels resting in Colony and Hudson's Bay Company quarters while ignoring the extent of buildings destroyed, crops ruined and settlers uprooted at Red River and the loss of Hudson's Bay Company furs and property at distant Athabasca. No doubt, also, the Earl would have wished to make an issue of jurisdiction because he would have agreed with the spirit of a resolution passed by the Council of the Southern Department of the Territory of Rupert's Land on June 7, 1817, questioning the authority of the Governor General of Upper and Lower Canada to send a Commissioner into Rupert's Land, "in the face of the Charter granted by King Charles II."

Clearly, Coltman did not allow new friendships to interfere with his sense of duty and as a parting gesture he arrested Lord Selkirk, Captain Matthey, Captain D'Orsonnens, Dr. John Allan and various others. True, he allowed bail but at what seemed like exorbitant figures, £6,000 for the Earl, £2,000 for Matthey and £1,500 for D'Orsonnens and Allan. Samuel Gale, the barrister from Montreal, and Col. Robert Dickson furnished sureties of £3,000 each for Selkirk, guaranteeing his appearance before the courts in Montreal on March 1, 1818.

Miles Macdonell seemed like the only man of local prominence who was not being arrested. The reason was plain; he had his arrest previously, faced the courts without conviction and was a free man. There was no point in arresting him again and so he was free to blunder along, doing nothing for the cause of harmony. He might have rendered a good service in the recapture of Fort Douglas but his service in the community was in doubt. Some people, including Samuel Gale, rated him a liability to the Earl, and said so. To Lady Selkirk, he described Macdonell as "Lord Selkirk's evil genius." He had something to say about the Macdonell "stupidity, arrogance and self conceit" which rendered his advice useless. Gale looked hopefully to the day when his Lordship would get rid of both Macdonell and Robertson and added:"I shall always think he runs much risk until then."[11]

Lord Selkirk could not get away from current troubles, some of them of his own making to be sure. Nevertheless, the three months at Red River made a pleasant interlude. He repeated that he would be happy to stay and forget about the House of Lords in London and the hostile people in Montreal.

He left the Settlement on September 9, promising to come back, but looking worn and pale. He regretted his failure to gain Coltman's endorsation for denial of N.W.Co. land rights within the Colony and for a qualified military force but he knew that with the de Meurons left behind, the Colony was not as likely to be destroyed again. The de Meurons might never be the best farmers but they were handy people to have around in time of trouble. He felt more optimistic about the Colony's future than about his own future. He would travel by way of Pembina, Fond du Lac and Upper Canada and there face the courts in an unfriendly climate.

CHAPTER SEVENTEEN

The War of Words in the East

While the bloodiest battle in Lord Selkirk's struggle to establish an agricultural settlement in the fur country was taking place at Red River and the Earl was on his way west, a war of words of some magnitude was breaking over Montreal. The rough-and-tumble North Westers were better with fists and guns than with pens but they had educated and voluble friends who could help them in moments of special need. The important missiles in this paper war were two in number, a critical treatise on the fur trade by Lord Selkirk, and a "Letter," which was more correctly a book, addressed to Lord Selkirk by Rev. John Strachan. Both were published in Britain in 1816 and reached Montreal almost together when the Earl was absent and making good his invasion of Fort William. At the same time, newspaper correspondents and editors were entering "the war" with verbal guns, mainly through the columns of the *Montreal Herald* and *Montreal Gazette*.

In the fur-trade city's atmosphere, the war was rather one-sided because citizens had more time, more patience and more support for the North West Company cause than for Selkirk's. It was not surprising in the light of the McGillivray Company's place of permanency in the business life of the community. The Earl and Countess of Selkirk and their three children, making a short stay in a big rented house, were more like transients who might depart at any time and never show again. Their rank gave them a certain prestige, of course, but William McGillivray's people had wealth and influence and friends, all of which could be useful in a quarrel.

To be sure, the Earl was making new Montreal friends, but slowly. He was quiet and reserved and unobtrusive; he was backward in penetrating the city's social life. Montrealers recognized him as a visiting gentleman rather than as a businessman and in their modesty, hesitated in drawing him into their activities. The Countess of Selkirk was a better "mixer" and in view of her longer residence at Montreal, became a more familiar personality. During the first months when the family was together, she enjoyed the experience of a Montreal winter, but after the Earl left for the West in June, 1816, to be gone for more than a year, she grew unhappy and became withdrawn. Before the second winter was over, she had reason to hate Montreal. She might have returned to Scotland but she wanted to be in Montreal when the Earl came back and she could serve a useful purpose by watching the political events in which he would be interested. The winter months were unusually cold; the snow deep; she was lonely and worried, but she possessed his quality of determination and persevered.

Selkirk could not be regarded as a fur trader but the fact was that he had had an academic interest at least for more years than many of the traders had been active. His interest, which exceeded his admiration, began when he was a young "knight" looking for "dragons" with which to engage. The slave trade presented a challenge, social injustices of the time another, and the fur trade still another. His meeting in Switzerland with Count Paolo Andreani, an Italian who had visited the North American fur country a few years earlier, sharpened his views about the trade, especially the manner in which the North West Company operated. The Count's information was not totally reliable and he might have been a misleading teacher, but the association made a deep and lasting impression upon the young Scot's mind. The result was that long before he actually penetrated the beaver country, his decision was to write an exposure to which he gave the title: *A Sketch Of The British Fur Trade In North America, With Observations Relative To The North West Company Of Montreal.* Although started before the Earl actually set foot upon the fur-producing territory, the Sketch was being printed and bound at a moment when he was seeing many of the evil aspects of the trade for himself and becoming more engrossed daily in fur trade troubles. He did not see the printed publication until the next year. Jean saw it and read it and observed the reaction of uneasiness it produced in Montreal. If the Earl had chosen to rewrite it at this later date, he could have made it more vivid and more convincing, by far, from the reports he had received and the exhibitions of fur trade methods witnessed.

Even as it was, he did not hide his suspicions of Company misconduct in the trade, malpractices like the abuse of liquor as an inducement in trading with the Indians, and the devaluation of Montreal money in the back country. By giving the Montreal dollar a value of only half, the Company could gain a big advantage on the turnover of goods sold to employees in payment of wages.

The Earl's Sketch turned out to be more a criticism of the Montreal firm's methods than a general description of the trade. He chose to accuse the highly vaunted Company of exaggerating the importance of its business. It didn't really generate new trade for Britain but simply "changed the course of the trade, bringing home by way of Montreal those returns which would otherwise have reached England by a different and more direct channel," meaning the Hudson's Bay Company and Hudson Bay.

The writer accused the North West Company of plundering the native people and resorting to violence when Indian customers turned to offer their furs to rival traders. There was the instance of a cruel revenge for such an offense, the shooting of an Indian and then, to make the lesson more memorable, the hanging of another. But Selkirk was not wholly convincing in this because the record of the years showed the Montreal Company winning and holding a very large share of Indian trade and Indian loyalty, something which was not consistent with Indian abuse as alleged.

He was probably correct in showing the North Westers as the more ruthless traders and the principal offenders in selling liquor to the native people. "Every impartial person acquainted with the Indian trade," he wrote, "is ready, to acknowledge that with respect to sobriety, orderly behaviour and steady adherence to their moral duties, the Servants of the Hudson's Bay Company are much superior to any other class employed in the same business."[1]

"Upon the whole," he added with obvious reference to the Montreal men, "it must be sufficiently evident that the extensive countries occupied by the North West Company are in a state which calls aloud for the attention of the British Legislature; and that the honour of the nation cannot fail to be tarnished, if the outrages now practiced be allowed to go on without effective checks or interference."

Among the North West Company sins to receive the Earl's written attention, of course, was that organization's attitude toward the formation of an agricultural settlement "in a district which had been exhausted of valuable furs by the extirpation of the beaver." Those selfish people who opposed his plan wanted, so obviously, to clutch the whole country for "the exclusive occupation of the savage Indians, the wild beasts of the forests and themselves." What he did not admit was that both Companies had men who despised the very prospect of settlement.

Asking if the fur trade as a whole was as important as claimed by its rulers, the Earl's answer was an emphatic "No." How could anybody be so prejudiced as to believe that a trade with gross returns never exceeding £300,000 should be allowed to condemn an immense territory, "possessing the greatest natural advantages . . . to perpetual sterility?"

Waxing boldly prophetic, he saw the western regions, which traders so selfishly wanted to keep to themselves, affording "an ample means of subsistence to more than thirty millions of British subjects." Were these immense resources of natural wealth to be forgotten forever, "for the sake of a trade to the gross amount of 200,000 or 300,000 pounds per annum?"

But if the Earl was disturbed by the "outrages" he saw at a distance at the time of writing, how much more would he have been horrified by what he saw and heard in the course of his journey to Red River! The crime list as he saw it was long, with such items as the 1815 destruction of the Settlement; the killing and starving of rival traders at Athabasca; the bloody affair at Seven Oaks; the murder of Owen Keveny; the threats against his own life, and so on. If he chose to make the list more exhaustive, Col. Coltman by the end of 1816 could have helped.

But everybody did not share his views and fears, especially after the seizure of Fort William. There were those Montrealers who believed or chose to believe that the Earl was the leading culprit, a meddlesome, scheming, lawless culprit, and that the North Westers were amply justified in the strong action they had taken.

If the McGillivray men read the Earl's denunciation of their Company's methods, they, as officials, offered no direct rebuttal. But they had friends who were ready and eager to counterattack. If words were bullets, those who opposed the Selkirk plan did most of the shooting.

Among the unidentified "snipers" was "Mercator," who sent most of his letters to the *Montreal Herald,* writing often and writing well. He could be relied upon to place Lord Selkirk in the worst possible light, commonly as the author of a clever plan to ruin the North West Company. "His Lordship's Polar Star is self interest, to which all public considerations and the rights of others are invariably sacrificed by him. No man who had not become callous could possibly have used magisterial authority for the systematic purpose of destroying rivals."[2]

It was all a great swindle, even the Hudson's Bay Company's claim to land granted to Selkirk, Mercator said. "Having in his youth studied some law, he was fertile in expedient, if not in chicanery, and lit upon that of getting the Hudson's Bay Company to give him a grant of 117,000 square miles of country, which was no great effort of generosity in those to whom it never belonged."[3] The point intended was that the British King granting the Charter in 1670 did not even have a claim upon the Red River prior to the Treaty of 1763.

The writer sounded very much like a McGillivray employee and may have reminded some Scottish readers of letters appearing in the *Inverness Journal* in 1812, over the name "A Highlander," actually the composition of Simon McGillivray, brother of the celebrated William.

That so many of those who wrote to damage the Earl's image did so without disclosing their identity might have given cause for suspicion. But humiliation made good reading and editors in Montreal certainly did not discourage it. Indeed, the correspondent probably expressed the sentiment of the editor when he wrote that "a British peer turning commercial speculator and land jobber, and leaving his seat in Parliament to wage war in his Britannic Majesty's dominions against a Company of British merchants is, even in these extraordinary times a little singular."[4]

The prize letter and the prize exhibit presented from the North West Company side was the long one — seventy-six printed pages — written by the Reverend John Strachan, Rector of York, Upper Canada, and later Bishop Strachan.[5] His precise motive in writing this "Epistle of Strachan To The Selkirkians," or to anybody who would read it, was debatable. Perhaps he really believed the Selkirk scheme was a swindle but his own words betrayed such a view because the decision to write the letter was made while he was still woefully ignorant of Red River and the Settlement plan. It appeared from his writing that he could even be persuaded that the Red River ran south. But Strachan, the Scottish immigrant with sharply chiseled features and sharp tongue, was rapidly becoming a man of force in both Upper and Lower Canada and there was no doubt about his ability to influence people.

It was a Strachan trait to take a firm stand on every issue, whether adequately informed or not, and quickly his name became one to capture attention across the country. An academic, an Anglican, an imperialist, a Conservative and an anti-American, he possessed all that was needed to make him a leading light in what was known as the Family Compact of Upper Canada, a smug little group which succeeded in perpetuating itself in positions of authority prior to the Rebellion of 1837.

Like most of the North West Company men, Strachan was a Scot by birth and from the time of arrival in Canada, was on good terms with Company leaders living in Montreal. William McGillivray could greet him like an old friend and the lady Strachan married in 1807 was the widow of Andrew McGill, bearer of a name standing out prominently in the fur trade. Indeed, the 300 pounds annuity the new Mrs. Strachan brought with her came, no doubt, from North West Company fur returns.

It was not surprising that Strachan found himself on the side of the North West Company when the Earl's western Colony became the subject of debate. His knowledge of Rupert's Land in general and Red River in particular was sadly deficient but with a declared wish to write a public warning or denunciation, he did not allow a lack of information to stand in his way. He knew something of Lord Selkirk's Prince Edward Island success in colonization, and more about the Baldoon failure. With the latter in mind, he might have been saying: "It's going to happen again but on a bigger scale." He might have been trying, also, to ingratiate himself with McGillivray, knowing very well that a public criticism of Selkirk's plan would bring delight to the Montreal friends. McGillivray did, a few years later, write to Strachan, to acknowledge gratitude.

If the clergyman about to write a criticism felt the need for more basic information, he knew where to obtain exactly what would be of greatest benefit; he wrote to his friend William McGillivray, the supreme being in the North West Company. The contents of the letter have survived:

"My Dear Sir: I have just received from our Friend the Priest, Lord Selkirk's prospectus and have some wish to write him a public letter on the subject as I conceive the whole to be a gross imposition on the nation and calculated to divert the stream of emigration from the Canadas and to cover those who go to Red River with disappointment and misery. There are, however, some things which it is necessary for me to know before I proceed, namely how far the proposed settlement is from Montreal, the nature of the water communication, whether it can be reached by the Lakes, how many carrying places or if any.

"Then the nature of the communication between it and Hudson's Bay and the distance, how long Nelson River is navigable during the season, whether there be carrying places in that direction and how many? What markets can be opened for the produce of the settlement, what kind of soil, how long the winter. ... Perhaps some other local circumstances worth mentioning may occur, whether the settlement does not immediately interfere with the Indian hunting grounds and whether they are pleased or displeased with it. ..."[6]

Then came the great letter, dated at York, Upper Canada, October 5, 1815. It was a far-ranging criticism of the Earl's North American efforts. The writer could not find much to discredit in the Prince Edward Island settlement program but he spoke scornfully about Baldoon, saying it was impossible "to behold with complacency a British Peer turning land speculator. ... For every settler brought into Upper Canada by your Lordship you received 200 acres of land, of which you were bound to grant him 50, making a net profit of 150 acres on each settler."

Of course, settlers going into a wilderness area required more generous assistance, as was recognized by the Imperial Government in dealing with the Loyalists coming from the United States after the Revolutionary War. They were given land, farming utensils and provisions. But the Baldoon people were given a burden of debt, the letter intimated, and it would be worse at Red River where remoteness would prove to be a serious liability. "The most fruitful valley in the world is worth nothing" if hopelessly isolated and it became a falsehood to say the Red River lands were equal to "those of Lower Canada and Nova Scotia, unless their situation be equally favorable."

It was simply ridiculous: "To charge £50 for every hundred acres in a place so remote, is to pillage the unfortunate emigrant; for if he had found his way to Canada, he would have received 200 acres for nothing, or at most £9, the price of survey; and instead of being cut off from all the world, he would have been in a good neighborhood and near a good market for his produce."

Why should Britishers run the risk of settling in the uncivilized surroundings of Rupert's Land when they could have good land and safer surroundings at less costs in the eastern areas? It became the pious hope, therefore, that the "letter" would "prevent any more from encountering the miseries of the polar regions."

The Prospectus, the writer insisted, placed the Earl once again in the category of a land speculator. In this, Strachan had a point but not as big a point as he chose to believe because the Prospectus was never given wide circulation and no land sales were made to the investors to whom an advertising pitch of the kind was normally directed.

Nevertheless, Strachan backed his condemnation of the Prospectus with plausible warnings. First, he would join with the North West Company in scoffing at the validity of the Hudson's Bay Company Charter which conveyed title to the lands in question and was revered by Company officials like the Ten Commandments. That Charter granted by King Charles II was conveyed "under gross ignorance of the geographical situation" and while it gave certain rights to soil and watercourses, it did not, according to Strachan, give any right of transfer and was never intended to extend rights or privileges as far inland as the site of the Settlement. If the dear settler at Red River did not have enough about which to worry, he could consider the strong possibility of the Charter being declared illegal and void, and all land transactions being canceled too.

As he searched for more with which to worry the Red River settlers, he noted that if the International Boundary were to be established at the 49th degree of north latitude, some of Selkirk's land would be alienated and settlers already located on the more southerly holdings would be left in United States territory. Not only that but the writer could see dangerous American influences clawing at the cultural throats of all people residing near the border. He came close to branding himself a British bigot when he yielded slightly to the Earl, presuming he was "too well acquainted with the depravity of the American character to desire any number of that people" in his Settlement. And even if successful in excluding those terrible neighbors from the Colony, there remained that threat of "contamination" from the south. Strachan was right in anticipating the most practical communication between Red River and the outside being by way of the United States, but he was not right in assessing the alternatives to it, namely, becoming American citizens or being cut off from all practical means of communication with the rest of the world.

For those readers who might ignore other warnings, there was the reminder that the country concerned was not much good anyway. True, Sir Alexander Mackenzie had had some favorable remarks for it prior to the proposal to colonize it but Strachan marveled fearfully that anybody would think it fit for farming; "Sir Alex. praises it only as a fine residence for uncivilized men, and the very circumstances which render it valuable to them detract from its value as a civilized colony."

The reverend gentleman thought he knew something about livestock also and he could see nothing encouraging about the prospects in the far West. The Indians who would set fire to a crop ready for harvest would kill farm animals. "It is notorious," he warned, "that the Savages, when hungry, will kill oxen, cows and sheep for a single meal, leaving the remainder of the carcase without regret."

Ignorance can be lamentable. Sometimes it is entertaining. When Dr. Strachan discusses the limitations in sheep and wool production on the western plains, he is likely to produce chuckles from experienced sheepmen. While Selkirk saw a good future for sheep, Strachan answered in these words: "The advantages of these plains for sheep walks may be justly questioned. The grass is extremely coarse, the bottom not close and foggy like English pastures; it will tend, therefore, in all probability, to alter the natural qualities of the sheep. Such plains are frequently unhealthy, and the wolves are innumerable. In Spain, the fineness of the wool depends upon the variations of climate which the Merinos enjoy in going from one part of the kingdom to the other, as the seasons change; nor is it probable that a climate infinitely more severe, and coarser food, without the advantage of changing, will make no alteration in the fleeces of these valuable animals."

After the famous "Letter" was written but before it went to the printer, the settlers who had deserted the Red River Colony in return for transportation in North West Company canoes to Upper Canada, arrived at York and John Strachan hastened to interview them and obtain statements for inclusion in a postscript. Here was testimony too good to miss, from men like Alexander Matheson, a Stromness man who came to Churchill River in 1813 and experienced the hard winter and long walk to York Factory before the snow melted in the spring. He could tell vividly of the hardships on the trail, the food shortages, the bleeding to correct snow blindness and the night camps in the snow. He added what others overlooked, that "Before leaving Churchill to go to York Factory, all were bled." But the Matheson testimony only confirmed the general suffering of the Kildonan people during the winter season, which nobody had ever denied, and said nothing of consequence about Red River. Still, he apparently said about what Dr. Strachan wanted to hear.

Strachan would remind readers that Red River land titles were insecure, that the Colony was so far removed from other British settlements that there could be no hope for assistance in case of an attack, that there was no market for grain or other produce, that there remained the strongest possibility of settlers being massacred by Indians, and that the Colony, if it survived, would never witness the fulfillment of the promises incorporated in the Prospectus.

Having drawn these conclusions, John Strachan wondered why any British would take the risk. "I would strenuously advise those who can live comfortably," he said, "to remain where they are; for the greatest success will not be an equivalent for the miseries they must suffer before this success is realized."

It should have been enough to discourage all but the most hardy and determined. It should also have been enough to demonstrate the folly of making strong and sweeping statements about a land of which the speaker knew little, enough to enterain those Canadians who saw Selkirk's Red River Colony surviving and becoming the cornerstone of a gigantic agricultural industry.

The North West Company circulated the Strachan "Letter" widely. It bespoke the Company's wishful thinking. There is no indication of Lord Selkirk making a direct reply but John Morgan Gray in his good book, *Lord Selkirk Of Red River*, tells that a libel suit was considered.[7] As it was, Selkirk had other troubles sufficient to keep him occupied — mainly in court — and if he had not been a man of extremely strong convictions, he might, after all the harassment suffered, have been inclined to agree with John Strachan, that it was a mistake.

CHAPTER EIGHTEEN

The Distressing Year in Court

Chief Justice Monk and Mr. Justice Bowen looked grave — as judges are supposed to look — and men whose lives would be affected by decisions soon to be handed down, carried expressions of worry. It was the opening day of Oyer and Terminer, February 21, 1818, and the Montreal courtroom, cold and dreary at the best of times, was colder and more crowded than usual.

But to anyone familiar with the leaders and personalities in the great Rupert's Land disputes, this courtroom scene bore a strong hint of an Old Home Week. Most of the prominent figures from both the Red River Settlement and the fur trade were there, either as accusers, accused or spectators. William McGillivray, wearing a fine beaverskin coat and the cultivated smile of a successful businessman, greeted some of those around him like long-lost friends, and carefully ignored others. He had an assuring wave of the hand for most men occupying the witness benches, unshaven men with the moderately dark complexions revealing hereditary compromises, and clothes fashioned to endure in the outdoors.

Lord Selkirk, with straight and slim figure, reddish hair and a boyish bashfulness, was there, this time as an observer. He looked more frail and sickly than ever. Just a month earlier, while returning from the West, he went far out of his way to face the ordeal of court at Sandwich, one of the Upper Canada seats of justice, just across the river from Detroit. For him there was more courtroom exposure to come, much more. That recent session at Sandwich was the first in a long series of legal battles which would make this the most unhappy year of his life. It would be a year to furnish a rather complete and unpleasant review of all the bizzare events from the onset of the Pemmican War, through the attacks upon the Settlement, to His Lordship's injudicious seizure of Fort William and repeated resistance to arrest. The year would bring a few judicial successes, an equal number of reverses and no end of frustration. The court procedures would be dreary and drawn out, like a bad winter.

It would soon be two years since the Battle of Seven Oaks and there was loud complaint about delays. McGillivray blamed Selkirk for failure to return promptly "to this Province [of Lower Canada] with the special

Commissioner to meet the accusations against himself and to establish his charges against others." Instead of recognizing this responsibility, he "went on a tedious and circuitous voyage for his own private purposes and did not get to Montreal until February."[1]

McGillivray was right; the Earl did not return promptly but his only legal obligation was to comply with Coltman's order to appear for charges at Montreal on March 1, 1818. He was in ample time to meet this date and he took the opportunity to present himself at Sandwich to face accusers on certain other counts laid against him.

In that January appearance at Sandwich he heard specific charges of theft of eighty-three muskets at Fort William, illegal entry at the same place on August 13, 1816, assault and false imprisonment of William Smith, and resisting arrest. The Court found insufficient evidence and ruled to require the accused to appear later, but set bail at a more reasonable figure, £350. Selkirk interpreted the Sandwich result as a first step toward the withdrawal of all charges. But it was too soon for such optimism.

His return to receive the warm embraces of Lady Jean and their children — Isabella, Daer and baby Katherine — after an absence of more than a year and a half, brought sheer happiness but almost at once he was caught up again by the demands of law. At home only a few days, he received a letter from Attorney General N. F. G. Uniacke, notifying that "the Government of the Province of Lower Canada has transferred to the Courts of Upper Canada for trial the cases of George Campbell, Louis Perrault, William McGillivray, Joseph Brisbois, Francis Fermin Boucher, Paul Brown, John Cooper, Hugh Bannerman, John Severight, Alexander Mackenzie, John McDonald, John McLoughlin, Allan McDonald, Simon Fraser, Hugh McGillis, Hector McDonald, Jean Baptiste Desmarais, Cuthbert Grant, Duncan Cameron, John Dugal Cameron, William Shaw, Peter Pangman [known as Bostonois] Robert Gunn and Seraphin Lamarre, accused of offenses in the Indian Territory."[2]

"The greatest number of these persons have been committed by your Lordship in your capacity of a Magistrate for the Indian Territories," the message continued, "and as you are in possession of the information and evidence necessary to support the several prosecutions, I beg leave to request that your Lordship will communicate the same to me in order that I may transmit it to the Attorney General of Upper Canada or that you will instruct the Law Office of that Province in support of their prosecutions."

Here was that "package of criminals" of which the Earl wrote in August, 1816, with a few more added to it. He was not to be allowed to forget that he was still prosecuting as well as defending. This shift of venue to Upper Canada pleased the North West Company people because it would bring the Court nearer to many of the witnesses they would be calling. And because it brought satisfaction to the North Westers, it brought objection from Lord Selkirk.

Manitoba Archives

The Selkirk house at St. Mary's Isle, Kirkcudbrightshire, 1911

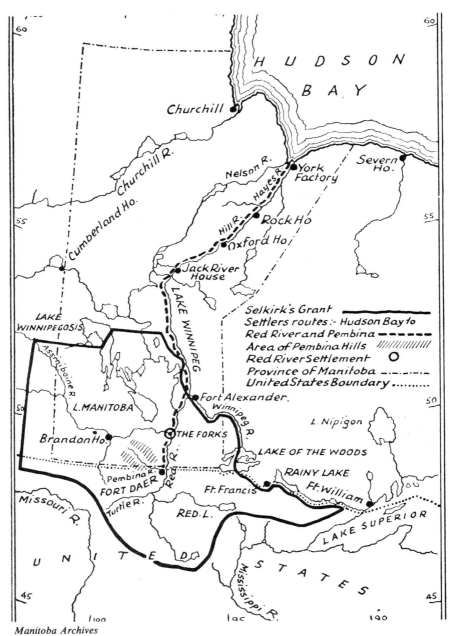

Map showing Selkirk's grant and the route taken by early settlers to Red River and Fort Daer

Manitoba Archives

Agricultural and household implements used by Selkirk settlers in the early 1820's: 1 and 2 - The sickles with which the grain was cut 3 - A fork used to lift a boiled round of meat out of the vessel or pot 4 - The flail with which threshing was done on the barn floor 5 - A chimney utensil used to arrange the burning wood - the sockets had short handles of wood. 6 - A garden hoe 7 - Yoke with which animals were fastened in the stable 8 - A mold in which candles were made.

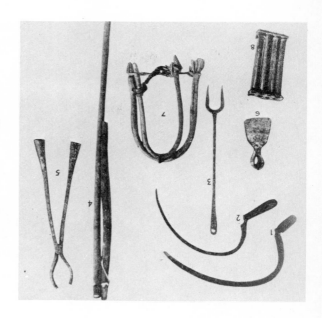

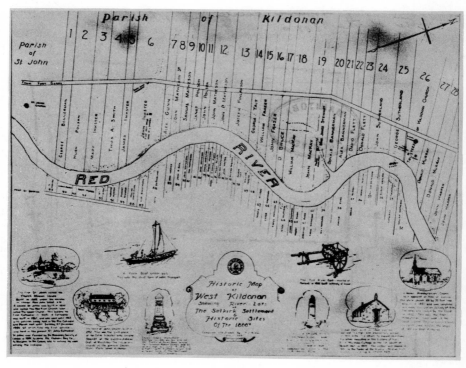

Manitoba Archives
Historic map showing river lots of Selkirk Settlement and historic sites of the 1800's

Quern, or hand mill, used by the settlers

Farm equipment in use in the early 1820's: 1 - Old ox harness 2 - Hollowed block and mallet for barley crushing 3 - The "quern" - flour grinder 4 - Seed basket for hand sowing 5 - Collar and harness 6 - Shoulder yoke for water carrying

Manitoba Archives

Types of Selkirk settlers in 1822: 1 and 2 - A Swiss colonist with wife and children from the Canton of Berne 3 - A German settler from the disbanded de Meuron Regiment 4 - A Scottish Highland colonist 5 - An immigrant colonist from French Canada

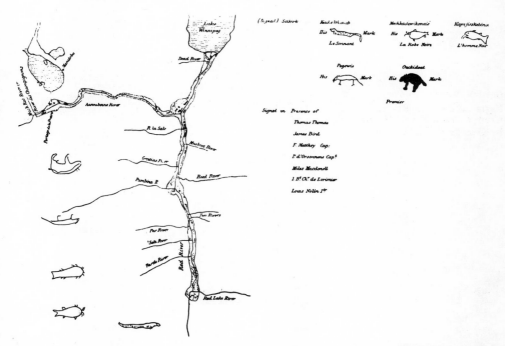

Manitoba Archives

Lands at Red River conveyed by Indian chiefs to Lord Selkirk in 1817

Hole cut in ice for cow to drink (from a pen and ink drawing by George E. Finlay, c. 1846-1848)

Farm house, Red River, 1846 (from a pen and ink drawing by George E. Finlay, 1846)

Split Lake and Nelson House brigade leaving Norway House

Watercolor by Peter Rindisbacher of Fort Douglas on the Red River

York Factory at the zenith of its influence in 1853. Of all these buildings, the depot in the center is the only one left. On the right is the summer mess house, and on the left the guest house.

Ministry of Industry and Tourism, Province of Ontario

One of the most imaginative historic re-creations in North America is Old Fort William at Thunder Bay, Ontario, which recalls Canada's fur trading era and the brief but lusty life of the voyageur.

The trials seemed to be assuming ever larger proportions. At the moment when the Earl sat as an observer in the courtroom at Montreal, more than a hundred charges ranging from larceny to murder stood against servants and friends of the North West Company and a smaller number against the Earl and his people. Murder charges alone numbered forty-two, nearly all against men who had participated at Seven Oaks. Nineteen men from the North Westers' side were charged with arson arising from the burning of buildings at Red River. Against Selkirk's people were five accusations of robbery, six of grand larceny, nine of stealing a house, one of malicious shooting, five of pulling down a dwelling, three of false imprisonment, two of murder and one — against Miles Macdonell — of assault.

Lawyers labored overtime and prospered. Their work was so multiplied that Attorney General John Beverley Robinson of Upper Canada, where most of the charges were now to be heard, would write that he was "perhaps the only member of the profession in this Province who is not engaged on the one side or the other of this extraordinary contest."[3]

If the Earl was unhappy about the turn of events and the mounting costs to him, why did he allow himself to be held like a slave to the courts? Much of the trouble was of his own making and it would have seemed quite proper for him to make an effort to settle out of court, especially if the opportunity was presented to him. By yielding just a little on principle, he might have seen the highly complex and costly involvement brought suddenly to an end.

Commissioner Coltman, true to his inclinations, favored a settlement by negotiation and tried to promote it. He was an honorable fellow and much respected by all who knew him but he was, by nature, a compromiser, a seeker for peaceful settlement more than a stickler for justice. Having conferred with William McGillivray, he believed he had a solution; by his Master Plan, the North West Company would retire completely from Rupert's Land, leaving the trade exclusively to the English Company and the Colony unmolested to Selkirk, while the Hudson's Bay Company would withdraw from the Athabasca area in favor of the North West Company, and parties on both sides would drop all charges before the courts.

There was much to be said for such a working arrangement and, after all, leaders on both sides had shown an earlier interest in some negotiated division of the trading area as a means of ending the costly and brutal competition. With the added advantage of full settlement of legal differences, this seemed like the appropriate time to move on it. It is quite possible that Andrew Colvile, in London, would have given support to the proposal but the idea did not reach him. It was placed before Lord Selkirk and there it met its doom. Coltman might be a compromiser but not Selkirk; he would never be one to exchange what he considered justice for expediency. He had too much of the spirit of the Scottish Covenanters and John Knox for that. He would see the business through, even though the trials ruined him financially and wrecked him physically — which they did.

At the February hearings, Lord Selkirk had reason to be moderately encouraged. Seventeen of those charged with the murder of Governor Semple were indicted. Against Miles Macdonell, the Grand Jury ruled No Bill on the charges of assault, false imprisonment and stealing a dwelling. But Colin Robertson did not fare as well and the jury brought back a True Bill of Indictment against him and four others for pulling down and destroying a house.

Cuthbert Grant, who led the halfbreeds and North West Company servants on that fateful day of Seven Oaks, was one of those against whom a True Bill of Indictment was found and an application for bail on his behalf was refused. A later appeal for bail was granted, much to Lord Selkirk's horror, and then, when Grant was wanted again, it was discovered that he had disappeared and was presumed to be somewhere far to the west.

Making his own appearance before the Court of King's Bench in Montreal, in conformity to the order under which he was bound by Col. Coltman, Selkirk found that his case, also, was being transferred to the Court of Oyer and Terminer in Upper Canada, where he would answer to the charges of resisting arrest in November at Fort William, a second resistance of arrest in the following March, resistance to a writ of restoration involving Fort William, and a further resistance to arrest at Sandwich. It looked like a reprehensible degree of resistance but still it was difficult to understand the law officers in choosing at that time to re-impose the original and seemingly ridiculous bail of £6,000.

Meanwhile, Selkirk's loyal personal physician, John Allan, rode from Montreal to Sandwich on a horse — well over 500 miles — to face his charge of resisting arrest, and was rewarded with acquittal.

Lord Selkirk hoped to have the charges confronting him brought forward to a special summer court at York but it was not arranged. For him, now, the main test would be at Sandwich in September and to that place Lord and Lady Selkirk, the two older children, Samuel Gale, the solicitor, John Allen and Capt. D'Orsonnens journeyed in late August, traveling mainly by riverboat and lakeboat. Under other circumstances, it would have been a happy outing but the uncertainty of the impending court and a new writ served on the Earl at Detroit were enough to prevent full enjoyment. If more were needed to produce uneasiness, the Earl's pallor and wrenching cough would do it. The new warrant was placed on behalf of James Grant who had been among the North Westers arrested two years earlier and who was now claiming trespass damages by the Selkirk party when en route past his Fond du Lac post.

There seemed no escape from the vengeful North Westers but the concern of the moment was at the Sandwich Assizes. The initial charge there was that of resisting arrest on the first instance at Fort William and in short order the Grand Jury rejected it. Attorney General Robinson was displeased and decided aginst presentation of the companion charge involving alleged assault and illegal arrest of Under Sheriff Smith. Instead, he advanced the hastily prepared charge of conspiracy to injure the North West Company. Some strange and ugly courtroom scenes followed, bringing credit to nobody.

Lord Selkirk found more sympathy from the Grand Jury than he might have expected, even though he objected publicly to two members who, he contended, were commercial agents of the North West Company. The Judge was unimpressed and it was soon apparent to the accused gentleman that he could expect no more than minimum understanding from the Attorney General. The latter's conduct infuriated the Earl and verbal exchanges became loud and shamefully unworthy. Selkirk's impatience and impulsiveness were probably symptoms of nervous exhaustion but that did not justify his attempts to take courtroom liberties, for which he was reprimanded by the presiding judge. Had it not been for the restraining influence of Samuel Gale, the Earl might have been cited for Contempt of Court. The undignified performance dragged on for several days until the Judge, for reasons most onlookers could not understand, terminated the proceedings by an abrupt adjournment.

The affair was thoroughly reviewed in the following weeks. Lord Selkirk, making a pretense of injury, complained to the Governor General: "Only one of the charges to which I had been bound to answer was brought forward; this indictment has been thrown out by the Grand Jury, and the others appear to have been dropped; but new charges which had been studiously concealed were brought forward, as if to take me by surprise. . . . Under all the circumstances of the case, I cannot think there is any obligation on me to remain longer in these Provinces, when objects of paramount importance call me elsewhere. I regret that I cannot attend the trials which are expected to take place at York, but I believe no material inconvenience can arise from my absence, as I leave persons who are capable of giving testimony on all points with which I am personally acquainted. . . . I have already put into his [the Attorney General's] hands the necessary materials for prosecution of all the individuals who were arrested under my warrants, and whose trials have been referred to Upper Canada."[4]

At about the same time, Dr. Allan, the Earl's physician and confidant, was writing to the Attorney General to clear up a few points which in his opinion were still being misconstrued. "Like an English sailor," he said, "I am accustomed to speak with frankness." He wrote with frankness, stating that "When you proceed to speak of Lord Selkirk and his people at Fort William, as if you were in possession of the evidence on both sides of the question, you will permit me to observe that you deceive yourself and may be led to do injustice to others."

Then, presenting the Attorney General with a capsule of the much-discussed events at Fort William, the versatile young doctor demonstrated how differently the same happenings could be seen and interpreted. It was one of the most significant statements made in the defense of the Selkirk action. In Allan's words: "Lord Selkirk caused Fort William to be entered of necessity in the execution of his duty as a Magistrate; he afterwards took up his abode in it to avoid the preparations which were made to attack him in the open plain. He could not go on to Red River that summer, for his own houses there had been burnt, the colonists were driven off, the season was advanced, and a body of the North West servants were at that time traitorously in arms, with the artillery provided by Government for the defence of the settlement posted on the River Winnipic in order to prevent the entrance of any but the North-West people into the country. He remained at Fort William instead of retiring to Lower Canada till the spring, in order to be nearer at hand to render the earliest assistance to the widows and orphans who had been expelled. He went forward with the first navigation in the spring to Red River, and by these exertions and by his conduct, he provided for the support of the surviving settlers, widows and orphans who returned to the Colony, and procured for the remains of the dead the charity of a grave, which had been denied them by the North West Company."[5]

The Attorney General, after seeing both Dr. Allan's and Lord Selkirk's letters written following the September assizes, chose to present his own views to the Lieutenant Governor, apparently trying to justify his own actions. He explained that his first Bill against the Earl for resisting "the execution of a legal warrant by an officer of justice" received scant attention by the Grand Jury and was turned down. He was prepared, he admitted, to find a feeling existing in his Lordship's favor but still found it difficult to understand so much sympathy for a peer of Great Britain who would commit crimes "which should have put any private individuals out of the pale of society."

After rejection of his first Bill, "in as short a time almost as must necessarily have been occupied in reading [it]", the Attorney General felt reluctant about presenting a similar one for resisting the Deputy Sheriff of the Western District who was at Fort William to execute a warrant of restitution and instead of being allowed to carry out his purpose, was subjected to the added indignity of being imprisoned for six weeks or until released by the special Commissioners. Rather than expose the administration of justice "to a second insult" by another rejection, he, the Attorney General, submitted the Bill charging the Earl with conspiracy to ruin the trade of the North West Company, "grounded principally on His Lordship's conduct at Fort William." What followed was the unfortunate and unforeseen adjournment, leaving the Earl, as the Attorney General feared, able to say that nothing could be brought against him, that he was there anxious to meet his accusers, "and ready to show the falsehood of their charges," and that he could "conceive himself no longer under obligation to remain in the Province."[6]

The four members of the Selkirk family returned to Montreal, realizing full well that the new trials at York would tempt the Earl to change his plans and attend. He wondered what infamy McGillivray's people would be attempting in his absence. But his wife, more worried about his health than she admitted, urged him to let Samuel Gale and John Allan maintain the watching brief while he went on his way to England. Gale, who was recovering from an illness, and Allan had remained behind at York, hoping the Earl would not subject himself to the strain of attendance but expecting he would be there. It was the prevailing opinion that he should be present but Gale, having worried about the Earl's emotional outbursts at Sandwich, was secretly happy when he did not appear.

The North West Company forces were well prepared for their defense and their leading attorney, Samuel Sherwood, from Montreal, directed his comments and cross-examination with brilliance. The Attorney General's performance in prosecution was mediocre. As one after another of the men arrested on Magistrate Selkirk's order appeared before Chief Justice William Dummer Powell, Mr. Justice Campbell and Mr. Justice Boulton, North West Company confidence mounted. The first of the accused to be called were Francis Fermin Boucher and Paul Brown, charged with the murder of Governor Semple, and the defense made much of the folly of even considering a Settlement at Red River where it would be an aggravation to the native people. Wasn't the whole idea conceived by the Hudson's Bay Company to ruin the North West Company? Then with the harassment of the Pemmican War, the destruction of Fort Gibraltar and the interception of the North Westers' mail, how could there be hope of averting a clash? Weren't the Selkirk people inviting trouble?

The tragic events of June 19, 1816, were described again and again with much debate about who fired the first shot and the real intent of the Cuthbert Grant followers who bypassed Fort Douglas and were traveling in a northeasterly direction when the Governor came to intercept them. As the defense told it, the mounted men from Qu'Appelle and Portage la Prairie had a double purpose and all legitimate: first to escort two cartloads of pemmican intended for the provisioning of an incoming brigade of canoes on the Red River, and second, to warn the canoe crews that Semple had his cannon set up to command all river traffic at his location.

Samuel Gale squirmed as he watched and listened, increasingly confident that few if any of the men charged under warrants from Lord Selkirk would be convicted. He longed to take an active part in the prosecution but this the Attorney General refused. It was Robinson's error, in the first place, to charge the Cuthbert Grant men with the murder of Governor Semple in whose conduct it was comparatively easy to establish provocative acts. Why did the Officer of the Crown not accuse these men with the murder of John Rogers, the man who saw the hopelessness of Semple's intervention and dropped to his knees to cry for the compassion that would save his life — and was then shot?

As it turned out, the jury returned to declare Boucher and Brown Not Guilty. So it was with those who followed, including "the Gentlemen Partners of the North West Company" who were named as Accessories Before and After the Fact in the murder of Semple. The list included Alexander Mackenzie, Hugh McGillis, John McDonald, Simon Fraser and John McLoughlin. The presiding judge gave the unmistakable lead, declaring that there was not "a scintilla of evidence against any of them."[7]

The Earl's absence certainly did not go unnoticed at the trials. "It was expected that the Earl of Selkirk would have attended the late Court of Oyer and Terminer, at which the trials of his charges against the North West Company took place," the *Montreal Gazette* added in its York report of the acquittals. "It would appear that His Lordship set out from Montreal on the 22nd ult., as was supposed, on his way to this Province, but a few days afterwards it was ascertained that he had directed his course to New York, and was expected to embark for England in a vessel appointed to sail on the 28th."

The business matters of "paramount importance," of which he wrote in the previous month, arose in part from an English communication telling that his seat in the House of Lords was in jeopardy. A peerage election was expected and Lord Selkirk, absent for almost three years, should be at home. Jean and the children were remaining at Montreal because his Lordship would be coming back as soon as business matters would permit.

The late warrant for his arrest served in connection with an alleged plundering at Fond du Lac was quashed, but still it was not the end of his legal tribulations. Two civil actions brought against him, both for false imprisonment, were not heard until the spring assizes at York in 1819. Strange as it seemed to all, including J. B. Robinson, with whom Selkirk had disagreed noisily, this man was invited to conduct the defense. Robinson, however, had arranged already to act for Mackenzie and Smith, the plaintiffs.

The alleged circumstances of detention were already well known, Mackenzie claiming to have been held in the "Black Hole" at Fort William where his addiction to liquor was encouraged and at which time he, as a partner of the North West Company, was induced to "sell" Fort William and much stock of goods to the Earl. The jury reached a verdict of Guilty and the plaintiff was awarded damages of £1,500.

The other case, that of William Smith, who, as Deputy Sheriff of the Western District, had attempted to arrest the Earl on a warrant for felony when at Fort William, was scarcely less unusual; the Under Sheriff, instead of being allowed to carry out the arrest of a Magistrate, was promptly lodged with other prisoners from March 19 to May 11, 1817. The defense argued that Smith's imprisonment was voluntary but that was difficult to accept and the jury found in favor of the plaintiff. Smith was awarded damages of £500, making his stay at Fort William fairly profitable.

The Earl, contrary to his intentions, did not return and the *Montreal Gazette* of May 19, 1819, quoting from the *New York Spectator* of the 11th, disclosed what friends of the family expected: "We understand that Lady Selkirk and family arrived this morning from Canada, and that they have taken their passage in the Packer Ship, *James Munroe,* for Liverpool."

For Lord Selkirk's failure to return, there was a very good reason.

CHAPTER NINETEEN

Warfare Ended

He was not running away from the courts — far from it — but in responding to certain demands for his presence in Britain, he was finding a certain satisfaction in irreverently turning his aristocractic backside to Upper and Lower Canada and the North West Company which was at the base of most of his troubles. He was saddened at leaving his wife and three lovable children in Montreal but they would be safe and he would return in a few months, hopefully with better health.

It would be good to see England and Scotland again, even in winter, although he was not looking forward with any pleasure to the ocean voyage from New York to Liverpool. He was not a good sailor at the best of times and at this season travel could be most disagreeable. It was disagreeable; for most of the voyage, the sailing ship reared and dipped on seas acting as if they held a grudge — like angry North Westers deprived of their pemmican. Nothing, however, lasts forever, not even toothache or seasickness, and there was comfort in the thought of Liverpool and St. Mary's Isle and familiar places and faces. The Mersey Estuary with its low clouds and heavy ship traffic was the first hint of home but Liverpool was clammy cold and even the normally bright and cheeerful St. Mary's Isle, in the absence of Jean and the children, proved to be a dreary place.

Right away, the Earl's doctor ordered him to bed, there to remain until he regained some strength and color and appetite — and overcame the recurring spells of rasping and exhausting coughing. It was the first of a new round of setbacks. While so confined, he received a report from Upper Canada, a mixture of good and bad. The cheering news was that he had been cleared on the charges of resisting the execution of warrants for arrest at Fort William and this brought double pleasure because it could be seen as the court's answer to the impulsive outburst from Colonial Secretary, Lord Bathurst, whose order on February 11, 1817, "to take care that an indictment be prepared against his Lordship," seemed to supersede the usual processes of law. The rest of the Upper Canada news was not as favorable: an indictment on the count of conspiracy to ruin the North West Company.

By this time, Selkirk should have become conditioned to the occasional rebuke from the courts, but it stung severely when the election for the peerage seat for which he was a candidate went against him. Being too long absent and then being ill when he should have been marshaling his supporters, he simply failed to gain enough votes. It should not have been surprising but it carried the disturbing hint that even his friends near home might have lost faith in him. It tended to confirm a fear that in this land renowned for British Justice where he expected to command more understanding for his actions than in the Canadas, most public figures remained under the spell of Lord Bathurst's premature but scathing denunciations.

One disappointment after another made him think his store of luck was exhausted, like over-trapped beavers on the Assiniboine. But after swallowing a succession of bitter pills, there was one small and sweet morsel of satisfaction when his brother-in-law, Sir James Montgomery, who married Elizabeth Douglas, sought through his chair in the House of Commons to reveal the truth about the festering North American dispute. Exercising a member's right, he moved for the tabling and then the publishing of all pertinent communications passing to and from the Government offices. The reply became public information under the title: Papers Relating To The Red River Settlement, 1819, and survived to become a valuable source of information for scholars and historians, but failed to make much of an immediate impression.

The return of Lady Selkirk and the children to St. Mary's Isle brought a ray of cheer, but Jean saw the deterioration in her husband's health and was shocked by the more frequent bouts of morning coughing and growing signs of respiratory bleeding. She set about steadfastly to curtail his activities, hoping this would conserve his strength. It was of no avail. The stubborn disease tightened its deathly grip on him and Jean, acting on medical advice, made plans to take him away for the winter and try the therapy of relaxation under the warm skies at the south of France. Her brother, Andrew Colvile, would look after the Earl's interests and keep him informed, especially with respect to developments at the Colony and in the Canadas. It was a good idea and the family took up winter residence at the quiet town of Pau, in the shadow of the Pyrenees Mountains.

Knowing that the Earl was a very sick man, and depressed, friends and relatives were casting about, anxiously, for anything that might help or cheer him. Dr. George Bryce told of the Earl's sister, Katherine, appealing to her brother's friend and classmate from the University of Edinburgh years, Sir Walter Scott, for a message. This, Sir Walter — also far from having good health at the time — was glad to furnish and declared publicly that he had never in his life known "a man of more generous and disinterested disposition, or one whose talents and performance were better qualified to bring great and National schemes to conclusion."[1]

Meanwhile, the two old and belligerent trading Companies continued to quarrel, coming closer and closer to open warfare. The Red River Settlement, having suffered much, was enjoying a respite but in the rich and remote Athabaska, where the North West Company aspired to a trading monopoly, almost every conceivable form of violence was tried. The Montreal men were the more aggressive and the more ruthless — also the more successful in obtaining business — and when servants of the Hudson's Bay Company received a rumor of a North West Company invasion from the northern trading region for the purpose of seizing the rival forts on the Saskatchewan River, Governor William Williams resolved to cripple the tormentors with cannons if nothing else would do it. His plan was to fortify the area of Grand Rapids, close to the mouth of the Saskatchewan River. In the spring of 1819, when Lord Selkirk's condition was taking a serious turn and the North West Company's brigades were setting out on the long journey to Fort William, Governor Williams was setting his trap by placing cannons and swivels at a location commanding the lower end of the rapids, and more cannons on a small boat on the lake. The latter, an improvised gunboat, was better known as "Williams' Warship."

When the North West Company canoes came down, on their way to Fort William, the gentlemen partners, with thought for their own safety, would walk the two miles around the rapids while the canoemen would "shoot" through rather than portage, then wait at the lower end for the gentlemen. For Governor Williams who knew the routine, it was a simple matter to seize cargoes and make prisoners of the officials. The prominent partners falling into his hands in that spring of 1819 made an imposing array, Benjamin Frobisher, John Duncan Campbell, John George McTavish, Angus Shaw and others. It was showing a total disregard for the Prince Regent's Proclamation of two years earlier but Williams, defiant and unrepentant, was reported to have said that he cared "not a curse for the Prince Regent's Proclamation." He would act on the authority of the Charter of the Hudson's Bay Company and as Governor he would do as he considered proper. He intended to drive out of the country, every "damned North Wester or perish in the attempt."

Most people agreed that the trade could not continue with so much nonproductive effort and late in the year, while Lord Selkirk was sequestered in the south of France, Andrew Colvile and Edward Ellice, two of the most influential figures in the English Company and Montreal Company respectively, were meeting in London for some highly confidential discussions about possible measures which would reduce the violence or remove the cause of violence. Coalition in some form would do it and Ellice, on behalf of his Company, was interested in obtaining a majority of shares in the Hudson's Bay Company. Colvile, never one to pass up an opportunity of a profit, was interested in making it possible for Ellice to achieve his purpose. The discussions reached the point where Ellice was offering an undertaking to halt all legal proceedings and claims for damages which his

Company and Company servants had against Lord Selkirk and his agents, it being presumed that Lord Selkirk's people would likewise surrender all their claims and actions against the North West Company. Secondly, Ellice would give the assurance which he knew the officials of the Hudson's Bay Company would feel honor bound to demand, namely, to promise the Red River settlers that they would receive "the same support which Lord Selkirk by his engagement with them had promised."[2]

Andrew Colvile thought well of the proposal and was prepared to present it at a meeting of the Committee of the Hudson's Bay Company, but before so doing he felt morally bound to consult his ailing brother-in-law. The Earl was not a director but his voice was strong and even on his deathbed he was emphatic in opposition to any compromise with the North West Company. Colvile should have known how Selkirk would react but on the chance that the sick man had grown weary of the troubles in which Company and Colony seemed to be constantly immersed, he would confer by writing. He might have saved himself the effort. Selkirk was sick but his convictions were unchanged. He would reckon it "immoral as well as disgraceful," he said in reply, if such a deal were entered into strictly from "views of pecuniary advantage." And as for giving up or selling the Settlement, "that is entirely out of the question. I know of no consideration that would induce me to abandon it. I ground this resolution not only on the principle of supporting the settlers whom I have already sent to the place, but also because I consider my character at stake upon the success of the undertaking and upon proving that it was neither a wild and visionary scheme nor a trick to cover sordid plans of aggression."[3]

Edward Ellice was pressing Colvile for some indication of probable reception of the scheme by the Hudson's Bay Company. Having received Selkirk's letter, Colvile wrote to Ellice on the last day of the year. "Lord Selkirk," he said, "considers that if the N.W.Co. were to acquire a preponderating influence in the management of the H.B.Co., his property in the Settlement and the people who have settled . . . would be completely at the mercy of that Association."[4] Colville might have added that the Earl was dying but his spirit was unyielding, just as it had been unyielding when Col. Coltman proposed a division of trading territory and a settlement of all current legal differences.

There was no complaint about the warm sun and kindly climate in the south of France but it wasn't enough. Lady Selkirk and the children waited in vain for that improvement in the Earl's health for which they prayed. The cruel disease commonly called consumption would not loosen its grip and the frail body became steadily weaker until release by death on April 8, 1820. "For several weeks his strength has been rapidly declining," Andrew Colvile reported, "and we were all prepared to hear of the fatal termination of his illness."[5]

The big question now: What will happen to the Settlement and the Hudson's Bay Company?

Fortunately for the Colony at Red River, effectively cut off from the rest of the world, Andrew Colvile vowed to be its guardian. He possessed both the resources and the ability to do it well. During the Selkirk illness, he assumed the major responsibility and directed the Colony affairs very much as the Earl would have wished. Now, out of respect for his late brother-in-law and affection for his widowed sister who shared the family loyalty to the Colony, Colvile was anxious to see the Selkirk policies perpetuated. The Settlement would have his best personal attention.

But there was no guarantee that Selkirk's stubborn objection to some measure of cooperation or union with the rival Company would stand long against the demands for economies. Actually, it did not survive more than a few months. Edward Ellice, who was willing to negotiate for a consolidation just weeks earlier, was still anxious to see the traders in both Companies abandoning their expensive conflicts, and equally anxious to see the partners in his organization sharing in the use of Hudson Bay, a shipping lane offering much greater economies than the long and slow canoe route via Fort William to Montreal.

It wouldn't have happened while Lord Selkirk was alive but now that his voice was silent, the principals from the two Companies — Andrew Colvile, J. Berens, Jun., and J. H. Pelly from the Hudson's Bay Company, and William and Simon McGillivray and Edward Ellice from the North West Company, began discussions and quickly came to an acceptable understanding. By March 26, 1821, less than a year after Lord Selkirk's death, an agreement was signed to provide for a union. It would give the two parties an equality in shares and an equality in profits and losses. In a coalition, one Company name would have to disappear. Many of the proud partners with Highland names were saddened to think of the North West Company ceasing to be a familiar force across the continent but it was to the advantage of all to retain the name on that much-discussed Charter granted by King Charles II in 1670. For obvious reasons, the old dispute concerning the validity of the Hudson's Bay Company Charter would cease. Those who formerly challenged the validity would now be among traders deriving protection and benefit and be at once defenders.

A certain number of shares in the new Company were to be set aside for servants, chief factors and chief traders. Everybody would feel the changes. People who had been enemies for years were now expected to forget their differences and work together. It would not be easy for men who tried to destroy each other to become suddenly friendly and forgiving. There would be new leaders, among them a young man with only a brief experience in the fur country but with unusual leadership and energy, George Simpson, shortly to become a familiar figure at Red River.

If Lord Selkirk had been alive, he might have blocked the plan to effect a union. He had his reasons. But however conscientious he might have been in opposing it, the union brought to the Red River community the best security it had known. There would be no recurrences of the destructive attacks suffered in 1815 and 1816. That was enough to warrant rejoicing along the river, even though all thinking people probably surmised that Red River's troubles were not all in the past. Moreover, there was reason to wonder if the Colony would ever again have such a friend and leader as its founder.

Those who suggested or argued that the late Lord Selkirk was engaged in colonization for the dollar benefits to himself should have been presented with Chester Martin's estimate of the net cost to the Earl of his eight-year association with the Red River Settlement: £114,000 or over half a million dollars. His influence in the Hudson's Bay Company did not survive for very long after his death, but in the western Settlement and in the broadening agricultural community, it was different; what he started at the Forks not only survived but gave promise of living forever in the Farming Empire of the West.

CHAPTER TWENTY

The Settlers Must "Walk Alone"

Red River was not out of trouble and danger. Like the child who gets measles, mumps and chickenpox, the youthful Colony seemed unable to escape a succession of disorders. The latest Colony affliction — striking while Lord Selkirk was facing the courts and tuberculosis — was a plague of grasshoppers, destroying nearly all crops in 1818 and 1819 and forcing residents to winter again at Pembina where they would be nearer the source of buffalo meat. Colin Robertson spoke too soon when he reported to Lord Selkirk on July 18, 1818, that "the old Scottish sentiment of Peace and Plenty is at last realized on the fertile plains of Assiniboia." Before he had sealed the letter, the hoppers were descending in countless and ravenous millions and the threat of famine loomed again.

Nor had the danger of North West Company-inspired attack passed. The trade war at Athabasca was at the peak of its intensity and it could erupt at Red River just as readily as at Grand Rapids where the Hudson's Bay Company Governor was preparing to become the aggressor for a change.

Among the last instructions directed to Captain Matthey by the ailing Lord Selkirk was to build a "hexagonal blockhouse" for the protection of settlers who might find themselves again under attack. Under frontier conditions, savage thrusts might come from any direction. Indeed, attack upon Company stores by the rebellious de Meurons was not being overlooked as a possible prelude to their departure from the settlement. Ironically, the settlers figured their old enemies, the halfbreeds, would be their allies in the event of a de Meuron onslaught.

Miles Macdonell, still unpopular but still strutting with an air of authority, bespoke the danger in a Proclamation "to the loyal servants of the Red River Settlement" who had come forward so splendidly in defense of lives and property. The affairs of the Colony were still in a troubled state, he declared, but he was now promising on behalf of the Hudson's Bay Company and the Earl of Selkirk that "in case any of you should be maimed or hurt in defence of your just rights, you shall receive a pension equal to that given in the British service."[1]

Poor Miles Macdonell! He was now like a harp with a broken chord. He had become a lonely figure and disgruntled. This deposed monarch was obsessed with the idea that he had not received salary payments and the land grants he was promised. Writing to Andrew Colvile who was handling the Earl's affairs during the latter's illness, he noted the good position paying £300 per year which he left when Lord Selkirk asked him to proceed to England in 1810. "I am now many years older, thrown out of every situation, my property neglected and wasted in my absence, and I have lost many friends by espousing to the interests of Lord Selkirk." He did have the justice to say in conclusion: "I have too great respect and attachment for the [Selkirk] family ever to give their enemies more room to exult by uttering a complaint."[2] But to his letter was appended a statement of estimated back salary with interest at 5 per cent and expenses, totaling £4,473 — 10 — 10, in addition to a request or claim for 50,000 acres of land.

Andrew Colvile wrote to Samuel Gale in Montreal, asking him to try to reach a reasonable compromise with Macdonell but adding politely that, as far as he could judge, "Miles has already been very much overpaid."[3]

The Red River population was changing slightly, with some departures and rather more new arrivals. A few settlers concluded recently that they had had enough of Rupert's Land hardship and danger and were giving up the struggle, moving to Upper Canada or the United States. It was a sort of natural refining process, however, and those who remained were the ones with an overplus of perseverance and the Colony character did not suffer. As some moved out in 1821, a contingent of Swiss moved in. The newcomers were only moderately well received. The agent who made the selections on behalf of the Colony was accused of taking some of the immigrants from Swiss jails and some from the "madhouse." He was reminded, also, that one member of the group died from overintoxication the day after arrival at York Factory.

But as with most immigrant groups or non-immigrant groups, there were the good and the bad. For many of the residents of the Colony in which the sex ratio was seriously out of balance, the bright spot in the immigrant band was the number of eligible girls. If the young ladies were looking for husbands, they came to the right place. The members of the Swiss party began arriving at the Red River Settlement on November 5 and on November 13, exactly eight days later, as Colony Governor Alexander MacDonell reported to Andrew Colvile, ten of the Swiss girls had married local men already "this week." He wished the incoming party had "more than double the number of girls."[4]

With the mingling of the newcomers with the de Meurons, the Swiss influence in the Settlement was immediately very strong. An inevitable result would be a change in the local "balance of power." Heretofore, the Scottish settlers had outnumbered the de Meurons and all others and had demonstrated their superior strength in occasional racial contests with fists. With some humiliation to erase, the de Meurons forced a new test of muscle before Christmas, with the Scots forced to yield some of their Highland conceit.

Some further racial comparisons were inevitable. By the assessment of George Simpson who was always brutally frank, the Swiss and de Meurons as settlers were neither industrious nor provident, and were constantly talking about leaving; the Scots, on the other hand, would never leave and never stop complaining, grumbling being "the characteristic of High-landers." He paid the Scots a further doubtful compliment, saying they were honest in their dealings, "except with the Company and the Executors."

With more huts and houses showing among the riverside trees, the place was gaining more of a community character. Dwellings by the autumn of 1819 numbered eight-eight, with ten more under construction. By the spring of 1822, the number of houses had grown to 126 and the count showed 160 gardens — more gardens than houses. The human population stood at 681, with three men for every two women.

Two Catholic priests, Father Provencher and Father Dumoulin, with encouragement and financial help from Lord Selkirk, arrived in 1818, and Rev. John West, Anglican, followed in 1820. It left the Kildonan Scots — nearly all Presbyterians — without a minister. The Highlanders did not approve of the three church leaders who arrived, as not one of them could speak Gaelic or conduct a service in Gaelic and this represented a serious ecclesiastical flaw. The majority of the Scots could not speak English but that did not prevent them from registering their complaints, one of them being that the Church of England parson was there without a congregation while the Scots had a congregation without a minister.

These people from Kildonan would do more than merely welcome a minister of their faith which Lord Selkirk said he would send; they would, according to a petition signed in July, 1819, build the reverend gentleman a church and build him a house. The petition was signed by twenty-one individuals, five of whom signified with an "X". The first name on the list of petitioners was that of William Laidlaw, the man who arrived to take charge of the experimental farm. But no minister had arrived. In the meantime, a building which could serve for both school and church purposes was erected for any group wishing to use it, about a mile below Fort Douglas.

The reason for Lord Selkirk's inaction in sending a Presbyterian minister to those who, in George Simpson's words, "cannot reconcile themselves to the Church of England forms," was very valid but still unknown to the settlers. News traveled slowly across the thousands of miles of waste spaces. Word of the defeat of Napoleon did not reach the Red River residents for a full year after the Battle of Waterloo, and they did not learn of Lord Selkirk's serious illness and death for half a year after his passing. But the delay did not blunt the anguish of settlers of all faiths and many were heard to moan the question: "What will happen to us now?"

The sad news was followed by an assurance from Andrew Colvile, speaking on behalf of the Lord Selkirk Estate, that the Settlement would receive precisely the same support and treatment that was provided while the Earl was active.

Then, almost at once, came the surprising and welcome news of union between the two old Companies which had been at each other's throats for years. Accompanying was a public pronouncement, echoing the Andrew Colvile determination to respect the wishes of the late Earl, that the Colony would not only be maintained but the former policies would be continued without any major changes. It sounded too good to be true: the strife between the Companies, in which the Settlement had been caught up most brutally and often, could now be at an end. If it was real, it was the object for which the people of all faiths had prayed.

Without the North West Company to fire their hatreds, the halfbreeds would no longer be a threat. The only remaining danger was in Indian attack and up to this time, the settlers had succeeded in maintaining a friendly relationship with tribesmen in the immediate area. Nobody could tell what the much-feared Sioux from the more distant south might do. They had a bad reputation for killing cattle being trailed through their part of the country and indulging in pointless murder. The atrocities seemed to strike close to the Selkirk people when former members of the Settlement, the Tullys, were victims near Lake Traverse, about sixty or seventy miles beyond Pembina. David Tully was a Scottish blacksmith hired to come to the Settlement in 1819 at £30 per year. He brought his wife and three children but after three or four years, decided to seek work farther south. It was soon after they had left the Red River community that the settlers received the sad news. The Sioux, having killed the parents and one child, kept the other two children until they were recovered by members of the United States military forces. A message from Fort Anthony advised Governor George Simpson that the two children were then in the care of a Lake Traverse halfbreed and would be returned to the Selkirk Settlement as soon as it was considered safe to be traveling with them.

But the Sioux did not normally come close to the Fort Douglas area and the settlers became more friendly with than frightened of the nearby Saulteaux and Cree, those Indians with whom Lord Selkirk had made a Treaty in 1817. Since the Earl's passing, the devoted Chief Peguis wrote to Andrew Colvile, thanking him for the annual payment of tobacco, consistent with the Treaty arrangement, and added a friendly note, saying he had contentment in his heart. He would not forget the Earl's instructions to him, he assured Colvile, to take the Colony under his protection. "I followed his wishes," the Chief wrote proudly, "and still hold the Colony under my care as an Eagle keeps its prey in its talons. . . . I shall hold sacred the promises I made."

The Earl's diplomacy was good, resulting in the cementing of a friendship which could serve the Settlement well. During the few years following, the annual payment of tobacco was augmented with a bonus consisting of a few kegs of spirits, supplies of powder and shot. The result for Red River was freedom from troubles with local Indians.

Among the changes wrought by the union came Governor George Simpson. Like a new barking dog in the community, he had to convince those around him that he would not bite but nobody was very sure. Still a comparative newcomer to the country, this short, serious, slightly pugnacious Scot had risen rapidly to fame and responsibility after demonstrating in his single year of service in the Athabasca region that he was made of tough fiber. Following the union, he was promoted quickly to the important post of Governor of Rupert's Land. He struck Red River like a tornado and while echoing Colvile's sentiment about helping the Colony, he let it be known that he would be seeking to prune poor and unproductive branches from the Hudson's Bay Company and the Settlement tree of operations.

At no time did George Simpson give reason for anyone to doubt his unusual capacity to be critical. In his long service to the Hudson's Bay Company, his record was unsurpassed and he deserved the title of "Mr. Fur Trade," but as those about him knew very well, he could see the worst in everybody. In one letter to Andrew Colvile, in the course of which he had reason to mention members of his own Company council, he had little of good to say about any of them: "MacDonell is disaffected . . . Thomas is timid and weak . . . Cook is drunken and without either body or mind . . . Pritchard is froth . . Matthey is discontented and designing . . . in short there is not one among them who has any pretension to the title he bears."

Although normally blunt, Simpson's honest opinion about the Colony remained in doubt. If he shared the sentiment of the traditional fur traders, he would have neither love nor patience for farmers but he could not openly go against the stand taken by Colvile. He was thus obliged to be a Colony supporter, outwardly at least. But in a letter to Colvile soon after the Red River Settlement came under his jurisdiction, Simpson gave a strong hint of prejudice, saying: "It is not my province to enquire into the object of establishing this settlement and I seriously wish it may meet the objects of its patrons, but I can assure you that it, at this moment injures the affairs of the Company very seriously and in my humble opinion will ultimately ruin the trade if very different regulations are not pursued."[5]

Here, most probably, were George Simpson's true feelings about the Settlement and if so, they represented another obstacle for the Colony. As time went on, he did try to overcome his fur trader's antipathy and give the Colony reasonable support. In any case, George Simpson was, for most of the next forty years, a force of great consequence in the Settlement as he was in the whole of Rupert's Land. He gave his views on every conceivable subject, generally loudly. Anyone reading Simpson's letters to Colvile would be enlightened about almost every happening in the area, and not always in delicate terms.

Colony Governors were targets for Simpson's sarcasm and not many remained in office for long. Alexander MacDonell, the last to be appointed by Lord Selkirk, stood accused of neglecting his Settlement duties, spending too much of his time trading horses with the Indians and reselling some Indian horses to the settlers with a profit to himself. He decided to retire and live on his property in the Settlement, and was followed by an ex-army man, Captain Andrew Bulger, an able manager but totally unfitted for frontier life. The result was that Bulger complained bitterly; he "was tormented day and night by mosquitoes; weak from want of nourishment and pestered by the clamours and threats of the people." He found this to be "one of the most miserable countries on the face of the earth." And Simpson who might have been his tormentor more than mosquitoes, added his view that Bulger was guilty of extravagance and "while there was rum in the Fort, he never went to bed sober."

Bulger was followed as Governor of Assiniboia by Robert Parker Pelly, in whose short regime the Settlement adopted an elementary code of law and order, registration of land titles and even a modest force of police constables. These developments marking a new state of maturity probably reflected the Simpson influence more than that of Pelly.

Nor did Pelly last very long and he was followed by the popular Donald McKenzie who was in office at the time of the tragedy of flood in 1826.

Simpson took up residence in the Colony and was drawn into more and more local affairs like the Tallow Company and the Assiniboia Sheep and Wool Company. Such involvement would be from business convictions more than sentiment. He was practical more than compassionate. The Indians, he believed, would have to be "ruled with a rod of iron to keep them in a proper state of subordination." And in dealing with the settlers, he would insist upon good business discipline. When he sensed waste and extravagance — the unpardonable sins — he advised the Company Committee against shipping in any more "fineries and luxuries." Citizens should be taught resourcefulness and thrift, especially the younger ones who were losing self-reliance; they should take a lesson from the older people who "if they have a hatchet, a hoe, a little ammunition and a few hooks and lines, can shift for themselves and be happy."[5]

It was Simpson's philosophy which Colvile was expressing in 1824 when he declared that Company paternalism had to end: "The settlers must now walk alone; having a stock of provisions from good crops and plenty of cattle, they may do very well if they are industrious. If they are not industrious, they must endure the whole consequences as best they can."[6]

It wasn't exactly in the spirit of promises made immediately after Lord Selkirk's death but it may have been more productive of valuable pioneer virtue than anybody realized at the time, cultivating independence and self-reliance. Anyway, although the Red River struggles were far from being over, there were better days ahead and the time-tested Red River settlers were to demonstrate how well they could "walk alone."

The Hayfield Experimental Farm

Rupert's Land in the second decade of the 19th century was about the last place any knowledgeable person would expect to find an experimental farm — even a modest one. The area was still without church or school but there on the west side of the Red and half hidden in trees was the new experimental farm which Lord Selkirk believed was needed to help reduce the high cost of inexperience on untried soil. Its task would be to test and demonstrate in a part of the world where everything was new. Mistakes seemed inevitable in new country but better that those errors be made on one farm than on a hundred.

As it turned out, the Hayfield Experimental Farm was not an overwhelming success. Neither was the initial effort to grow wheat in the West. Nobody contended that the farm accomplished all that its planner expected or intended, but as the first institution of its kind in all of British North America — perhaps on the entire continent — it deserved to be remembered for its purpose, if not for its performance. Here was the clearest evidence of forward thinking on the part of the inventor, Lord Selkirk. It was also one of the last programs of his planning.

Modern Canadians are familiar — or should be — with the complex Canada Experimental Farm System which had its origin when Hon. John Carling, Minister of Agriculture in Sir John A. Macdonald's government, instructed William Saunders to conduct a survey of the service in the United States. The report to the Minister, tabled in the House of Commons on April 15, 1886, outlined a proposal for a Canadian program. Parliament acted briskly, authorized the establishment of five experimental farms with Saunders as the first director. Work went forward at the Ottawa site chosen to be the Central Experimental Farm, and simultaneously, land was being acquired for farms at Nappan, Brandon, Indian Head and Agassiz.

It meant that the Experimental Farm System, as Canadians have come to know it, had its beginning more than a hundred years ago; but to be well noted is the fact that the infant West had an introduction to experimental farms more than half a century before the first farm was started at Ottawa. The Red River effort to assist the settlers by means of experimental farms was easy to criticize but the plan in its inception was worthy of praise.

Lord Selkirk selected the site, west of Fort Douglas, when he was at the Colony in 1817; but the decision to embark upon the program was made earlier and the Earl's choice of a man to be manager of the farm was already on his way to York Factory. The appointee, William Laidlaw, was a young man of enterprise who had farmed successfully in Scotland. Selkirk's instructions to him were to develop this Red River property as a dairy farm and make it useful as a public demonstration. The money needed would be forthcoming.

Laidlaw arrived at the Settlement after freeze-up in the autumn, burdened sufficiently to try any ordinary human patience with the most uncongenial and uncooperative traveling companions in the form of seven pigs for the Settlement, the first of their race to reach that place. Had he done nothing more than deliver the pigs under the most difficult conditions early winter could impose he would have earned a place in history.

Of course the settlers should have pigs as well as cattle, sheep and horses, even though members of the swine family seemed particularly foreign to this western land. Transporting the selected specimens across the Atlantic presented no great problem because the masters of sailing ships often carried pigs to consume waste and furnish fresh meat on long journeys. But conveying these, the most obstinate of farm animals, from York Factory to Red River was an undertaking presenting the most extreme difficulties, especially when the season was far advanced and frozen lakes and rivers could put a sudden end to travel by canoe.

But Laidlaw saw this as the first test of his stewardship and was determined to finish what he had undertaken. Proceeding from York Factory, the pigs — by this time weighing about 100 pounds each — were cooped up in a section of the canoe, which worked well enough. Daily, however, he became more aware of the danger of his boat being arrested by ice. Before reaching Jack River, winter weather brought all travel by water to an abrupt end and Laidlaw knew he must abandon the precious porkers or transport them by sled. Obtaining the necessary sleighs and toboggans and dogs to provide motive power, he wrapped the pigs in buffalo robes to prevent them from freezing, then tied each one down to the sled. The pigs protested with squeals to be heard for miles in the frosty atmosphere, and the hungry sleigh dogs, lusting for a taste of pork, had to be muzzled to prevent them from attacking.

Supplies of pig feed carried all the way from Scotland were running low and Laidlaw sensed the danger of losing his pigs through starvation — until he reached Jack River where he found an abundance of fish available for pig feed. He gave instructions about cooking the fish before feeding but apparently the helper did not obey orders and fed frozen fish which, in Laidlaw's opinion, accounted for the deaths of three animals. The remaining four, however, still carefully clothed in buffalo coats, reached Fort Douglas to command as much attention as if they were Bengal lions. There they stood, the only members of their race in half a continent and, in terms of effort, surely the most expensive pigs ever bought for breeding purposes.[1]

Having delivered the pigs, Laidlaw's task was to become the leading farmer, starting with raw land and no improvements whatever, no helpers and no means of power. It would not be easy. To add to the difficulty, he would be under the critical eyes of people like Capt. Matthey, Alexander Ross and Miles Macdonell who were not totally immune to jealousy. Wisely, he lost no time in going to work. Taking some experienced axmen, he proceeded to Pembina to cut trees for building logs. The logs were dragged to the river's edge, there to be left until they could be rafted down to the Forks in the spring. In this he was acting ahead of instructions Lord Selkirk was writing to him, to take experienced men to Red Lake or Roseaux River to cut and square pine and spruce logs and have them ready for floating to the Settlement because the new experimental farm would need various buildings: stables, houses, a mill and workshops.[2]

The land chosen for the farm was, according to Laidlaw, excellent for the purpose and he wrote enthusiastically to Lord Selkirk: "I am vastly pleased with the situation your Lordship picked upon for the farm. . . . This is certainly much superior to any place formerly thought of for it. I have only planted nine bushels of potatoes and two gallons of barley this season, merely for a trial. The soil appears to be excellent. I have not seen a place in R.R. so much adapted for a farm as it is. What a beautiful place it may be made for a sheep walk. Nothing can beat it; it is so finely sheltered and watered. There is an immense quantity of the best natural hay I ever saw in my life, which has induced me to call it Hayfield. If your Lordship wishes to change the name. . . . I intend to cut about 4,000 to 5,000 stone of hay in case we should be fortunate enough to get some cattle."[3]

Having expounded glowingly about the setting and the hay, Laidlaw then offered some reasons for the limited progress in the first season. As of July, 1818, he had only six acres of new ground turned over with the plow, having been handicapped by shortage of help and shortage of field power. At midsummer he was obliged to travel to York Factory and expected the plow to be kept in use during his absence. But all evidence of industry vanished at Laidlaw's departure and on his return he found only two acres had been added to the field of plowed ground. His men offered two reasons for the poor showing: first, the loss of four horses, and second, the plow's lack of strength and resulting inability to stand up in the heavy gumbo sod. But Laidlaw was making a new and stronger plow from iron brought from York Factory the year before. Plow improvement was in itself a useful service because, as Laidlaw noted: "There has never been a plough made at R.R. fit to turn the plain properly."

While he was making a new plow, he was directing a hunt for the lost horses and succeeded in finding three of the four. Although it was now late in the season — too late for good breaking — he brought a fresh determination to the task and in order to have two plows at work, he hitched the three cattle at the farm — a bull and two cows — and found the result most satisfactory, "the steadiest yoke I have yet seen at Red River," he said of them. In this way, he brought his fertile but difficult gumbo land for the next year's crop to sixteen acres.

One of Laidlaw's bright ideas for the new farm was a buffalo park. It would be an attraction and at the same time serve as a center for an attempt to domesticate the wild creatures and experiments in hybridization. He had one buffalo heifer on the farm at the time and intended to use the winter months to obtain more.

Laidlaw's report for 1819 was not very favorable, mainly for reasons beyond his control. The new farm house was destroyed by fire on the previous 30th of November, although another was under construction. The newer one would be 30 feet by 24 feet at the ground, with 8-foot walls.

Crops which started well in the previous year — bringing surprise that such splendid growth could be realized "from one turning of the soil" — were cut down savagely by the clouds of grasshoppers. But in spite of this setback, Laidlaw was able to recover enough potatoes for the 1819 planting, also enough wheat and a small amount of barley. Regretfully, he had neither beans, peas or oats for seed, but as the following season turned out, it didn't matter about the lack of seed because practically nothing survived the grasshoppers anyway. When Laidlaw saw the new crop of hoppers hatching in superabundance and heard from Peter Fidler that the insects were not as numerous at Brandon House on the Assiniboine River, he resolved to take his limited seed to that place for the 1819 planting. The season for sowing was already late, and by the time he was ready to plant at Brandon House, that district had the grasshoppers also although not quite so severe as at Red River. From three bushels of barley, five bushels of wheat and an unstated amount of potatoes planted, Laidlaw recovered slightly more than these quantities in the harvest and with what he was able to get from Lac la Pluie, he had enough seed for the experimental farm fields in 1820.

By working his three horses, two cows, one bull and the buffalo heifer, Laidlaw must have had the strangest assortment of experimental farm power in history but it served his purpose on the sixteen acres of cultivated cropland. Surely no other director of an experimental farm was ever obliged to conduct his cultivation under more and greater difficulties.

He wanted more cattle in order to put dairying to a test but there was no alternative to waiting for a herd to be driven from St. Louis. The herd was being delayed. The only favorable cattle news was that "the two cows which came up from York factory last summer have each a fine quey calf doing finely, and I believe both are in calf again." And the pigs were doing well but many more were wanted to meet Colony needs.

One of Laidlaw's worries was jurisdictional. From the time of his arrival he failed to find a harmonious working arrangement with Capt. Matthey, the former de Meuron who was ultimately placed in charge of the Colony.

Matthey insisted that the experimental farm was part of the Colony and therefore within his sphere of supervision. Laidlaw argued that the farm was an independent unit, completely outside Matthey's authority. In writing to Lord Selkirk, Laidlaw appealed for a letter to define areas of management because Capt. Matthey had been "very officious and intermeddling" where he had no rights. "I told him I acknowledged no authority from him, nor will I, and that I was determined to abide by the instructions I had formerly from your Lordship." Laidlaw might have mentioned one reason for the farm's failure to survive: "I am debited with everything and get credit for nothing."[4]

The 1822 farm inventory showed three houses, one for the manager and two for servants. The manager's house was imposing enough and could show nine glass windows and two parchment windows, and had an inventory value of £199. It was good enough to make most other facilities appear inadequate and mean. Other items on the list: one stable valued at £20, one byre at £15, one ice house, three horses, two oxen, two cows, two calves, one bull, one boar, three plows, one set of harrows, one set of horse harness and one set of ox harness. Planned for early addition were a horse mill for threshing and either a windmill or a watermill to be decided after studying the "lowest rapid on the Assiniboine."

It was a modest inventory. For an experimental farm intended to become a model dairy establishment, the presence of two cows, two calves and one bull would certainly invite questions. Whether Laidlaw was to blame or not, the Hayfield Experimental Farm was not advancing to furnish the leadership such an institution would be expected to provide. The manager's critics, however, should have remained silent until they had taken proper stock of the obstacles.

Laidlaw departed; the management fell to Alexander MacDonell, who was unenthusiastic, and the farm's prestige fell. George Simpson, whose criticism was unfailing, supposed that MacDonell saw the farm only once a month and the seven servants were "allowed to have things their own way." The farm "as now managed cannot possibly clear expenses." Simpson, whose first love was the fur trade, could never give either the Colony or the experimental farm the benefit of a doubt and after seeing the farm servants acting as their own bosses, he reported to Andrew Colvile that the place was probably "a scene of plunder" all along. Grain produced there, he was sure, would cost double what it could be bought for elsewhere in the Settlement. He was glad to find that Captain Bulger, who followed Alexander MacDonell as Colony Governor, had given Mr. Kempt the use of the farm for his private use at no cost, thus ensuring against maintenance charges to be directed at the Company or Estate.

Simpson was now recommending that the Hayfield Experimental Farm be sold to "an old Canadian," Battosh by name, who could be induced to purchase. The said buyer would pay £300 for the farm and buildings, £250 at time of purchase and the balance in two years. Battosh was described as "an active and industrious old fellow who will gain a living on it by keeping an Inn and a kind of butcher or flesh market." As Simpson viewed the deal, it would be a useful economy measure — and that was what counted most.[5]

Alexander Ross looked back and heaped more criticism and scorn on the experimental farm. He made note of the fine house lost in the fire and the good stables looming as an extravagance on a dairy farm with no cows to milk and no oxen with which to plow. He had a point.

It was an inglorious end for a highly vaunted experimental farm, but regardless of the sudden demise, nobody could say convincingly that the idea as conceived by Lord Selkirk was not a good one. And had he lived longer to exercise the wise leadership of which he was capable, the place might have lived up to its high purpose.

But the merit in an experimental farm was apparently not in question and the desire was present to try again. Strangely enough, the second such farm, although still looking like a Selkirk legacy, was promoted by George Simpson and thereby had the backing of the Hudson's Bay Company. The Northern District Council, presided over by Simpson, directed Chief Factor McMillan on July 3, 1830, to establish "an Experimental Farm at or near Red River for the purpose of rearing sheep and the preparation of tallow, wool, hemp and flax for the English market."

The farm was located beside the Assiniboine River, three and a half miles back from the Red. According to his diary, Robert Campbell, who became the Assistant Manager, placed the farm between two creeks and extending two miles back from the river. Most of the preparatory operations depended upon Campbell and he moved with his tent to the building site at the 1st of May, 1831. In the months following, he had as many as forty men building, plowing and making hay.

Alexander Ross, the historian, was more benevolent toward this farm and wrote that "cows of the best breed were purchased," and a "princely dwelling" was erected. Nevertheless, Ross expected the venture to be another failure. He was largely correct; the farm lasted six years — about the same span of life as the first experimental farm had experienced. It ended with a loss to the Hudson's Bay Company of £3,500. But again, the farm played important parts in two major projects, it provided accommodation for the imported stallion, Fireaway, and then, by its very existence, it was instrumental in the importation of the sheep flock driven from Kentucky in 1833.

Two experimental farms failed to last more than six years but the Lord Selkirk concept which gave rise to the first one lived on and produced a third effort, this one initiated by the Hudson's Bay Company in London. The motive was increased production more than experimentation. The new enterprise would raise sheep on a large scale, it was hoped, also flax and hemp. This hope of producing for export was simply and clearly a projection of what Lord Selkirk had proposed on many occasions. Even the products were the ones Selkirk had named so often.

The farm, started in 1838, was situated close to Upper Fort Garry, on the north side of the Assiniboine. In design, it was the most ambitious of the three pioneer farms and twenty acres of cropland were prepared in the first year. A flock of sheep containing 300 head was placed with a shepherd brought from Scotland. Taking a further idea from the late Lord Selkirk, the London committee undertook to do some colonizing and sent out thirteen workers with families to obtain their introduction to the country by living on the farm. If the opinion of Alexander Ross be accepted, the immigrants for this experimental farm were disappointing, "notorious beer drinkers," could neither "work nor eat without the beer pot at their lips."

Again an experimental farm had a short life but there must have been some significance in the fact that an increasing number of those who followed Selkirk believed that his concept was prophetic and the agricultural infant in the West was worthy of an experimental farm.

CHAPTER TWENTY-TWO

The Buffalo Business

For settlers with Old World traditions, farming in the absence of livestock was nigh unthinkable. "It's no' a farm wi'out a coo," a Scot might be heard to say. But what could newly arrived residents at Red River do about it when the nearest available breeding stock was removed by hundreds of miles of country made forbidding by harsh travel and hostile tribes?

Rupert's Land, as Europeans found it, could show only two races of domestic animals, horses and dogs. With a special longing for cattle, it was to be expected that resourceful people would wonder if the huge buffalo herds could be made to furnish more than pemmican. Thoughts would turn to domestication. After all, if the cattle and buffalo races were related, why would it not be possible to crossbreed them and use the hybrid progeny to supply meat, leather, oxpower and even milk, just like the domestic parent?

Lord Selkirk, with the inquiring mind of a scientist and ever conscious of the needs of his settlers, was proposing planned attempts to domesticate and hybridize even before his people were settled, and was supporting the ideas with orders to put them to the test. The Government of Canada which, many years later, conducted long and costly breeding experiments with the hybrids called cattalo, first at Wainwright and then at Manyberries, might well have dedicated the project to the Earl as the first person to advance the idea and try to do something about it. In his enthusiasm, this man saw the possibility of the buffalo progeny filling the settlers' needs for both cattle and sheep by furnishing "wool" as well as meat, power and milk, thereby relieving the necessity of importing costly livestock from Britain or elsewhere.

Writing to Miles Macdonell in 1813, Selkirk bemoaned the absence of cow's milk for family needs and noted that settlers would be reluctant to use "mare's milk." He then challenged Macdonell to consider domesticating not only the prairie bison but the northern reindeer and the "musk buffalo." The wool of the latter, he mentioned, was likely "to prove of great value."[1]

Macdonell succeeded in obtaining some buffalo calves but reported only failure in raising them. "Several were caught and brought to Fort Daer last spring but they died from want of milk. I hope to have better success another year."[2]

Selkirk was not letting Macdonell forget. Ever in his mind was the hope of finding a rewarding product for export, perhaps buffalo tongues in a salted state, buffalo tallow or buffalo robes. In a letter in the next year, after warning that no cattle could be sent out in the forthcoming season, he repeated his wish that "the buffalo may be domesticated in a better and more effective manner." His latest idea would entail taking a large body of mounted men to the plains, "and when you find a herd of cows, spread your men into an extended line and drive the herd before you gently without alarming them unnecessarily, and follow them day after day until you bring them to the plains near the Settlement, where a few men must be employed to watch them constantly to prevent them from straying away and prevent them from being hunted and disturbed. By degrees they will grow less wild, especially if in the winter they are supplied with hay, and may probably admit a cross of a European bull."[3]

He was writing like an "old hand" with the wild livestock rather than like a novice who had never seen a real live bison, but the proposal was not an improbable one. There is no indication of it having been tested.

After another year, Selkirk was displaying impatience although not giving up. Now he was modifying the earlier directions, suggesting that riders try to gather a big herd to be held loosely by herdsmen north of Portage la Prairie. If the wild things rejected an attempt at domestication, there would still be reward in having meat supplies available at relatively short distance from the Settlement.[4]

Miles Macdonell's departure from the Colony was followed by a lapse in interest in capturing bison stock but it was revived when William Laidlaw became manager of the experimental farm. Huge herds came close to Pembina in the spring of 1818, appearing to Laidlaw "more crowded than ever I saw Kyloes on the mountains of Scotland." Employing horses and dogs, he ran down some of the calves easily enough but keeping the young things alive after being bitten by pursuing dogs was not easy. Only one calf survived but at midsummer, this one was doing well and had become quite tame, following the man who fed it "like a dog." More optimistic than Macdonell, Laidlaw said "There is not a doubt but that they can be domesticated easily."[5]

Laidlaw said he would get more of the wild calves, and did. The heifer of which he wrote was working in harness when two years old and doing her share of the farm plowing. Disappointingly, "the English bull on the farm" was inclined to snobbery and refused to associate with the bison female. The experimental farm now had two other buffalo specimens, both yearlings, on pasture and hired helpers were making additional quantities of hay in anticipation of capturing more in the next winter.

By this time, the idea of making more use of buffalo stock was gaining favor with the people on the little farms. The long-expected herd of cattle from the south had not arrived and the wild animals were receiving more covetous attention. Increasing numbers of the settlers were ready to accept Alexander MacDonell's opinion that the buffalo, when trained, would prove to be "good milkers as well as the best workers and if this be so, they are the best stock, being the most hardy and adapted already to the climate."[6]

John Pritchard had a good report for Andrew Colvile, informing him that the settlers in 1820, had "18 domestic buffalo which are as tame as European cattle and any quantity might be procured with very little trouble." Pritchard, ever the promoter, had the bright idea that a pair of buffalo calves — a male and a female — should be sent as a present to Colvile, perhaps in recognition of his helpful interest in the Settlement. He was not the Governor of the Hudson's Bay Company until many years later but his voice was strong and as executor of the Selkirk Estate, he was the best possible liaison between Company and Colony. Still, there was no indication that Colvile wanted two buffalo calves or had a means of keeping them. It didn't matter to Pritchard; he would give the London executive a chance to judge for himself "how far superior in point of strength the bison is to your English ox for agricultural purposes."[7]

Pritchard, at the same time, notified Colvile that five pounds of musk-ox wool were going forward to him. "I request you to send one pound of it to my brother, William, and he will endeavor to ascertain its value."

Before he could hope to have a reply from Colvile concerning the proposed gift of the animals, Pritchard had the calves in captivity at Pembina and was reporting them "exceedingly tame and in fine condition." In due course, the two wild specimens were on their way and Alexander MacDonell, as Governor of the Colony, wrote to assure Colvile that if anything had happened to prevent the young bison from arriving in safety, he (MacDonell) could "send another couple next year." Unfortunately, the complete story about the adventures of two young prairie bison in England in 1821 — the year of union between the Companies — is not known.

The gesture of forwarding the calves coincided with the peak of interest in domestication because Red River in the next year received the big herd of cattle from the south. But as interest in domestic bison fell, settlement attention turned sharply to buffalo "wool" and the opportunities it held. The dream of producing a distinctively choice grade of sheep's wool for export to the British market was not realized. Perhaps this strictly North American product now to be marketed by the Red River Buffalo Wool Company was the one to bring fame and fortune to the struggling Settlement. Although the birth of the Buffalo Wool Company coincided approximately with the death of Lord Selkirk, there was reason to believe the Earl was the author of the idea. He certainly subscribed to it. John Pritchard, whose name became linked most prominently with that of the company, was its manager and promoter.

Here was the demonstration of a pioneer maxim: what's at hand is the best substitute for what isn't available. Having been unsuccessful in obtaining the sheep in needed numbers, Red River citizens found themselves meditating on the thick and moderately fine undercoat of the buffalo. It was called hair, properly, but why not call it "buffalo wool" and persuade the British spinners to use it and declare its goodness?

Hair and wool are not the same at all. The latter possesses scales and crimps or waves giving it special value for spinning. A fine and strong yarn could not be produced from straight hair fibers. But nobody at Red River was in a mood to let technicalities defeat their purpose. The new company, financed by the sale of shares at £100 each, would be the only one in the world with buffalo wool for sale and when the British spinners and manufacturers accepted it, huge profits would stream toward Red River.

John Pritchard, on behalf of the new company, asked for a grant of land on which to build a plant and Andrew Colvile on May 25, 1820, instructed Colony Governor Alexander MacDonell to "Measure off and deliver to John Pritchard, Esq., for the use of the Buffalo Wool Company a lot of one hundred acres in a convenient situation." Colvile, wishing to have a voice in the affairs of the enterprise, directed one condition, that the Buffalo Wool Company would accept as shareholders "such persons as may be nominated by the Executors."

Pritchard devoted his full time and energy to the new enterprise and urged buffalo hunters to bring their stocks of hair and hides from the slaughters to the company's plant at Pembina, located there until the permanent facilities were ready at the Forks. The company would pay one shilling, sixpence per pound for the hair or wool and six shillings each for hides. A good skin, Pritchard found, would yield six or seven pounds of hair, of which two or three pounds would be of the quality for export as wool. The remainder would be "fit for coarse cloth, blankets and mattresses. Besides, there is a quantity of hair from which we intend to make rope." Captain Matthey, going to England shortly, would carry samples, "some of which I think are equal to the finest that have ever visited the London Market."[8]

By June, 1821, Pritchard had some sale goods ready for shipment — not as much as he had hoped to have but enough for a good public demonstration — about 700 hides, 300 pounds of "fine wool" and 1,000 pounds of the coarse fraction which he was satisfied to call hair.

Until the British manufacturers passed judgment, great optimism prevailed and the capital was spent lavishly. One of the few to remain skeptical was the sagacious George Simpson who told Andrew Colvile that "Pritchard and his Buffalo Wool Company make a great noise. He is a wild visionary speculative creature without a particle of solidarity and but a moderate share of judgement. If that business were properly managed I have not a doubt of its turning out well."[9]

The first bad news came to Red River in March, 1824, Colvile reporting to Pritchard, saying: "I am sorry to say the result of the sale of last year's importation of wool is not at all encouraging. . . . I fear the wool will not answer your expectations. Success will depend on what you can make of it by converting it to cloth which you can sell in the Settlement. If you can show to the satisfaction of Governor Simpson and the Council that you can make a profitable concern of the leather and cloth business out of which you can extinguish your debt, I have no doubt they will be disposed to assist."[10]

It was indeed a sad turn of events but there remained a spark of hope because Lady Selkirk at about this point in time became interested in the project and espoused the cause with a refreshing determination. It was the resurrection of a loyalty to her late husband's cherished venture. The British spinners and millers might have drawn their conclusions and despaired of further worry about buffalo wool but suddenly they were being summoned to re-examine this strange product and attempt again to use it in some manner likely to create a profitable demand.

Lady Selkirk sent samples of the wool to various authorities on woolen goods and asked for reports on tests. She wished to see garments having a special appeal to fashion-conscious women in London and Edinburgh and elsewhere. The leading shawl makers were urged to consider all possibilities in producing something pleasingly different. The best shawls were made in Edinburgh from yarns spun in England. They were all invited to try again. Spinners, dyers and weavers agreed to cooperate. Even the manufacturer who specialized in blending wool and silk was brought into the consortium and Lady Selkirk was assured that the very best effort was being made to make Red River buffalo wool a success.

But difficultires and obstacles were too obvious and too numerous to be ignored — short staple; presence of occasional coarse fibers; failure of the wool to take dyes lighter in shade than brown, black, scarlet and crimson, and the unmanageable character of the wool when used without silk. Nevertheless, the joint attack upon the problems proved that presentable shawls could be turned out with the major difficulties reduced to two, the first to generate a market or demand for the finished products and the second to turn the goods out at prices which would attract buyers. The cost, inevitably, was high.

The first finished shawls were sent to Lady Selkirk and she wore them in high society, hoping to start a fashion rage. A few ladies whose husbands held interest in the Hudson's Bay Company condescended to wear the indelicate things but generally, the response was negative. Three sample pairs of ladies' stockings were made — "beautiful goods" as described by the manufacturer — but nobody became excited about them. Buffalo wool stockings didn't sound appealing and won no friends.

One of the concluding letters in an extensive correspondence between Lady Selkirk and representatives in the industry, was on October 21, 1826, when James Ogilvie of Edinburgh wrote to her Ladyship, admitting failure. He recognized that Lady Selkirk and others beyond himself had spent much time and money in trying to overcome the obstacles the buffalo had created in Britain. He had never applied himself with more interest, he said, never had more correspondence on an aspect of the woolen trade. But in spite of the best of efforts, the shawls and stockings upon which the future of the great Buffalo Wool Company depended, were still rough in appearance, high in cost and lacking in whatever it took to make milady want them.[11]

It marked the end of an operation but not the end of the buffalo chapter in the lives of the settlers. Cattle were ultimately driven over the long trail from the south to satisfy the persistent longing for milk and beef and ox power, and the bankrupt Buffalo Wool Company was something the investors wished to forget, but reliance upon the wild herds as sources of pemmican did not diminish.

The native people were expert buffalo hunters long before the settlers arrived upon the prairie scene, and in transmitting their skills to the newcomers they proved to be good teachers. Before the Selkirk people were long in the country, the annual or biannual buffalo hunt became a gigantic community institution in which all residents, young and old, male and female, natives and others, went out together under a single command. Possessing some of the character of a Harvest Festival, this outing in which every adult had a part, grew in importance and lasted almost as long as the wild herds lasted.

It was almost like an army maneuver, both in size and organization. According to Alexander Ross, 540 Red River carts screamed on dry axles on their way to the hunt in 1820, and the number grew — 820 in the year 1830 and 1,210 in 1840. In that latter year, when the roll was called at Pembina on the evening of the third day out, the count revealed "1630 souls," the 1,210 carts, hundreds of oxen and horses and 542 dogs. The kill in the hunt of that year was about 2,500 bison and the outing from the departure from the Settlement until back with the supplies of pemmican, lasted two months and two days.

On every annual hunt, participants paused at one of the first evening campsites, where carts were arrayed in a big circle with tents erected at the center, to elect their captains and leaders, and approve rules of conduct by which the expedition would be governed: No buffalo to be run on the Sabbath day; no party to fork off or attempt to hunt by himself; nobody to run buffalo before the general order given by the chief captain, and all the people to submit strictly to the rules of good order in camp. Infractions would bring severe penalties.

Unless the participants took 800 or 1,000 carcasses, it wasn't considered a successful hunt. Such numbers represented much work, especially after the killing. All members turned out for the skinning and dressing and then, while the noble males retired to celebrate their success, the women and children were left to perform the less glamorous task of drying the meat and making pemmican. It was expected that the carts would return with 100 pounds of the highly-prized pemmican for every buffalo felled. It was Henry Hind's estimate that Red River people — settlers and Métis — between 1820 and 1840, took about 652,000 animals from the mighty prairie herds.

One way or another, buffalo business over more than fifty Red River Settlement years, was big business.

CHAPTER TWENTY-THREE

Cows for the Colony

"The cattle are coming," settlers shouted-for joy when it was known that the herd driven from St. Louis would arrive later on that day, August 28, 1822. Half of the residents in the Colony trekked along the river trail toward Pembina to meet the herd and enjoy the thought of once again having milk and butter and cheese on their tables. They had waited long and not always with patience for cattle in worth while numbers, knowing very well that trying to farm without cattle was like trying to operate a canoe without a paddle.

Cattle were not totally unknown — just scarce. The struggle to get them had been difficult. It was eleven years since Miles Macdonell and his band of workmen arrived at the Forks, bringing with them the two young cattle — Adam and Eve — which they discovered unexpectedly at Oxford House. They were such rare specimens at Red River that many of the natives gazed for the first time in their lives upon the species.

As far as anybody knew, the total population of domestic animals in the area later defined as Manitoba, Saskatchewan and Alberta, consisted of a few thousand Indian-owned horses and dogs, five cattle, no sheep and no pigs. In addition to Adam and Eve, three other cattle — one bull, one cow and one calf — were owned by the North West Company at its Souris River post, and these Peter Fidler bought for the Settlement, paying 100 pounds for them in the spring of 1813, thus bringing all the known cattle in the country to Red River.

Presumably, Adam and Eve were taken from England as calves and the two adult cattle at Fort Souris would have been brought from Fort William as calves.

Lord Selkirk, with sizable farming interests at St. Mary's Isle, was well aware of the crofter's regard for livestock and intended to send eight head of cattle with Miles Macdonell in 1811, thereby having a small herd to greet the settlers when they reached Red River. But the practical problem of space for cattle, feed and fresh water for a voyage lasting up to two months, discouraged the idea and the *Edward and Ann* sailed away from Stornoway, leaving the cattle behind on the quay.

The tiny herd of five cattle assembled at the Settlement experienced more of misfortune than success and failed to contribute much to community needs. Only two of the five were females of breeding age and neither of the adult males survived very long. The bull acquired from Souris River brought a bad temper — suspected as being the North Wester's dislike for anybody connected with the Hudson's Bay Company — and had to be destroyed. It did not seem serious because there was no apparent need for more than one bull. But then, as bad luck would have it, Adam, with philandering notions, strayed away and was never again seen alive, leaving the cattle count at two cows, one calf and no bull.

Although it was recorded clearly that Adam disappeared and nothing was seen of him until his dead body was observed riding on a cake of ice during the breakup in the spring, his name reappeared in correspondence; it was confusing to find Captain Matthey writing to Lord Selkirk in August, 1818, mentioning a scarcity of horses and oxen and adding that "were it not for poor wounded Adam and old Eve, we should be badly off for draft animals." Presumably, the Adam mentioned at this later date was the bull calf born to Eve in 1814, a son of the original bovine Adam. He had been wounded by gunshot earlier in the year, leading Colin Robertson to praise him as the "only animal we had to depend upon for hauling provisions; indeed he was better than four horses."[1] It would have been less confusing if he had been called Adam II.

It was discouraging and except for that bull calf born to Eve, there was no addition to the herd until January, 1817, when Lord Selkirk's soldiers coming from Fort William and Lac la Pluie to recapture Fort Douglas brought with them one bull, one ox and three other cattle which had been the property of the North West Company. The right of the soldiers to take the cattle was certainly in doubt but the animals were repossessed by their original owners and slaughtered in the next year, hence doing nothing of lasting benefit for the Colony.

Between breeding failure and strife in the Settlement, the local people were making no headway with cattle. Distressed by the reverses, Selkirk wrote early in 1819 to John McDonald, Midmills, acknowledging the necessity of "restoring the herd," and asking him to purchase four heifers, calves of the previous year, preferably in the Orkneys. The Island cattle, it was admitted, were "not handsome" but they were hardy and had the reputation of being good milkers, which was an essential consideration. It could be told that arrangements had been made with the Committee of the Hudson's Bay Company to send these cattle by the ship *Prince of Wales* to York Factory.

Having made an arrangement about purchase, the Earl then wrote to Alex Cuddie, asking him to take charge of the cattle in transit and giving him detailed instructions about feeding. Supplies would be provided to allow for a feed allowance of two pounds of oatmeal and four pounds of hay daily for each heifer, and one turnip per week. And if for any reason, the feed resources were found to be inadequate on the voyage, Cuddie would have the authority to slaughter one heifer, thereby extending the feed stocks available for the heifers remaining.

As he had done on other occasions, the Earl again seized the opportunity of obtaining positive information about the effect of a long voyage on young cattle; he ordered that each heifer be weighed at the time of departure from Stromness and weighed again on arrival at York Factory. Why miss the chance of a scientific test from which useful data might be drawn?

The trip was of moderate length and Cuddie wrote from York Factory, conveying the information requested:

The black heifer weighed 203 lbs. at Stromness, 224 lbs. at York Factory, a gain of 21 lbs.

Lesser red heifer weighed 210 lbs. at Stromness, 208½ lbs. at York Factory, loss of 1½ lbs.

Large red heifer weighed 229 lbs. at Stromness, 225 lbs. at York Factory, loss of 4 lbs.

Red and Black heifer weighed 275 lbs. at Stromness, 311½ lbs. at York Factory, gain of 36½ lbs.

For the four heifers, there was a net gain of 52 pounds.[2]

It was found impossible to take the four heifers to Red River in that season and the only alternative was to winter at York Factory and feed the heifers on hay from the coarse northern grasses. The result was not favorable; the next letter concerning the cattle was from Alexander MacDonell, Selkirk's agent at the Colony, reporting that "Two of the queys left at York Factory are dead and the other two are on their way up."

Two cattle from Oxford House, five from Lac la Pluie which ended in slaughter, two from the Orkneys and so on, represented a determined effort but was achieving little if anything. Losses were matching the slow gains and the few beasts surviving looked lonely and were doing practically nothing except in keeping alive the memory and the desire for milk and butter. Something on a bigger scale would have to be done and Lord Selkirk knew it. He considered driving a flock of sheep and a hundred or more cattle from his Baldoon Settlement by way of Detroit and Chicago to Red River but the War of 1812-14 terminated the plan when part of the livestock became unwilling and unauthorized rations for United States army invaders. It was the thought of driving cattle and sheep from Baldoon that led to Selkirk's inquiries about obtaining breeding stock from the south. He made contact with some American dealers and drovers. Early in 1814 a letter was sent on Selkirk's behalf to Robert Dickson, a fur trader who became the Earl's agent at Michilimackinac, announcing a wllingness to place an order for a herd to be driven from somewhere deep in the south to Red River. "The route must be by the plains, on the west side of the Mississippi, through the Sioux country," the letter warned.

The Earl's wish was for "100 young milk cows and four or five bulls but not to exceed one thousand pounds [sterling] for the whole expense,

including purchase and the expense of driving. . . . According to Arrowsmith's map the distance appears to be between 700 and 800 miles. If the
animals are carefully driven, they may certainly travel 15 miles per day
through grassy plains. . . . It is probable that the expedition may require 10
weeks. The winter sets in on Red River about the end of October, from
which Mr. D. can judge whether there is time to accommodate the business
this autumn [1814]. . . . Capt. Macdonell can be advised and he will come to
meet the herd. . . . If a parcel of sheep can be sent at the same time with the
cattle, it will be desirable to have any number from 50 to 200 ewes — rams
are not wanted. . . . Lord Selkirk takes it for granted that men may be
engaged who are acquainted with the Sioux language."[3]

By the time Dickson received the message, it was too late in the season to
act upon it.

Selkirk, on returning from Red River to Montreal in 1817, traveled by
way of Prairie du Chien and there had conversation with French Canadian
Joseph Rolette who was prepared to take any cattle driving assignment, at
his price. He wanted $100 per head for cows and oxen — any number —
delivered at the Settlement. He proposed a herd of 100 head. If the Earl
would confirm a deal, Rolette would drive the cattle from St. Louis to
Prairie du Chien during the summer, winter at that place and drive on to
Red River in 1819. In his opinion, "it would be impossible in one season to
take them from St. Louis to Red River in good order." Without undue
modesty, he believed he was "The only man in this country who will
undertake such a job."

This would be a $10,000 contract, twice as much as the Earl was prepared
to budget. But if Rolette would deliver forty cows and four pairs of oxen at
the stated price, Selkirk was prepared to place the order, with certain
stipulations: "that the oxen shall be strong and well broken and that none of
the cattle shall be above four years old. . . . As to the cows, I am not so
anxious about them being large as of good form and a breed for milk. And I
prefer the dark colors, black, brindled, brown and dark red without any
spots of white. . . ."[4]

Selkirk and Rolette did not come to terms. The latter's price of $100 per
head was too high, Selkirk believed. Drovers could buy cattle for less than
half of that at St. Louis and make a fair profit by delivering them at $70.
Nevertheless, he would still pay up to $100 per beast on a small herd
representing not over the $5,000 figure. What he was trying to tell his
representatives was to obtain as many cattle as possible for $5,000.

He mentioned also that he would like to have the cattle drover, whoever
he might be, bring "three or four breeding mares and a strong and
handsome kind of wagon, and a stallion colt one year old." It would be well
if the mares were in foal to a superior stallion. This was not an order, merely
a desire.

Another point for the information of anybody considering a drive: a
contract would demand delivery "at the Settlement," but in the event the

drivers were unfamiliar with the country, they might make a halt somewhere near the headwaters of the Red River until some of the settlers could come out to direct the cattlemen to their destination.

When the Earl returned to Scotland, the exchange of letters was inevitably slow but at this point a new name appeared among those who could be considered candidates for a cattle delivery contract, that of Michael Dousman, a Michilimackinac trader who could turn his hand to any task likely to yield a dollar of profit. On hearing about this man, Selkirk asked Col. Robert Dickson to discuss the matter with him and obtain an indication of prices. Again the Earl specified that the total expenditure must not exceed $5,000.

A few months passed and Selkirk wrote directly to Dousman, confirming an interest in obtaining cattle for Red River and repeating that he would not enter into a contract exceeding $5,000. He admitted a willingness to be flexible on the number of cattle and price per head as long as the total cost was within the said limit. One-eighth of the herd might consist of work oxen, with the balance made up of young cows and heifers — one, two and three years of age. The money would be paid when the cattle were delivered at Red River and there would be a bonus: "I will also, on the safe delivery of the cattle, assure a lot of 100 acres on the R.R. to each of the drivers and 500 acres to the person who conducts the expedition."[5]

A copy of this letter was sent to Robert Dickson but before it reached him, the affable Dickson, said to be "foolishly careless in money matters," had entered into a formal contract with Dousman for the purchase of 100 cattle to cost a total in excess of $8,000, also some mares which would make the total expenditure almost twice as much as the Earl said he was appropriating. With Dickson's letter, reporting what he had done, was a copy of the contract, making the Earl very angry.

The agreement, signed at Michilimackinac on June 28, 1819, "between Robert Dickson, agent of his Lordship, the Earl of Selkirk . . . and Michael Dousman, Merchant of the Island of Michilimackinac" called for 76 good milk cows, 20 good oxen and 4 bulls, "to be delivered at Big Stone Lake, so called, near the headwaters of the River St. Peters." The delivery price for cows would be $80 each, for bulls and oxen, $100 each.

The agreement provided, also, for "a number of breeding mares not exceeding six and one stud horse" but no price figures were mentioned, except to declare "the original cost and all reasonable charges incurred in moving them to Big Stone Lake." The horses would be moved with the cattle but at the risk of Robert Dickson — which meant at the risk of the purchaser, the Earl.

As for settlement, it was agreed that "in payment for the said cattle, 500 pounds Halifax currency shall be advanced at the signing hereof and the balance at the time of delivery." In the event of Michael Dousman being unsuccessful in purchasing and delivering as required by contract, the advance payment of 500 pounds would be refunded with interest and, conversely, if the final payment were not made at the time of delivery, as agreed upon, the amount of the balance owing would bear interest in Dousman's favor.[6]

Then, adding to the confusion of Dickson having committed Selkirk to a contract the Earl would not have authorized, Dousman, legally or otherwise, sold his interest in the agreement to Adam Stewart who was one of the parties formally witnessing the initial signing. Stewart, also a Michilimackinac man, then wrote to the Earl to explain his new position — or perhaps just to introduce himself.

"In the month of June last," Stewart wrote, "Col. Robert Dickson entered into a contract with Mr. Michael Dousman for the delivery of 120 head of horned cattle at Big Stone Lake. Mr. D., after making the contract was fearful of the consequences of his not being able to purchase and forward the cattle . . . he offered me the contract which I have taken off his hands. I shall leave this place for St. Louis in a few days, where I intend to purchase the cattle and drive them as far as Prairie du Chien this fall and from thence to the place of delivery in April or May next. The drove will probably reach Big Stone Lake by the 15th of May. I would therefore suggest to your Lordship the propriety of you writing to the Governor of the Colony to dispatch some person to meet me at the said lake 15th May. I could have delivered the cattle this fall at the Lake but Col. Dickson was of the opinion that a sufficient quantity of hay could not be procured in time. In consequence of my being obliged to winter the cattle at Prairie du Chien, it will cost me at least $1,000 more than I expected. I hope your Lordship will be disposed to give me a farm somewhere on the Red River."[7]

If Stewart had read the contract properly, he would have realized that the Earl had already promised a farm for which he could qualify. A man in Selkirk's position would be familiar with requests for contributions and handouts but he would still be surprised that Stewart, almost every time he wrote, was asking for something more than was written into the Dousman agreement. Probably he did have some extra costs but it was his idea to buy the contract from Dousman. He was supposed to have paid Dousman $1,800 for the contract and he said he paid Joseph Rolette at Prairie du Chien $600 for wintering the cattle en route to Big Stone Lake. On the question of wintering the cattle, Stewart's story was somewhat garbled. At one point he gave the impression of holding the cattle in upper Illinois when he was warned of a serious feed shortage at Prairie du Chien, hence paying in two areas for the wintering. In view of this misfortune bringing additional costs, Stewart told the Earl that unless his Lordship would take more than the 120 head named in the contract, losses would be high. As if trying to shame the Earl into a still larger investment, he said he was "unwilling to believe that you will suffer me to lose by the contract."[8]

With the Earl now on his deathbed, Andrew Colvile was undertaking the direction of all affairs pertaining to the Red River Settlement and while he was determined to act with sympathy toward the needs of the residents, he was basically a businessman and one who could be totally uncompromising with anyone appearing to seek unjust gain. He was well aware of Selkirk's instructions to keep the total expenditure for cattle at less than $5,000 and reprimanded Dickson for entering into a contract which was so obviously contrary to the Earl's wishes. "Whether he [the Earl] got 20 head of cattle or 100, he would not give more money than the $5,000," he wrote to Dickson. "I cannot conceive, therefore, on what principle you should have felt yourself at liberty to enter into a contract to the extent of $10,000."

Nor was that end of Colvile's reprimand; Dickson should not have paid 500 pounds in advance, especially when he had no guarantee that the sum could be recovered even in the event of failure to deliver. Now that Stewart had the contract and Dousman, presumably, had the 500 pounds, who would be expected to reimburse in the event of inability to produce the cattle?

And another clause in the contract was annoying Colvile. Dickson should not have consented to take delivery of the cattle at any point short of the Settlement. Cattle at Big Stone Lake were still far from their destination and much of the country between the lake and the Settlement was fraught with danger from Sioux Indians. Indeed, Colvile could see scarcely any good about the agreement and if the 500 pounds had not been paid, he would be ready to reject the entire deal as one based on an instrument for which there was no proper authority. But Dousman had the deposit and Colville could only hope for a reasonable number of cows and bulls and oxen to show for it.

But Dickson who was being criticized for his indiscretions was not the only person with reason to worry. The confusion mounted on every hand and reached Red River. The cattle were supposed to be at Big Stone Lake in the summer of 1820 and Alex MacDonell, on June 27, sent William Laidlaw to that distant point deep in Indian country to meet the herd. Laidlaw remained at the lake until the 20th of July without seeing cattle or hearing from Stewart. He suspected the Indians had prevented the herd from reaching this place. Apparently some Sioux had been recently murdered by Americans and the Indians had become suddenly more hostile. It seemed likely the Sioux had decided to stop all Americans — with or without cattle — from traveling through their country.

The fact was that Stewart's troubles prevented him from even reaching the area of major Indian hostility. His decision to winter at Prairie du Chien was a mistake. Apparently, in spite of the report of him wintering in upper Illinois, he did drive on to Prairie du Chien where the supply of hay was totally inadequate and the big herd, said to number 284 head, starved to death — all but nineteen of the cattle. It was a serious loss but Stewart should have sent word to Big Stone Lake where he knew the settlers' representatives would be waiting.

But Stewart was not a quitter. Instead of giving up, he was planning to return to St. Louis for another herd with which to fill the contract nearly everybody was growing to dislike.

The second herd, driven north in 1821, numbering 175 head, reached Prairie du Chien late in the year and encountered Sioux Indians, both angry and hungry. The Indians took most of the cattle and the rest of the animals died there.

While Stewart's second herd was falling into Indian hands, Joseph Rolette, with whom Lord Selkirk had had early correspondence, succeeded in taking a small herd to the Settlement, strictly as a private venture. Of the little band of twenty head delivered in that autumn of 1821, Rolette sold a few cows to eager settlers at prices ranging from 25 to 30 pounds, then offered the balance by auction, and saw them sell at more moderate prices. Alex MacDonell bought eleven cattle and one horse; among his purchases were two white cows for a total of 26 pounds, three oxen for 52 pounds, one branded cow for 13 pounds, one black cow for 18 pounds, two bull calves for 8 pounds and one horse for 6 pounds.

"The Swiss people are keen for cows," MacDonell noted and with obvious impatience over Stewart's failure to bring in the big herd, he was recommending that a contract be negotiated with Alexis Baily, the driver who brought the Rolette herd.[9]

Most observers were sure that Adam Stewart, after losing two herds and two seasons of work, would give up. They were wrong. They had failed to assess properly the Stewart determination. He went again, and with the experience gained in the course of previous failures, brought the third herd to the Red River Colony on August 28, 1822, amid jubilation such as the Settlement had not known. The Swiss sang native songs; the Germans danced on the river trail and the Scots made boasts that sounded as if they had fought the Battle of Culloden over again and won it.

Andrew Bulger, now Colony Governor, wrote at once to Andrew Colvile to report the great event, the delivery of 170 cattle "in very good condition," 120 of which the Colony was bound by contract to take. "The remainder have been brought on speculation and will be disposed of, I suppose, by auction. I am at a loss how to distribute those which belong to us, there being very few persons who are able to pay for them and all being equally anxious to be supplied."[10]

Bulger, on behalf of the executors of the late Earl, then signed the official receipt, acknowledging the delivery "from Michael Dousman." It seems strange that Dousman had to be named at all at this point. The ultimate success was due to Stewart's perseverance and the skill of the drivers, Louis Musick and Frederick Dickson. The receipt recognized 96 milk cows, 1 bull and 23 oxen and to guard against loss of memory, it restated the prices agreed upon four years earlier, namely $80 each for cows, and $100 each for the bull and oxen. It would bring the cost of the cattle to $10,080.

Bulger's acknowledged problem in distribution of the Colony cattle was not difficult to understand. With fifty cattle more than the Colony authority was required to take, there was the risk that settlers choosing to buy privately from the drivers would secure the best animals and succeed in obtaining them at lower prices than those fixed by the contract. Anticipating this danger, Bulger rode out to meet the incoming herd but discovered that some of the Scottish settlers were ahead of him and had, sure enough, selected sixteen of the choicest animals. Having picked their cows and agreed upon an attractive price, they gave orders on the Colony account for payment and drove the cattle to their various farms.

Bulger was furious. The Scots had outsmarted him but he demanded redress. He summoned the drivers and all who bought cattle and announced that until the cattle were returned to the Stewart herd and he had made his selections to satisfy the agreement, he would have no part in the transactions whatever and would pay no bills arising from cattle bought privately. His threat brought cancellation of the advance sales and he then cut out the 120 head he was prepared to accept and for which he would authorize payment.

Then came the tricky problem of distribution without being accused of racial or other bias. But the man who had taken his practical education in the army wasn't likely to waste much time in weighing justice. He was forthright in what he thought to be fair and seized some priorities which satisfied him even though they looked like prejudice to many of the people. As he reported the allocations: "I began with the married men of the de Meurons, to whom Lord Selkirk made promises of cattle in writing; next I considered the Scotch families which had been the longest in and suffered the most for the country; then the married Canadians from Montreal. . . . These being served I was induced, in the hope of reconciling [the Swiss] to the country to give a cow to each of them that had a family. I supplied the three German families and then the unmarried men of all countries who appeared to have the strongest claims on Lord Selkirk. No one was allowed to choose; I adopted a kind of lottery. . . . There are still some settlers who require to be supplied. It will not be in my power to satisfy them this year but the sub-contractors have offered to bring from 150 to 200 head to the Colony next spring at the following prices: good milch cows at 40 dollars each, oxen at 50 dollars a head. They will bring these cattle to the Colony provided I will agree to take 60 of the cows, the remainder they will dispose of as well as they can. I have not given them an answer but I consider it to be good for the Colony."[11]

When Bulger mentioned "giving" cows to certain groups, he meant selling at the contract price and the only thing he gave was credit. Still, the settlers who received cows or oxen were thankful and wanted more. The complaints were mainly from Bulger, as always, his objections being about the people around him, "dishonest paupers such as the majority are." And Adam Stewart continued to present complaints, the latest being his loss of about $4,000 in carrying out the contract which he had seen fit to purchase from Michael Dousman. He was also looking, quite properly, for the deed to 500 acres on the Red River which the Earl had promised to "the person who conducts the operation."

After debating with himself about the propriety of committing the Colony to a further purchase in the next year, Bulger entered into a loose contract with the two drivers, Musick and Dickson, to take sixty more cattle for 1823 delivery. The two cattlemen, having become more expert in long-distance driving, came through in October of the following year with 210 head. By this time, Bulger had departed and his successor, William Kempt, accepted the sixty cows and two bulls of Bulger's ordering, most reluctantly, and gave the drivers a receipt good for payment by the Selkirk Estate.

The executors, displaying ever more caution about expenditures, protested loudly at another purchase with inadequate authorization. Colvile said his colleagues were "most anxious to put a stop to all further outlays beyond the necessary establishment and that upon the most economical scale." To George Simpson, Bulger's order for the sixty additional cows was "madness in the extreme," but the settlers were not complaining and the two cattle dealers had no difficulty in disposing of the entire herd of 210 and even came back in 1824 with still another herd for private sale to settlers whose needs were finally being met.

Regardless of the disputes created by the incoming herds, the cattle changed the lives of the Red River inhabitants almost as much as the acquisition of horses changed the lives of the Plains Indians.

Now that cattle numbers were becoming sufficient to meet all local needs, a new question was raised: "What do we do when cattle numbers exceed our needs?" It was obvious that beef or meat of any kind was too perishable to be exported from remote Red River. There could, indeed, be too many cattle, but George Simpson, who was normally unenthusiastic about anything in agricultural production, had an idea for the movement of highly perishable meat from the Settlement to York Factory — let the cattle carry their own beef as far as the shore of Hudson Bay. To implement the proposal, the cattle would be raised in any number at Red River to the age of three or four years, then broken to work like oxen and started north about the month of October pulling sleds or stoneboats. Each animal would haul freight to the amount of 200 or 300 pounds, possibly dressed flax for export, possibly just feed for the cattle in travel.

By way of preparation, feeding stations at twenty-mile intervals would be set up along the route, with a native servant located at each. He would put up hay in season and work to improve the trail at other times. The traveling cattle would reach a different station each night. No shelters would be provided and the cattle would be tied to trees and fed hay. Hopefully, the cattle would reach York Factory in March. After grazing on the coarse northern grass along the rivers all summer, they would be ready for slaughter. The beef would be salted and hides and corned beef would then be shipped to London. It was a new and strange enthusiasm for Simpson but he even permitted himself to see beef as a profitable line, ultimately surpassing beaver skins.

But export of beef was a false hope. The only surviving advantage — a big one — was the assured supply of cattle for home needs. Never again were the settlers without and the herds brought in 1822 and later represented foundation for an industry.

CHAPTER TWENTY-FOUR

The Long Wait for Wool

Red River wives and mothers, almost without exception, were on good and understanding terms with spinning wheels but the precious implements carried tenderly from Scotland or elsewhere beyond the Atlantic had been idle for too long. The reason was obvious: the lack of wool. What the prairie bison contributed — call it hair or wool — was tested hopefully but the resulting yarn was coarse and weak and unsatisfactory. The settlers wanted sheep in the way they wanted cattle and Lord Selkirk was well aware of the need and the desire and tried earnestly to accommodate. There could be no better evidence of serious intent than the provision at great expense of the little flock of twenty-one Merinos sent out with the first settlers in 1812.

The choice of breed was dictated by quality of wool — the world's finest — and it carried a hope that the sheep would not only furnish wool and mutton and possibly milk for home use, but also that much-discussed article for export. Selkirk believed a program of rigid selection in breeding stock would be attended by such excellence in fleece quality that the Red River label on a bale of wool would identify it as the best in the trade.

It did not work out as planned. Probably the settlers were not prepared for such aristocratic stock requiring more care than the Highland Blackfaces, and between disease, predator dogs and Indians craving a taste of mutton, the flock became smaller rather than bigger. The sheep that numbered twenty-one at arrival in 1812 were down to fifteen in 1814 and eleven in 1816, and were continuing to dwindle.

The Earl, by his proposal to drive a flock of 200 sheep from the Upper Canada Settlement of Baldoon, proved willingness to spare neither cost nor effort. It would have been a trail journey of more than 1,400 miles and a person can only speculate about the probable numbers of animals which could be expected to reach the Forks. But the outbreak of the War of 1812-14, bringing the usual wartime plundering, saw many of the Baldoon sheep "entering the United States Army."

The proposal for a sheep drive from Upper Canada was abandoned but not the idea of a drive from some other distant point capable of furnishing the much-wanted foundation. In the meantime, Lord Selkirk declared faith in the idea which had led to the failing effort of 1812; he thought well enough of the purpose and principle involved to decide upon repeating it. Although he did not live long enough to see it carried out, those who followed in authority obtained and sent the sheep. Andrew Colvile, in 1821, wrote to Alexander MacDonell, reporting that: "The fifteen ewes and five rams of Merino, producing the finest wool will be sent by the ships. They have been imported from Saxony at some trouble and considerable expense and it is expected Mr. Laidlaw will take due care of them. . . . When the intercourse with the Mississippi is safe and when sheep can be procured at a price not exceeding 40 shillings each, delivered at the Settlement, one or two hundred ewes may be procured. If they get the pure Merino rams and if all the ram lambs are cut out of the crossbreds for four or five generations, the wool will become as fine as the original Merinos. The dry soil and dry climate of Red River are admirably adapted to produce fine wool. Long, low, covered sheds kept clean and dry will be best for winter and the easiest protection against dogs at night. In Saxony, where great pains are taken for the sake of the wool, they always house their sheep in wet weather."[1]

But again there were pitfalls and an important part of the sheep consignment did not reach Red River. The animals, male and female, were landed at York Factory in good condition and to ensure the best possible protection from dogs and other predators, the five rams and an equal number of ewes were placed on a small island in the Hayes River where they remained for five or six days. Then the unexpected happened: the river level rose several feet in a short space of time and all the valuable rams and some of the ewes were drowned. The people at Red River would be smitten with disappointment; Andrew Colvile would be disgusted and angry that such a thing would be allowed to happen. Fortunately, George Simpson was at York Factory and averred that it did not result from neglect; it was just more of that bad luck which seemed to plague the pioneer efforts to secure breeding stock. The survivors — ten head and all ewes — reached the Colony in November "in fine order." Sheep numbers there were still inconsequential but Alex MacDonell lost no time in making a plea to Colvile for more rams.

The MacDonell appeal would not reach London until late in the next year, and then another year went by. The surviving ewes were growing older and growing lonely for male company and only in early 1824 did Colvile advise of the committee's instructions to send a young ram "in from Fort William by the express canoes of this year if possible, which I hope will enable you to preserve the breed of sheep."[2]

At midsummer the ram arrived from Fort William, but by this time, the shipment looked like an exercise in futility. The Red River sheep, it seemed, could not overcome the succession of bad luck and now, faulty management could be added to the list of misfortunes. Colvile had to be a most patient man but on receiving an explanatory letter from Robert Parker Pelly, he probably gasped: "What next?" According to Pelly, the ram arrived well enough but an undisclosed number of ewes died from some disorder during the winter and "others look sickly." By his own admission, Pelly, as Governor of the Colony, had apparently given up with sheep. He was induced, he said, to sell the remaining ewes "to the German doctor who has four or five yet living and I have transferred the ram to him for £3." This was the ram for which the people at Red River had waited for three years and was then delivered at rather great cost.

After twelve years, the Colony had fewer sheep than when it started with the original Merino band. Anybody could have found reasons for giving up with this class of livestock, especially after the Stewart cattle were delivered. But sheepmen are a persevering breed and instead of abandoning the idea, many of the settlers were ready to gamble with more and bigger schemes. The next proposal came from Chief Factor Colin Robertson whose reputation was for big ideas more than practical ones. In George Simpson's view, he was "an uncertified bankrupt," not likely to be worth "a guinea should he live to be 1,000 years."

This time he was promoting something to be called the Assiniboine Sheep and Wool Company and of which he would be the manager. He hoped to obtain a grant of 1,000 acres from the Selkirk Estate, also a capital advance of £1,000. He would obtain sheep and shepherds from the United States and would soon have large supplies of mutton for sale to local residents and large amounts of wool for export. Fortune would follow, just as sure as Indians followed the herds of buffalo. But Robertson's scheme did not advance beyond the planning, partly because of Simpson's refusal to support it. It was just another wild Robertson dream and Simpson advised Colvile against granting the land being requested.

After only two more years, however, the skeptical Governor Simpson was promoting a sheep scheme bearing some resemblance to that advanced by Robertson. It did bear testimony to one important point: that by the accepted Red River view, sheep had to come, regardless of the cost in errors and misfortunes. Colvile had expressed the opinion that only a large flock could be profitable and Simpson's idea was to raise £1,000 of capital with which to purchase a big flock in the south, perhaps at St. Louis, paying not over 40 shillings per animal. When reporting progress on June 14, 1826, he could show subscriptions from himself and five other parties, totaling £475, as follows:

George Simpson	200 Pounds
Donald MacKenzie	100 Pounds
James Bird	50 Pounds
James Sutherland	50 Pounds
Catholic Mission	50 Pounds
Protestant Mission	25 Pounds
	475 Pounds

Plans were being made to authorize a St. Louis man to buy and drive the sheep to the Settlement in the next summer, but consistent with the record of misfortune attending hopes for Red River sheep, the flood disaster of 1826 brought all such plans to a halt. The scheme was revived, however, and by the revised calculation, the sheep would be delivered in 1828. That was the optimistic view; the pessimists could have reasoned that the history of failure with sheep pointed to more of the same and they would have been right. The flock, well on its way, fell a victim to the Indians. It was George Simpson's unpleasant duty to report to Colvile. He was grieved to say it, he admitted, but the sheep "along with some oxen and horses were dispersed and destroyed by Sioux near Lac Travers last summer on their way to this place and we understand the contractor, Wilson, and his people saved themselves by flight."[3]

Those who subscribed capital, notably George Simpson and Donald MacKenzie, lost heavily but before a year passed, Simpson was again presenting a proposal, this one for a still more ambitious program to begin with a big flock to be driven from somewhere in the region of St. Louis. It may have been his reasoning that "One of these times we must have a change of luck." He issued a prospectus for a joint stock company but before it had time to advance very far, the second experimental farm was being authorized and a decision was made to place with it the custodian role for the incoming sheep.

This time there would be no American contractor and no American herders; men from the Settlement would be chosen to travel the necessary distance into the south and southeast, buy the needed sheep and drive them home to Red River. Men of the Colony would do everything in the huge undertaking, even to facing the untold dangers. But there were men in the Settlement who had years of youthful experience with sheep and men who were not easily frightened by risk of danger. William Glen Rae, a clerk in Hudson's Bay Company service, accepted the leadership of the searching, buying, driving expedition. Among those to travel with him was J. B. Bourke, a retired Company clerk who had seen action at the Battle of Seven Oaks. Probably the most useful person in the party was Robert Campbell who grew up on a Perthshire sheep farm and whose diary furnished the best account of the journey and the problems.[4] Campbell was already associated with the new experimental farm, with the title of Assistant Manager. Since early in the spring, he had been living at the farm, having moved to the site about three or four miles west of the mouth of the Assiniboine, before the first building had been erected. Occupying a tent, he spent the summer directing building operations, clearing land and breaking. Now he was a member of a party of ten men — likely the most knowledgeable member — traveling with two carts carrying supplies, and eight saddle horses. Departure from the Settlement was on November 8, 1832, a time when winter could be expected to strike at any minute.

Residents along the river had two very valid reasons for wishing the travelers a safe and successful journey, first because the men were friends and neighbors and second, because their mission held another hope for those who dreamed of sheep for their pastures and wool for their spinning wheels.

There was much uncertainty about travel in November but the party started boldly, following the river trail as far as Pembina, then varying directions moderately to improve the chance of escaping the attention of the unpredictable Sioux Indians. While in the region of these natives — the most feared of all the prairie tribesmen — the travelers allowed themselves no time for loitering. Hurrying to pass the area, they were taking to the trail at three o'clock in the morning, stopping briefly for breakfast at eight. They would travel until sundown when they would stop for supper, then push on for another two or three miles to be safely removed from the spot where curls of campfire smoke at supper time might have attracted hostile Indians and conveyed a tempting impression of white men made defenseless by sleep. As the members of Rae's party were informed later, a Sioux war band did follow them and gave up the pursuit only after three days.

There was another reason for hurrying: the Red River men hoped to reach St. Peter's Post on the Mississippi, opposite Fort Snelling, in time to catch one of the last riverboats of the season going to St. Louis. It would have hastened them on their way. Arriving on December 1, however, they were a few days late for the boat. Ice was beginning to form on the river and the ground was now covered with snow. Abandoning the carts, they transferred their provisions and supplies to sleighs and pressed on.

After a few more days of travel, following the Mississippi, the river water seemed to become more navigable and the men adopted canoes. But the ease of water travel with the current did not last long because only a short distance below Prairie du Chien, ice was again becoming a hazard. Another change was necessary and having left their horses behind, the men had no choice except to continue on foot. They crossed the Illinois River, traveled through Jacksonville and reached St. Louis on the third day in the new year, 1833. They were now, they estimated, about 1,500 miles from home by the circuitous way they traveled.

Now to locate and buy the sheep! For several weeks they pursued the search in the countryside around St. Louis but they made no purchases. The only sheep they saw were not for sale or priced beyond what they considered reasonable. At a moment when the men were feeling discouraged, Rae and Campbell received a friendly hint: "You'd do better in Kentucky."

Now, where was Kentucky? The men from Red River did not know but were informed that to go there, they would travel across Illinois in an easterly and southerly direction. It would mean a few hundred miles of added travel but the men of the party accepted what they believed to be necessity and set out for Versailles where sheep were indeed more plentiful than at St. Louis, and more reasonably priced. Purchases were made in rather short order and with a flock of 1,100 ewes and lambs bought at from five to seven shillings per head, also a few rams, Rae and his helpers were eager to begin the long and uncertain drive to Red River. As a precautionary measure, however, they delayed long enough to shear all the adult sheep, expecting them to travel with more comfort and more speed.

The drive began on May 2. Naturally, the sheep did not want to go. Perhaps they sensed dangers even more than the men. Perhaps it was just characteristic sheep cussedness such as appears whenever the animals are being driven in unaccustomed directions. Although travel was slow during those first days on the trail, Rae and Campbell were able to enlarge the flock by the purchase of 270 more ewes and lambs, bringing the flock to the substantial total of 1,370 head.

After more days of trailing, progress seemed satisfactory and Campbell wrote that they were covering between ten and twelve miles per day. But it was too early for predictions and as time was to reveal, the trail held unsuspected troubles. There were rivers to cross, with every individual in the flock registering objection. There were sore feet for which the men carried no cure. There were flies to torment both sheep and men. There were rattlesnakes lurking in prairie grass, accounting for the death of as many as five sheep in a single day. But the worst and by far the most costly curse of all was the speargrass encountered almost everywhere after passing Peoria. The javelin-like and barbed seeds of this native grass were maturing sufficiently to be easily detached from the parent plants. Collecting on fleeces as the sheep walked through the tall grass, the seeds worked their way into the wool and did not stop when reaching the tender skins. Penetrating the tissue, the barbed spears caused severe irritation and left openings to the flesh inviting flies and the growth of maggots.

After crossing the Mississippi at Rock Island, Rae ordered a halt for the purpose of shearing. It would be the second time in one season and it would test Rae's theory that shorter wool would reduce the accumulation of grass spears. The prevalence of maggots made the second shearing a repulsive task and, unfortunately, it proved to be a complete waste of time. It did nothing to remove the speargrass annoyance and the second-cut wool brought no monetary return. When Rae tried to sell the wool at Rock Island, those who might have been purchasers apparently concluded that the sheepmen could not take the wool with them and if it were left behind, it would be available at no cost to anybody who would take it. As second-cut wool, the fibers would be short and it would not be worth much but in failing to find a buyer, Rae's men tried to burn it. As they no doubt discovered, wool does not burn very readily, one of the points in its favor over vegetable fibers for garments.

Instead of holding the flock on some spot of "clean grazing" until the offending spears dropped to the ground, the men drove on, thereby leaving themselves open to criticism. The sheep became steadily weaker. A few more died every day. By July 7, according to Campbell's diary, the living sheep numbered 675 head — just about half of the original flock of two months earlier. By August 25, only 295 remained.

At this point the drivers were back in Sioux Indian country, with reasons for worry. Sure enough, they came face to face with a war party which might very well have ended the drive. Earlier in the summer, George Simpson advised Andrew Colvile that the sheep would reach the Settlement by August, "unless Rae and his party get scalped." The Governor added that he had taken certain precautions to prevent the scalping; he said he had employed an American postmaster, Raignville by name, who was supposed to be in good standing with the Sioux, and who would accompany the drive from St. Peter's to the neighborhood of Pembina. It is very doubtful that Simpson's action had any influence upon the natives. In any case, the band of amused Indians confronting the flock, instead of falling greedily upon a resource of mutton, just gazed with fascination upon these animal creatures, the like of which the Sioux had never seen. Rae distributed some presents and drove on.

Proving that there were still forms of trouble not yet encountered, Rae and his men now ran out of food supplies for themselves. With some sheep remaining, of course, complete famine was impossible and Campbell mentioned slaughtering a sheep "for our kettle." Then fortune seemed to have a smile for the sheepmen; a boat from the Settlement reached the drivers at Grand Point, high on the Red River, bringing supplies of much-needed provisions and news from home. As the boat was about to return, some of the lame sheep and lambs were placed on it, making it possible for the remaining part of the flock to be driven somewhat faster. Finally, after an absence of almost a year, traveling all the time, the men arrived at the Settlement on September 16, driving a weakened flock totaling 251 head, less than one-fifth of the ewes and lambs starting the drive.

Most residents rejoiced to see even the greatly reduced number of sheep, but some grumbled because the losses were so high. It was unfortunate but when the magnitude of the drive and the multiplicity of hazards were considered, the wonder was that sheep in any number were delivered. Had they been doing it again, Rae and Campbell would have avoided some of the mistakes which proved costly in sheep. They might have purchased fewer sheep at the higher prices asked at St. Louis and thereby shortened the drive; they certainly would have considered a halt for a few weeks at midsummer to escape the worst of the speargrass season. It was possible, too, that the men should have driven more slowly.

It was easy to criticize the methods employed by the drivers but Red River had 251 sheep—probably the hardiest part of the original flock—with which to found an industry. The sheep were delivered to the experimental farm, there to remain under the care of Robert Campbell who was destined in other ways also to make a distinguished frontier record. The weakened sheep recovered quickly and adapted readily to the new surroundings. Next year there were 400 sheep on the farm and from this flock, other Red River settlers obtained breeding stock, making the shrunken band of 251 head delivered at the end of a four-and-a-half-months' drive appear more and more like the "taproot" of farm flocks in Manitoba and farther west.

Oh for a Horse to Pull My Plow!

To prepare the first ground for wheat planting, Miles Macdonell and his workers worked laboriously with spades and hoes. They had no alternative. Given a choice of power for the purpose, they would have taken horses, most certainly, and oxen would have been an acceptable second choice. Without draft animals in sufficient numbers, settlers were seriously handicapped and Red River people felt the shortage of both horses and oxen for more than a decade.

The proposals to bring breeding horses from home communities overseas were rejected as impractical. Bringing sheep in the sailing ships was awkward enough and who would undertake to convey horses over the dangerous river route from York Factory to Red River? Moreover, it was known that the prairie Indians had horses and from them the newcomers to the country expected to buy to meet their needs.

Unfortunately, getting horses from the tribesmen was not as easy as anticipated. In the first place, the Plains Indians had not been long in possession of horses — less than a hundred years — and did not yet have as many as they wanted for themselves. Secondly, the Indian-owned horses were small and unattractive to people with fond memories of the improved European breeds. And finally, as Red River residents discovered, there was a peculiar risk in buying horses from the Indian people; it happened too often to be entertaining that the horses bought during the day were stolen away during one of the nights following.

Horses were really "old-timers" in these parts. They evolved over millions of years right here but for reasons unknown, they became extinct on the Americas and remained so until reintroduced by the Spaniards who followed Columbus. Animals escaping from their Spanish masters found it easy to adapt to the wild state and gave rise to the Mustang strain, from which the native people obtained some of their first horses. Nothing changed the Indian way of life as much as the ownership of horses and when one tribe had them, it was imperative for neighboring tribes to have them. Thus the great Indian pastime of horse stealing was born and its popularity was unsurpassed.

After being stolen from one tribe to another, northward, the first horses of the new strain were seen in the valley of the Bow River about 1730, roughly eight-two years before the settlers came to Red River. It was not a long time but long enough for the native people to become expert horsemen and long enough for the horses to become climatized, uniformly hardy, sure-footed and resistant to many forms of horse disease. They appeared as runts and unprepossessing but they were strong for their size and might have been exactly what the settlers needed, whether they realized it or not.

As it was, horse numbers at the Settlement rose and fell — like April temperature readings. The Colony by 1816 had twenty-one horses, then it had none. One of the reasons for fluctuation was thieving, although it was not as prevalent as farther west. James Sutherland was writing from Qu'Appelle in late 1815, for example, telling of Indians having "thieved our horses, 24 in number. They were two days gone before we missed them and then had no horses [with which] to pursue them. This will greatly retard our work as we must entirely depend on dogs for all our journeys as well as for hauling wood and meat."[1]

Among the Plains Indians who refused to take the concept of private property very seriously, horse stealing was an intriguing recreation, the best of all sports. It called for skill and was sufficiently dangerous to be challenging. In spite of what the missionaries said about it, how could it be such a sin when it was the right and privilege of the victim of a theft to try to steal back his horses?

Early in 1818, when the Settlement was still rehabilitating after the tragedy of Seven Oaks, the lack of horses was recognized as a major handicap. There were only six horses to serve the growing Settlement. So great was the horse famine that the milk cow and herd bull and even the semi-domesticated buffalo were harnessed for purposes of plowing at the experimental farm. The Hudson's Bay Company, with sizable stocks of horses at North Saskatchewan posts, was criticized for "supplying us with very few horses."

William Laidlaw, with an acute instinct for horse trading, hoped to relieve the critical shortage by making an expedition into Indian country to the west. "It is my intention," he wrote, "to go up towards Qu'Appelle in the fall of the year with two men and take some liquor and trifling articles with us." With these he was sure he could procure "good horses at a moderate rate."[2]

Laidlaw had been at Qu'Appelle earlier in the year looking for horses taken by the attackers in 1815 and 1816 but the trip was not particularly rewarding; of the lost property he recovered one horse, one saddle and three dogs. At the same time, he saw many Indian horses and commented: "If I had liquor and some trifling articles with me at the time. . . . I could have got 50 horses."

The most effective relief came in June, 1819, when the Company gestured by sending fifty-two horses from the Saskatchewan — presumably from

Fort Edmonton where a big herd was maintained for freighting — and these, according to Alexander MacDonell, "were divided among the Settlers and Mr. Laidlaw's farm."

But even this hardy Indian stock was not immune to equine disorders and disease struck during the winter months; in Alexander MacDonell's words: "Our people lost 16 horses out of 23 that I left them — died with a disease hitherto unknown." MacDonell continued with an unintended hint of starvation: "The snow was so high they could not scrape the ground as usual. The freemen were obliged to cut trees for them, and their horses lived on trees for a month."[3]

The experimental farm in 1820 was still without more than three horses, still hitching cow, bull and buffalo female when three horses could not do the job.

It is not clear to which particular horses MacDonell was referring when he mentioned the twenty-three he left with the settlers. He too was given to horse trading and even in his position of Governor of the Colony, he was not above some profitable dealing. George Simpson was critical, said he left himself open to censure for trafficking in this way, buying from the Indians "at low prices and selling to the settlers at enormous advance, thereby pocketing a large profit."

The power situation improved slightly after Adam Stewart's cattle were delivered on August 28, 1822, because a few horses and twenty-three oxen were included in the drive. For the next few years the imported oxen and colony-raised oxen were more conspicuous than horses in the farm fields. The settlers loved horses and wanted horses but the availability of oxen and the general utility of those critters under frontier conditions where work animals were obliged to live entirely on grass and hay were much in their favor. The ox was slow and unlovable but he possessed the ability to "live off the land."

But settlers lost none of their inherent sentiment for horses. They were grateful for the semi-native horses they acquired in small numbers but were not inspired by them unless they happened to get some superior buffalo runners or something fast enough to win local races or big enough to be hitched with oxen in pulling a plow. The best of these native mares were mated with a stallion brought with the Adam Stewart cattle, bringing noticeable improvement in size and type. Still the memory of Scottish Clydesdales and English Thoroughbreds and Hackneys did not fade and farmers let their yearnings be known to the Rupert's Land Governor, George Simpson.

The Governor, catching the message, communicated it to the London officials, saying: "Some plan must soon be fallen upon to increase our stock and improve our breed of horses, as they are becoming very scarce and of such small growth as to be quite unfit for our work. Until of late years we could get as many from the Indians as we required, but now the Indians have few or none for themselves, and instead of providing us as heretofore, steal those we rear from our very doors, although they are guarded by armed keepers."[4]

Either Simpson had a tip about the committee's intention or he possessed the brand of faith reputed to "remove mountains" when, in 1830, he issued instructions for the gathering of the best mares procurable for a special breeding program aimed at type improvement. Twenty-five mares were assembled at Fort Carlton and twenty-five at Athabasca River. The lack of a superior stallion appeared as an obvious weakness in the plan until the Company committee in England made a crucial decision and communicated it to Simpson on February 23, 1831. Deputy Governor Nicholas Garry forwarded the message, saying: "We shall send a stallion of a proper breed by the ship to York Factory. We should think the Experimental Farm at Red River the best place to commence raising horses for the service."[5]

A breeding stallion from England held great possibilities for good, also the chance of bitter disappointment. What did the Deputy Governor mean by "a proper breed?" What did he know about breeds and horses? How small was the chance of a stallion reaching York Factory without dying and if he did get that far, was there any hope of transporting him the rest of the way to Red River in safety? It took no imagination to see a well-grown stallion as very dangerous cargo for a canoe or York boat on the tricky northern rivers. Nevertheless, the gift of a stallion was a fine gesture and the citizens of Red River were eager to see what the committee selected. Knowing the conditions of river travel as they did, they dared not be optimistic but they could hope.

George Simpson replied to the Company officials in London, assuring them that the horse would be kept at the experimental farm and a band of selected mares would be brought to the same place. There was still no information about the stallion's breeding and characteristics. He was coming as a sort of a surprise package but late in the summer the mystery animal arrived at York Factory in good condition. Then, after more weeks of travel, he was brought to Red River, none the worse for the long journey and the primitive state of transportation.

Men, women and children from up and down the river turned out excitedly to see this equine aristocrat, of which they had so little detailed information, and to welcome him.

At once, all questions about the horse were answered. The stallion's name was Fireaway and he was a representative of the Norfolk Trotter breed, whence came the English Hackney. The old Norfolk Trotter or Norfolk Roadster, with Arabian blood in its veins, was stoutly built and found favor as a general purpose or utility breed. For the requirements at Red River, Fireaway was an excellent choice. Glad to plant his big feet on firm ground, the stallion stood like a statue with head held high, ears erect and tail carried with a stylish flourish. He was beautiful in spite of the hardships of a long journey. His bright bay coat glistened in the autumn sun and men who remembered how to "chin a horse" said he stood 16 hands.

His stoutly made body with good muscling pleased those people who were thinking about plowing and the claim that he could trot more than fifteen miles an hour pleased all others.

For Red River horse lovers, it was a great day and in due course, George Simpson reported to the Governor and committee in London with words of praise to cheer the English hearts: "The stallion sent out last year reached the Settlement in perfect safety and in high condition, and will soon give us a better breed of horses. He is looked upon as one of the wonders of the world by the natives, many of whom have travelled great distances with no other object than to see him."[6]

The selected mares were brought to the experimental farm as planned and in time there were foals bearing the stamp of their respected sire, strong, active, spirited, and they developed to the satisfaction of the most fastidious horsemen. At two or three years of age progeny were broken to saddle and then to harness, and settlers agreed they then had the best buffalo runners the country had seen; the young horses seemed to possess the stamina of their mothers and the speed of their father. They were no less distinguished as roadsters and were versatile enough to be better at field work than any horses before them. Admiration for both Fireaway and his offspring became louder rather than fainter as the years passed.

There was one serious problem in having a superior horse or superior horses at Red River: the people who believed good horses were for stealing, would not leave them alone. The attempts to steal Fireaway were so numerous that an armed guard was kept with him for twenty-four hours per day at one period in his Red River sojourn. Discriminating horse thieves who couldn't get away with the sire would settle for nothing less than his sons and daughters.

The Fireaway experiment was an unqualified success and the fame of the stallion and his get lived in Red River memories for more than half a century. When Rev. John McDougall, in 1864, drove from Fort Edmonton to Fort Garry to obtain supplies and some livestock, the purchase about which he boasted was a horse for which he paid a premium, simply because it was said to be a descendant of Fireaway.

Horsemen wishing to know the rest of the story about the great Fireaway may be disappointed. Questions about how long he lived and where he went from Red River must remain unanswered. Nobody in later years knew the answers or nobody would tell. One account had it that the stallion was sold at a high price to go to the United States, another that thieves were ultimately successful and whisked Fireaway across the border. According to still another story, the stallion's reputation as a breeder left the English producers of Norfolk Trotters wanting him back and prepared to pay well to recover him.

It will seem strange that so little is known of the stallion's later years and yet so much is acknowledged about his greatness as an individual with substance and quality, and his breeding successes which changed the character of Red River horses and helped the settlers to triumph in their cropping endeavors.

It was a compliment to Fireaway that the Hudson's Bay Company, some years later, chose to repeat the gesture of providing the Settlement with a high-class stallion. This time, in 1848, Captain Pelly, with Company authority, bought the English Thoroughbred stallion, Melbourne, for £210, also a gray Thoroughbred mare, an Ayrshire bull and two Ayrshire cows. The five Bluebloods from the English and Scottish livestock communities were sent forward to York Factory by the ship *Prince Rupert,* all under the expert care of Thomas Howsom Axe, who was engaged for three years at a salary of £30 per year and a bonus of £5 if all his charges reached York Factory in good health. Axe qualified for the bonus and the animal aristocrats were then part of the freight cargo departing York Factory in four York boats on August 28.

As described by Donald Ross, it was "a troublesome and dangerous cargo." Nobody could doubt it. The boats, like oversized canoes, were built to carry bales of furs and suffered damage from the heavy feet of the five head of cattle and horses. But the essential point was that Thomas Howsom Axe and his animals arrived at the Settlement in good health and settlers who gathered to witness the spectacle were pleased.

The success of the undertaking was limited but the five purebred animals could not be denied the distinction of being the first representatives of their respective breeds in the country; the horses were the first Thoroughbreds and the cattle were just as clearly the real pioneers of the Ayrshire breed. They had a chance of a great future. Twenty selected cows were assembled at the Settlement for a breeding program and twenty of the best mares were brought from Fort Pelly. The hope was that the Fireaway breeding success would be repeated. But the pattern was not the same. Fortunes began to turn. In the year after arrival, the Thoroughbred mare produced a promising foal but before the summer ended, both mare and foal were dead. Melbourne then kicked the high-priced English groom and broke his arm and local people insisted upon making comparisons, saying that Fireaway was a better horse than Melbourne. Eden Colvile, as Acting Governor of Rupert's Land, was losing his enthusiasm and ready to recommend selling Melbourne for "what he will fetch." Writing to Sir George Simpson, the Acting Governor said the animals were a bad speculation. "The settlers have sent just 17 mares to the horse, though the price of him was reduced to one pound with a shilling to the groom. He covered about 60 mares belonging to the Company but they were so wild, never having been handled, that I understand more than half of them are not in foal. . . . My opinion is that the horse should be sent next season to St. Louis, and sold for what he will fetch, and I think a good price may be obtained for him."[7]

The advice was not taken. Instead, Melbourne was transferred to Fort Pelly and used extensively for breeding at that place which became the principal horse breeding station.

The Ayrshire cattle lost their identity and failed to measure up to expectations. Likewise, Melbourne failed to match the success of Fireaway but his influence on the horse population of the country was very subsantial, and between the two imported stallions, the Settlement and the country had more and better horses.

CHAPTER TWENTY-SIX

How Are the Crops?

It would have been easy to blame the soil and climate for the recurring crop failures in the first eleven or twelve years of the Colony. The poor record was enough to discourage all but the most stubborn settlers. Some of the immigrants gave up in 1815, more after the grasshoppers in 1819 and 1820, and still more after the devastating flood of 1826. But the resolute and hardy ones remained to complete the test.

Lord Selkirk, like a "voice crying in the wilderness," said the soil was good. Not only was he right but his words were understatements because the Red River Valley soil, on which he was locating his people, would rank with the most fertile in the entire world, although it took a long time to convince the people who did not wish to be convinced, George Simpson among them. Simpson, as late as 1857, could see no future for the country Selkirk had so courageously championed, except in producing furs.

His words are worth noting. In February of that year, the opinionated Simpson — by this time, Sir George — faced a Select Committee of the House of Commons in London for the purpose of sharing his knowledge of the country with members trying to determine if the Hudson's Bay Company license for territory beyond Rupert's Land should be renewed. After thirty-seven years of close association with the Northwest, he should speak with authority. He made his replies with typical assurance. Asked to explain his "impressions of the character of the Territory of the Hudson's Bay Company in point of soil and climate, particularly with reference to its adaptation for the purposes of cultivation and colonization," Simpson answered: "I do not think that any part of the Hudson's Bay Territory is well adapted for settlement; the crops are very uncertain."[1]

It was unfortunate for Simpson's reputation as a man of judgment that he did not end his testimony at that point. The questioner asked about the area to which he made reference and Simpson replied: "I mean it to apply to Rupert's Land," meaning, by the geography of today, Manitoba, Saskatchewan and most of settled Alberta. Yes, the district of Red River was included, and when asked: "Why so?" Simpson made the amazing reply: "On account of the poverty of the soil, except on the banks of the river."

If Simpson was basing his observations about crops being "very uncertain," on the record of the first decade of the Settlement, he would have been correct but by 1857 — some forty-five years after the birth of the Colony, crops had become moderately reliable and the richness of the soil should have been no longer in question.

True, there was crop failure in most of the first ten years but never from "poverty of the soil." The fact should have been well established by 1857 that the soil on which the Settlement was located was deep and packed with the sediment of an ancient lake. It had a gumbo quality making it heavy to plow and difficult to cultivate but was still one of the most fertile expanses of agricultural land in the world. Nature played some unkind tricks on settlers in those early years but no part of the cropping troubles could be attributed fairly to Sir George's alleged "poverty of the soil."

The choice of winter wheat rather than spring wheat for the initial planting at Red River led to the first failure, and was simply an error in human judgment. It was of a kind to be expected in an untried country. Similarly, the disruptions from outside attack in 1815 and 1816, which saw settlers fleeing from their small acreages of seeded cropland maliciously trampled into the ground by the invaders, were strictly the result of human conduct. Although the attackers tried to destroy the crop in both years, there was substantial recovery in 1815 and settlers returning late in the year found their small fields presenting wheat ready for harvest.

Estimates of crop return in that year differed widely. John Halkett believed that 1,500 bushels of wheat and "a large stock of potatoes" were recovered. Peter Fidler, whose assessment should be respected, said the crop was "partly" saved and yielded "400 bushels of wheat, 200 of barley and 500 of potatoes."[2] And Robert Semple, soon after arriving at the Settlement on November 3, mentioned the first spectacle to gladen his eyes, "12 or 14 stacks of corn, a sight perfectly novel in this country." The stacks, he estimated, would yield about fifty bushels each, bringing the total grain return to Fidler's figure. Semple saw the necessity of budgeting the estimated 600 bushels of grain and notified Selkirk of his intention to hold back forty bushels for the next season's planting and rationing the remaining 560 bushels or about 28,800 pounds by his computation at two pounds per day for each of 120 people. At the rate of 240 pounds of consumption per day, the supply would last exactly four months.[3]

In the next year — the year of Seven Oaks — the settlers were still in exile at harvest time and nobody knew if the crop matured to a harvestable state or not. For all practical purposes, it was another failure because nothing was recovered.

The crop of 1814 was said to be damaged by early autumn frost but Miles Macdonell's figures showed it far from a total loss. Indeed, if Macdonell was accurate, the wheat return of "23 kegs of 10 gallons each after 19 quarts sown," meant a 28-bushel harvest from less than one bushel planted and should have been seen as a good yield under any circumstances. It revealed also that the 1814 cultivation for grain was still not more than an acre.

The frost enemy is shown to have appeared early in Western Canada's agricultural history but was certainly not confined to the early years of settlement. It remained for decades — at least until the introduction of the relatively early maturing Marquis variety — as the principal obstacle to successful cropping. Visiting Red River for the second time in the experience of the settlers, it struck in 1817, and its occurrence in late August or early September continued to be the most common of heart-breaking cropping experiences for much of the ensuing century — certainly throughout the homestead period. Colin Robertson, after saying the crop of 1817 was spoiled by frost, went on to give the return in that autumn as 99½ bushels of wheat, 11¼ bushels of barley and 308 bushels of potatoes. The total would be needed for the next year's planting and Alexander MacDonell gave instructions "to all the people not to eat any."

Then came the memorable grasshopper years, 1818, 1819 and 1820, when the insects in hordes struck without warning and without mercy, mowing down every green thing and leaving the settlers speculating if the vermin had come to stay. They were enough to inspire some extravagant language. Captain Frederick Matthey claimed the hoppers "dug the earth to eat the stems of the potatoes under ground. In some places they were two and three inches thick on the ground."[4]

Fortunately, however, the wheat on about seventy-five acres and barley on about twenty-five acres were so far advanced that the insects could not make a totally destructive impression and even after invading blackbirds took what they considered their share, the crop was moderately rewarding. Matthey said the potatoes "on the Scotch side" were very fine. He could add that in potatoes and wheat the people were fairly well supplied for seed for the next year. He failed to note that some of the wheat seed was from the diligent gleaning by hand on the part of Red River wives and mothers who went into the fields after the grasshoppers departed for the season, and gathered individual heads which the insects had missed. Thrift, ever a virtue, was deeply ingrained in the settler group. Altogether, as Matthey mentioned, the settlement secured "three respectable stacks and hoped for a return of 500 bushels of plump and heavy grain."

But the gleaning effort was wasted because the hoppers came again in larger numbers. Again, it was for Matthey to embellish a little. The insects, he said, began breeding "most furiously about the beginning of September when they laid their eggs in small holes within one or two inches of the surface of the earth. . . . In the beginning of May the first young ones made their appearance. They were coming out of the ground like froth out of the bunghole of a cask full of fermenting fluid. The beginning of June brought forth fresh miriads of new born ones who destroyed everything that attempted to pass out of the surface of the earth."[5]

This time the grasshoppers really took everything and even gleaning by hand was unrewarding. With a larger human population and more livestock to feed, some of the leaders wondered if they would be back to almost complete reliance upon the buffalo before the winter was far advanced. More settlers arrived from the Orkneys in 1818 to aggravate the impending food shortage, also a starting flock of six chickens needing grain feed from Sault Ste. Marie. The founding flock was followed by a shipment from overseas, described as "an abundant supply of poultry, geese and ducks which I hope we shall convey in safety to the settlement."[6]

All of this would increase the requirement for grain. The settler population after the arrival of the Orkneymen was 151 Scots, 45 de Meurons and Swiss and 26 Canadians, totaling 222 people to be fed.

In spite of grasshoppers, land sales increased, with small lots of the 50- to 100-acre size, with 10 chains of river frontage, selling at $2.00 per acre, and the buyer undertaking to make his home on the property. Parcels of 500 acres, with 10 chains of river frontage for every 100 acres included, were priced at $1.50 per acre, provided the purchaser promised to bring to the land one man servant or two women servants — potential settlers, of course — in addition to his own family. And by taking 1,000 acres with 8 chains of river frontage per 100 acres, a buyer could obtain same for $1.00 per acre and an undertaking to bring, in addition to his own family, not less than four men servants or eight women servants not under eighteen years of age.[7]

At the end of the 1819 season when the grasshoppers had finished their evil work on another crop, there was neither food for the people nor seed for the next year. Settlers made the familiar trek to Pembina, resigned to subsisting for another winter on buffalo meat and fish. It was the altogether too common postscript to crop failure. And William Laidlaw, manager of the experimental farm, still having disagreements with the small-of-stature and officious Alexander MacDonell, undertook in December to travel on snowshoes to Prairie du Chien beside the upper Mississippi River, for the purpose of purchasing seed wheat for the next spring's planting. He found the wheat and bought 300 bushels at ten shillings per bushel, hoping to raft it back to Red River when the streams were high in the spring. Because the water was not as high as expected, he was obliged to leave some of the seed behind. He succeeded in bringing 250 bushels to the Forks at Fort Douglas, a little late for the best seeding, but the grain was planted anyway, early in June.[8] When all expenses were tallied, the expedition was said to have cost Lord Selkirk £1,040 sterling, or about $20 per bushel. As the season advanced, the grasshoppers were back but in reduced numbers and the meager crop was harvested — about 2,000 bushels of wheat which was little enough from 250 bushels of seed bought at such an exorbitant price in both currency and effort.

The attitude that gave rise to the "Next Year Country" thinking in the West, seems to have had its origin about this time. The year of 1821, everybody was saying, would be better. But it wasn't better; it was worse and George Simpson wrote to Andrew Colvile, reporting: "The grasshoppers, I am extremely sorry to say, continue their destructive influence. The crops have been seriously injured, in many parts wholly destroyed. . . . I cannot recommend any more settlers from Europe, far less from Canada, until we see if the grasshoppers disappear."[9]

Actually, the Colony was closer to starvation in the following winter than in any previous year. The situation was made worse by the almost total failure of the hunters to reach the buffalo herds. The Settlement had more people to feed and many of them owed their survival to a diet of sturgeon during the winter months and the roots of "Indian potatoes" in the spring of 1822.

Even though the crops had been poor, Simpson believed the failure of the buffalo would do more good than harm by "stimulating the people to agriculture." There were various incentives to succeed in cropping. Leaders talked about the shortage of grain to meet the rising food needs, but there was another demand, arising from a shortage of grain for distilling, and liquor was scarce. That would never do. The Scots blamed the Swiss for drinking too much of the available brew and the Swiss blamed the Scottish for the same crime. George Simpson was torn between two opinions. If the settlers indulged in distilling, the Company could buy its liquor requirements for the trading posts without the heavy expense of bringing it across the Atlantic. "In the course of a year or two," he wrote optimistically, "Red River will furnish abundance of liquor; all the Scotch and most of the Swiss settlers understand distillation. They already possess the implements and make no secret of their intention to use them the moment their crops admit of it."[10]

A year or two later, however, Simpson had a change of mind on the subject. Distillation was getting out of hand and he feared that if crops were good, liquor manufacture might become a dominant and dangerous home industry. Drunkenness was increasing and he declared his intention of imposing restraints. He was shocked to find some of the people trafficking in liquor. Bootlegging was having its birth on western soil, as Simpson disclosed; he reported selling 800 gallons of rum in this year, 1824, at eight shillings sixpence per gallon while some of the settlers had resold it for as high as four pounds per gallon. It represented a huge profit which Simpson no doubt coveted.

Settlers might have furnished themselves with "implements," as Simpson called the stills, but otherwise, mechanization in the agricultural community was far away. The most advanced piece of equipment in that area, where grain was being cut with sickle and cradle and threshed by flail with help from prairie wind, was a windmill. But because of weight and complexity, it remained unused for years. Its assembly was too much for these people who were wholly unfamiliar with machines. George Simpson wrote in 1821 that the iron mill was in storage at York Factory and likely to remain there unless "handy men" were sent from England to cope with it. "I would recommend it be returned," he said. Two years passed; nothing was done about the windmill and Simpson wrote again: "The large mill, I think, should be sent home; here it is eating itself up in rust."[11]

It was not the end of the story about the West's first piece of machinery. Heavy and awkward as it was, the mill's parts were forwarded to Red River and a man, Mitchell by name, was brought from England to erect the mechanical monster. But Mitchell's skills were overrated, also, and George Simpson wrote with obvious impatience and disgust:

"Mitchell has been employed in erecting a corn mill to be wrought by oxen or horses which will give about 17 or 18 bushels of grain per day. He had a thousand difficulties and objections to set about a windmill and I have reason to believe he never did and cannot put one of that description together. The fall he arrived in this country I took great pains with him at York to select the pieces of the windmill machinery to be forwarded to the Settlement and the pieces he did select were carefully forwarded and are now here but they turn out to be the machinery of a sawmill, and all the pieces belonging to the cornmill have been returned. I am now firmly of the opinion that no more machinery should be sent from England and that the people should be allowed to grind the best way they can. Every second or third settler has a small hand mill or quern which is all that can be required. Flour cannot become an article of export as it would not pay the expense of transportation."[12]

Up to this time, the few plows in use had moldboards of wood, made by the Colony carpenter rather than the blacksmith and not very satisfactory. Many of the novice croppers remained loyal to the hand spade and the grain yields of 1824 seemed to confirm their good judgment. The crop of 1822 escaped the grasshoppers but suffered from hungry birds and then furnished between 5,000 and 6,000 bushels of wheat and barley. The next year was remembered as one bringing hail and drought to plague the crop.

Finally, there came the year of the bumper crop, 1824. It was an appropriate reward for perseverance and it remained in pioneer memories very much as 1915 was the never-to-be-forgotten year for many homesteaders of later times, when yields exceeded anything known before. R. N. Pelly, as the new Governor in the Colony following Bulger, was puzzled to know what to do with the 20,000 bushels he believed he saw in the harvest. In keeping with traditional economics, he dropped the price from seven shillings sixpence per bushel to five shillings per bushel for wheat, and from five shillings to three per bushel for barley. The Company might have taken more flour but there was still no mill in the Settlement.

It was a test year for a new iron plow made in the Colony from metal brought from York Factory. The most revealing point was that the wheat grown on plowed ground yielded forty-four bushels per acre and that grown on land worked with a spade and hoe gave sixty-eight bushels. The moral should have been clear enough: "If you're going to grow wheat, you should shun the new-fangled gadgets like plows." Nevertheless, the big yield of that season stimulated such interest in crop expansion that the Colony Governor was instructing his carpenter to make sixteen new plows to be sold to the settlers.

Lord Selkirk's idea of growing flax and hemp was partially revived in this year, with Nicholas Garry sending seed and instructions for cultivating and preparing the salable part of the product for export. "I hope you will be able to introduce it," he said.

Most significantly, that year of 1824 brought the first big crop in the twelve years of the Settlement and the next year would have been favorable had it not been for the ravages of mice which appeared in numbers that seemed to challenge the laws of normal reproduction. It was recalled as "The Year of the Mice."

It was still too soon to suppose that the Settlement had tasted all the forms of destructiveness the country was capable of serving. Headway was being made but it was like that of pilgrims journeying to Jerusalem, taking two steps forward and one in reverse. In those first twelve years there had been grasshopper plagues, frost, famine, warfare, arson, plunder — and more to come. Except for the Battle of Seven Oaks taking a heavy toll in human life, the biggest tragedy of the early years, both for crops and settlers, was the flood of 1826.

For years thereafter, any mention of "The Flood," was likely to invite the question: "Which Flood?" It had to be either the Old Testament Flood that transformed Noah from a landlubber to a sailor, or the Red River flood of 1826. The latter, unlike the former, came without warning and settlers occupying their small homes close to the normal high-water mark, were ill-prepared. There may be doubt concerning the exact depth of the water in Noah's time but much is known about the flood of 1826 which saw the water level reaching six feet higher than the memorable Red River flood of 1950, the second highest in recorded history. There was a local legend about still deeper floodwater in 1776 but no details survived and more will never be known.

The inundation of 1826 was cruel and costly. The Red River level rose nine feet in one day, May 2, and continued to rise. Overflowing its banks, river water entered the homes, driving settlers to higher ground. As they withdrew, they saw their houses, stables and pole fences being lifted by the rising water and borne away by the swollen current. One of their number who believed he would be safe and secure in making his bed and temporary living quarters on top of his haystack, discovered the fodder would float too and he was carried away toward Lake Winnipeg. Other settlers retreated until reaching Stony Mountain or Bird's Hill, from which point they could view the river, looking more like a lake with a spread of up to fifteen miles.

John Pritchard, who left the best eye-witness account of the Battle of Seven Oaks ten years earlier, was able to make another contribution to western historical records. He told about the spring breakup with its fury and noise like thunder on April 30, and described the great chunks of ice rearing like an outlaw bronco, shearing off the tallest poplar trees and the stoutest bur oaks, "like grass before the scythe." He was then among those obliged to abandon farms and homes and continue the flight as rising water pursued them.

The water continued to rise until May 21 when hardly a house remained in the riverside Colony. Francis Heron, a Hudson's Bay Company employee, according to his diary, saw forty-seven houses carried away in the space of half an hour on May 5.

George Simpson believed it was "the death blow" to the Settlement. To this man with growing attachment to the fur trade, it was difficult to know how much of this was wishful thinking. In any case, he saw the tragedy of it all, saw the settlers facing the threat of death from starvation, disease or drowning. He was grieved to say at the moment of writing at mid-June: "There is scarcely the remnant of a settlement to be seen, the face of the country being no longer visible except at a few elevated spots to the tops of which the inhabitants have retreated as the only salvation from a watery grave and what was once a boundless expanse of the most beautiful plains now exhibits one extended sea or lake.... In short, Lake Winnipeg now extends to Pembina.... The poor colonists I found in the greatest consternation and distress. I could not advise them to remain in the country as in that case they would immediately come upon me with demands for clothing, ammunition and all other supplies on credit. I therefore kept the people to the freedom of their own will. To the useless and disaffected I held out no encouragement to remain, on the contrary offered them such facilities as we could render to enable them to withdraw. But to the Scotch and other well-disposed settlers, I held out every inducement that did not involve the Company, the executors or myself in responsibility. After mature deliberation, they resolved to give the Colony one more trial without extracting a single promise or consideration from me."[13]

At the end of May when the flood water showed the slightest sign of receding Pritchard saw impatient settlers starting over the trail that would take them just a little nearer their homesites, eager to begin again. Those who recalled previous returns to the river after being driven out by attackers who wanted to destroy all hope of agriculture and colonization in this fur country were reminded of the plagues visited upon Pharaoh in the times of Moses, and hoped there would be no more.

Not until the middle of June was it possible to plant anything, by which time it was too late for most crops. Moreover, except for a bag of wheat stored in a church belltower that survived the flood, seed supplies like most other possessions were lost. But a few seeds were obtained from other posts and these along with potatoes were planted in spite of the lateness of the season.

John Pritchard returned to his former homesite after an absence of twelve weeks and when writing his recollections, was sitting "under a shed of boards," the best shelter he could find. Some of his former neighbors were not returning; they confessed to having had enough of frontier rebelliousness but he was among those preparing to build again, hoping to have a better roof over his head before the winter weather returned, hoping also for better planting conditions in the next spring.

All plans for improving roads, expanding in sheep, and growing specialty crops like flax had to be suspended. Simpson, returning from the East earlier in the spring was carrying nine gallons of flaxseed which he intended to distribute among the settlers for test purposes. The experiment was not abandoned, just delayed one year. It had been Lord Selkirk's cherished idea and Simpson was becoming enthusiastic enough to be offering premiums for the growing of both flax and hemp. A scutching mill was built in 1833 and Simpson said it was just a matter of time until "large quantities will be grown in the settlement as this soil and climate are bound to be highly favorable for these crops."

Simpson was wrong. Flax and hemp did not become the economic saviors he expected. Nothing in crops produced early miracles but wheat, barley, oats and potatoes became very much more reliable. For half a century after the flood year of 1826, the Settlement had ample of wheat and meat for local needs and some to sell to the Hudson's Bay Company. Until a treadmill operated with horses or oxen was set up, all grinding was by means of the hand device known as a quern, an ancient piece of equipment, the basic parts of which were the upper and nether stones. The upper one had a handle and the lower one was stationary. Grain admitted between the stones was crushed sufficiently to meet the frontier need in bread-making. Ultimately, the windmill came, then a waterwheel and still later a steam-driven mill for grinding.

But production was still for home use only. The colonists had not found that illusive article for export and did not find it for exactly fifty years after the awful flood. It was a long time to wait but finally, Lord Selkirk's dream came true. It was not a product from flax or hemp, or buffalo wool from Pritchard's company, or beef fat from the Tallow Company which collapsed in 1833. It was nothing more novel or spectacular than wheat and in 1876, the first shipment was sent away by riverboat, a total of 857 bushels and 10 pounds, all the wheat the West of Canada had to sell. It was enough to gently open the floodgates for the flow of millions and millions of bushels of the world's best bread wheat from the Selkirk country and beyond to help feed the world's hungry masses. It was too bad Lord Selkirk and his early colonists were not present to see the mounting torrent of bread grain crossing the Red River eastward between the Forks and Point Douglas, the best possible confirmation of their faith in western soil and what it would grow.

The End of a Chapter

Nobody in the Settlement was thinking seriously about a twenty-fifth anniversary of the birth of Lord Selkirk's Red River enterprise. Instead of being directed at birthdays, thoughts and conversation along the river were occupied by the startling news of the sale of the Selkirk territorial empire, known as Assiniboia, back to the Hudson's Bay Company, its original owner.

Exactly twenty-five years earlier, 116,000 square miles of this land, thought to have no value except to buffalo hunters, were transferred to the Earl, the total money consideration being ten shillings. Most people at that time were unimpressed, either because of personal interest in the fur trade or because they thought the scheme was an irresponsible dream of a wild visionary.

Concerning this recent transaction of 1836, the settlers had not been consulted and they were upset, more from fear of consequences than from the slight of being ignored. They wondered how reconveyance would affect their fortunes and it was easy to find reasons for pessimism. It would not escape them that the Selkirk scheme at its infancy was almost exclusively a child of the Earl and even Company officials were either quietly hostile or crassly unenthusiastic. Now, with many former North West Company servants occupying positions of authority, it was to be expected that old animosities toward agriculture and settlement would survive and latent hopes for liquidation of the Settlement would be restored.

The idea of purging the fur country of its menacing community of sodbusters and homebuilders, even at this late date, did not escape Company officials but two factors ruled against serious change: first, the insistence of members of the Selkirk family that the Colony's future be safeguarded, and second, the Colony's changing personality and growing importance in furnishing provisions for Company men in far-flung trading posts. Rather suddenly it was a Colony of a very different stripe.

In consequence, the reconveyance was carried out with no immediate impact, one way or another, upon the lives of the settlers. The transfer embraced less than the original 116,000 square miles because a redefinition of the boundary placed a portion of the Selkirk property within the United States. In any case, the return of the area marked the end of an important chapter in the history of western agriculture and settlement but only the first chapter.

Bearing date of May 4, 1836, a document was signed to the effect that the Selkirk heir surrendered his land and accepted payment in Hudson's Bay Company shares. The deal was initiated by the Company rather than the seller and the new Lord Selkirk acceded to the wish and accepted payment in the equivalent of £84,000, determined by a formula based on aggregate costs, interests and profits earned. The young Earl, with whom the financial arrangements were made, pointed out that the figure was actually determined from costs and interest only because there was no profit.[6]

That the Hudson's Bay Company wanted to repossess the Selkirk land was a good sign; it was an acknowledgment of a new sense of worth. The Colony had not become a source of money dividends but it was beginning to look like a good investment for the future and it could serve as an immediate symbol of proprietorship, capable of enhancing the Company in the eyes of British critics. The Company officers were much aware of the need for some improvement in its image. The manner in which Lower Fort Garry was being constructed to stand for a thousand years at the bottom of St. Andrew's Rapids, reflected the desire to give the impression of permanency. Built to George Simpson's specifications, the Lower Fort was on a site less vulnerable to floods than was the case at the Forks and as seen at the time of the reconveyance, it could share the distinction of solidarity with the less conspicuous Fort Prince of Wales at the mouth of the Churchill River.

The formal transfer at the twenty-five-year point afforded a proper time for general review and reassessment. By now the riverside community, showing more certain signs of surviving, was in a position to claim some proud distinctions. Hadn't it withstood the most savage attacks upon its right to exist? Wasn't it a portrayal of one of the boldest of all North American experiments in agriculture and settlement? Hadn't it been part of a most unrelenting search for local industry? Up to that time there was nothing quite like the Red River effort and the Colony, at its twenty-fifth birthday, stood as the finest possible monument to its founder, Lord Selkirk, who gave of his wealth and health to make it live.

The struggle was not over, not by any means. Many people were still skeptical of the area as a place for agriculture, choosing to take the pattern of crop failure in the early years as support for the fur traders' warnings. Agricultural disappointments had indeed come in many shapes: the unresponsiveness of the bison to domesticate or cross, the failures with flax and hemp and some other selected crops, the persistence of the grasshoppers, the extreme difficulties in establishing flocks and herds, and so on. It would take much persuasion to dislodge a widespread conviction that "seven-eighths of British North America is doomed to eternal sterility." Why not accept the country for what it was known to do so well: produce beaver pelts and buffalo skins? It would be the simple and easy policy.

It took a courageous and persevering person to challenge that concept and test the new one. The Earl was the one to do it and persuade the many others needed to carry out the experiment. Some of those who embarked upon the test gave up too soon. The wonder was that others suffering from the varied onslaughts did not quit also, most of all Lord Selkirk. But perseverance had its reward and the agricultural fortunes improved until by the year of the reconveyance, farming people were planting with confidence unknown during the first decade.

At the departure of the de Meurons and the Swiss following the flood of 1826, settlement population fell by 243. It left only the Scottish and Canadian families along with those classified as natives, a hardy and determined stock, and by this year of 1836, they were finding the reward of a new sense of security. Life was changing. Although self-government was still far away, the Company was moving to better government by expanding the local authority known as the Council of Assiniboia. Although still an appointed body rather than an elected one, its enlargement made it more aware of public needs and public views. The reorganized Council included many familiar names, John Pritchard, William Cochran, James Sutherland, Robert Logan, D. T. Jones, James Bird, Alexander Christie, William Cook and John Clarke. Before the end of the year, still more well-known personalities were added: Alexander Ross the sheriff and historian, Donald Ross, Dr. John Bunn, Andrew McDermott, Bishop Provencher, Captain George Cary and, most surprising of all, Cuthbert Grant. Nothing symbolized changing times and forgiving ways as much as the appointment of this man who was for years after the Battle of Seven Oaks considered to be the Colony's archenemy.

The search for industry likely to provide something to sell and export had been unceasing since Lord Selkirk selected Merino sheep from Spain in the hope of making Red River a supplier of the world's finest wool. The search resembled that conducted by towns and cities in later years. Early Calgary, for example, was pinning its faith on an oatmeal mill, then a tannery and a cigar factory. In the same way, the Red River community struggled to find industrial reward in the Buffalo Wool Company and heard about a few high-cost shawls selling to Lady Selkirk's London friends for twenty-five pounds each prior to the company's collapse, then in the Tallow Company of 1833 that would ship beef fat to Britain and make its shareholders wealthy. But the tallow enterprise lost about one-quarter of its cattle from wolves, weather and mismanagement in the first year and it, too, headed for bankruptcy. They were part of the growing pains of a struggling community; they were mistakes which did not have to be repeated. .

The search for industry continued in spite of the succession of reverses. And Simpson, far from giving up in his hope of finding a better and broader economic base, was proposing a School of Industry, mainly for the purpose of teaching boys and girls to spin and weave. He had six spinning wheels and three looms ready for use by the pupils in 1833 and expected twenty-four children to be employed.[2] At about the same time, the industry-minded Simpson was boasting hopefully of the discovery of "a coal mine on the Assiniboine, about 150 miles above the settlement."[3] That distance would place the coal discovery a few miles west of present-day Brandon, but it was a false hope and produced more of longing than burnable fuel and Fort Garry did not become a rival to Manchester.

Again, the most rewarding industry was found in the unspectacular home market for produce from the soil. Population was growing again and many Hudson's Bay Company men, coming to the age of retirement, were electing to settle for their years of ease right there at Red River. Moreover, the Company was looking more and more to the settlement for food supplies needed to provision the scores of trading posts stretching far to the west and northwest, wheat, barley, potatoes, corned beef, smoked hams, lard, butter, cheese, onions and cabbage. If the judgment of Alexander Ross is accepted, the quality left much to be desired; the grains suffered from too much association with mice and the butter, at times, was so rancid that it was fit only for lubricating axles. But there being no alternative supplies, consumers gained nothing by complaining and seemed glad to get any supplies.

The new order marked by the transfer of the Selkirk holdings back to the Hudson's Bay Company should have made the rejuvenated Colony appear more than ever as a monument to the Founding Father. It was not too soon to recognize the monumental character of what he had done and regret that during his lifetime this nation-builder received more of abuse than honor. Although nobody could speak with assurance, Selkirk's friends believed the intense opposition he encountered after 1815 materially shortened his life. A man of gentle mien, it was difficult for him to withstand the rebuffs of falsehood, accusation, litigation and even threats upon his life.

It is not suggested that his motives were entirely those of a Francis of Assisi. Perhaps a fabulous fortune was in his thoughts but nobody could question his desire to help needy people. Nor could anyone deprive him of the distinction of being Canada's foremost colonizer. And instead of making a fortune in carrying out his plan, he lost a fortune. According to Chester Martin, eminent Selkirk scholar, the Earl's losses amounted "in eight years to £114,000" or roughly half a million dollars.[4]

The point is that in those eight short years, he made an enduring imprint upon the destiny of a nation. How much more he might have done if he had lived for an average span of years invites speculation.

Naturally, his death was a blow to the recovering Colony which needed his support. The Selkirk Estate, presided over by the efficient Andrew Colvile, declared to maintain the Earl's beneficent traditions but things were not the same. In one sense, however, the passing was not without benefit because it seemed to remove certain obstacles to the union of the two rival trading companies, and union in turn removed or reduced the principal opposition and threat of violence confronting the Settlement.

True, the Earl came to Montreal in 1815 furnished with proposals for a new and more amiable business arrangement, one which would have eliminated the bitter and costly conflict. But after hearing of the North Westers' brutal involvement in the destruction of the Colony, he could not bring himself to face William McGillivray for even a business discussion. His study of the fur trade had left him with distrust for the North West Company at the best of times and after what he had heard of an attempt to destroy his beloved Colony, he became uncompromising in his hatred.

Of course, the animosities and the ultimate sins were not all on one side. The North West Company men who believed firmly that the Colony was a scheme to destroy their trade, and those who later felt the gross indignity of arrest with charges ranging from conspiracy to being accessories to murder, could not love Selkirk. North West Company enmity became Montreal enmity and even Britishers heard more about the man's mistakes than about his purposes. Canadians and Britishers seemed strangely willing to forget him.

The singular initiative and imagination brought to the infant western agriculture, decades ahead of any similar efforts, have been treated on other pages; they alone would justify the concept of "monument." But as a concluding note let there be added words of recognition of the immeasurable part Selkirk's Colony played in shaping Western Canada's political destiny. The agricultural impact should be obvious enough but was the Selkirk experience not a powerful force in safeguarding the British connection in the Northwest?

At a time when Canadian governments were indifferent and United States interests were seeing Rupert's Land and contiguous areas as essential parts in the fulfillment of the American dream of Manifest Destiny, the West's future was most uncertain. As historians know, it reached the point of the United States House of Representatives hearing formal bills for annexation of that territory which is now Western Canada, with provision for the organization of the newly acquired country into states. Only with the proof of productivity furnished by the Selkirk adventure and the people who became settlers, did the young Dominion of Canada find enough interest in the West to acquire the area and thus block American expansion in this direction.

It is difficult to escape the concluding thought that only Lord Selkirk had the vision to see beyond the fur trade and the confidence to use his own money in betting on an agricultural alternative.

Notes

(The abbreviation S.P. stands for Selkirk Papers.)

CHAPTER TWO   In the Beginning
1   George Bryce, *The Life of Lord Selkirk,* Centennial ed. (Toronto, Musson Book
        Co., undated [ca. 1912]).
2   Robert Chambers, *Life and Works of Robert Burns,* rev. by Wm. Wallace
        (Edinburgh, W. and R. Chambers, 1896).

CHAPTER THREE   The Great Canadian Colonizer
1   Colonial Office Records, A Transcript, No. 293 (London, Public Record Office,
        March 31, 1802).
2   *Ibid.* (April 3, 1802).
3   Alexander Mackenzie, *Voyages from Montreal* (London, 1801).
4   Lord Pelham, Memorandum dated May 27, 1802 (Colonial Office Records,
        1802).
5   Selkirk, Letter to Lord Hobart, July 6, 1802 (Colonial Office Records, 1802;
        Ottawa, National Archives).
6   Selkirk, *Observations on the Present State of the Highlands of Scotland, With a
        View of the Causes and Probable Consequences of Emigration* (Longman,
        Hurst, Raes and Orme, 1805).
7   Lorne C. Callbeck, *The Cradle of Confederation* (Brunswick Press, 1964).
8   Selkirk, *Observations on the Present State of the Highlands.*

CHAPTER FOUR   The Threat of Farmers in Fur Country
1   Selkirk, *A Sketch of the British Fur Trade in North America, With Observations
        Relative to the North West Company of Montreal* (London, James
        Ridgway, 1816).
2   *Ibid.*
3   *Ibid.*
4   *Ibid.*
5   Sir Alexander Mackenzie, Letter to Lord Selkirk, June 27, 1808. S.P.
6   *Ibid.,* Oct. 29, 1808.
7   Hudson's Bay Company Minute Book, Meeting of Feb. 6, 1811 (Winnipeg,
        H.B. Co. Archives).
8   *Ibid.*
9   *Ibid.,* Meeting of May 15, 1811.
10 *Ibid.,* Meeting of May 1, 1811.
11 *Ibid.,* Meeting of May 30, 1811.
12 *Ibid.*
13 *Ibid.,* Meeting of June 13, 1811.

CHAPTER FIVE   The Vanguard Party
1 Selkirk Diary, 1803-04 (Ottawa, Public Archives of Canada).
2 Miles Macdonell, Letter written at Nelson Encampment to Wm. Auld, Dec. 25, 1811. S.P.
3 Selkirk Memo, Dec. 10, 1815. S.P.
4 Letter to the Editor, *Inverness Journal,* June 21, 1811.
5 Miles Macdonell, Letter written at York Factory to Lord Selkirk, Oct. 1, 1811. S.P.

CHAPTER SIX   Into the Stream of New World History
1 Miles Macdonell, Letter written at Nelson Encampment to Lord Selkirk, May 29, 1812. S.P.
2 Miles Macdonell, Letter written at Nelson Encampment to Wm. Auld, Dec. 25, 1811. S.P.
3 Miles Macdonell, Letter written at York Factory to Lord Selkirk, Oct. 1, 1811. S.P.
4 Miles Macdonell, Letter written at Nelson Encampment to Wm. Auld, Jan. 21, 1812. S.P.
5 William Auld, Letter written at York Factory to Miles Macdonell, Nov. 3, 1811. S.P.
6 Miles Macdonell, Letter written at Nelson Encampment to Lord Selkirk, June 19, 1812. S.P.

CHAPTER SEVEN   The Big Push to Red River
1 Miles Macdonell, Letter to Lord Selkirk, June 19, 1812. Macdonell Papers (Ottawa, Public Archives).
2 *Ibid.,* Dec. 25, 1811.
3 Miles Macdonell, Letter written at York Factory to Lord Selkirk, July 4, 1811. Macdonell Papers.
4 *Ibid.,* Oct. 1, 1811.
5 William Auld, Letter written at York Factory to Lord Selkirk, Oct. 1, 1811. S.P.
6 Selkirk, Letter to Miles Macdonell, date indistinct, 1811. S.P.
7 Selkirk, Letter to William Auld, June 18, 1812. S.P.
8 Selkirk, Letter to Miles Macdonell, 1811. S.P., pp. 168-180.
9 Selkirk, Letter to Wm. Auld, June 18, 1812. S.P.
10 Selkirk, Letter to Miles Macdonell, 1811. S.P., pp. 168-180.
11 Selkirk, Letter to Miles Macdonell, June 13, 1811. Macdonell Papers.

CHAPTER EIGHT   Red River, At Last
1 Miles Macdonell, Letter to Lord Selkirk, July 17, 1813. S.P.
2 *Ibid.*
3 Selkirk, Letter to Wm. Auld, June 18, 1812. S.P.
4 Selkirk, Letter to Miles Macdonell, June 20, 1812. S.P.
5 *Ibid.,* June 5, 1813.
6 Capt. Matthey, Letter to Lord Selkirk, Aug. 30, 1818. S.P.
7 Miles Macdonell, Letter to Lord Selkirk, July 17, 1813. S.P.
8 *Ibid.*
9 John Macdonell, Letter written from Fort William to Miles Macdonell, July 18, 1812. Macdonell Papers.

CHAPTER NINE   The High Cost of Macdonell Arrogance
1 Miles Macdonell, Letter to Wm. Auld, Feb. 4, 1814. S.P.
2 Selkirk, Letter to Miles Macdonell, April 12, 1814. S.P.
3 William Auld, Letter, Sept. 26, 1813. S.P.
4 *Ibid.*
5 Miles Macdonell, Letter to Lord Selkirk, July 17, 1813. S.P.
6 Miles Macdonell, Letter written at Fort Daer to Alexander Macdonell, April 18, 1813. S.P.
7 Alexander Macdonell, Letter written at Pembina to Miles Macdonell, April 18, 1813. S.P.
8 Miles Macdonell, Letter to The Gentlemen Agents of the N.W.Co., Fort William, June 1, 1813. S.P.
9 Wm. McGillivray, and others, Letter written at Fort William to Miles Macdonell, July 22, 1813. S.P.
10 John Spencer, Sheriff, Proclamation issued Jan. 8, 1814. S.P.
11 Miles Macdonell, Letter to Wm. Auld, Feb. 4, 1814. S.P.
12 William Auld, Letter written at Brandon House to Miles Macdonell, April 15, 1814. S.P.
13 Miles Macdonell, Letter to the North West Company officers, June 18, 1814. S.P.

CHAPTER TEN   The Sutherland Settlers
1 Selkirk, Letter to Miles Macdonell, undated. S.P.
2 Miles Macdonell, Letter written at York Factory to Lord Selkirk, Aug. 31, 1813. S.P.
3 Archibald MacDonald, Letter to Lord Selkirk, May 22, 1814. S.P.
4 *Ibid.*
5 Miles Macdonell, Letter to Lord Selkirk, July 25, 1814. S.P.
6 Archibald MacDonald, Letter written at Red River to Lord Selkirk, July 24, 1814. S.P.

CHAPTER ELEVEN   Planned Destruction
1 Selkirk, Letter to Miles Macdonell, April 12, 1814. S.P.
2 *Ibid.*
3 William Auld, Letter dated Sept. 26, 1813 (other particulars missing). S.P.
4 Miles Macdonell, Letter to Lord Selkirk, July 24, 1814. S.P.
5 Selkirk, Letter to Miles Macdonell, Dec. 21, 1814. S.P.
6 A. Edwards, Report, Aug. 27, 1814. S.P.
7 W. B. Coltman, Report Relative to the Disturbance in the Indian Territories, *Papers Relating to the Red River Settlement* (London, 1819), p. 159, 1819.
8 *Ibid.*
9 *Ibid.*
10 Miles Macdonell, Letter to Lord Selkirk, Sept. 10, 1813. S.P.
11 James Smyth, Letter written at Fort Daer to Duncan Cameron, Dec. 22, 1814. S.P.
12 Duncan Cameron, Letter to Archibald MacDonald, April 3, 1815, *Statement Respecting the Earl of Selkirk's Settlement upon the Red River in North America* (London, John Murray, 1817).

13 *Statement Respecting the Earl of Selkirk's Settlement.*
14 Selkirk, Letter to Miles Macdonell, 1813. S.P.
15 James Whyte, and others, Letter to Lord Selkirk, June 24, 1815. S.P.
16 Cuthbert Grant, and others, Note to James Whyte and James Sutherland, June 25, 1815. Peter Fidler's Journal (Ottawa, Public Archives).
17 *Statement Respecting the Earl of Selkirk's Settlement.*

CHAPTER TWELVE   Robertson to the Rescue
 1 Simon McGillivray, Letter to Archibald McGillivray, July 2, 1815. S.P.
 2 Miles Macdonell, Letter written at Winnipeg River to Lord Selkirk, July 2, 1815. S.P.
 3 Warrant against Miles Macdonell, Sept. 15, 1815. S.P., p. 1698.
 4 *Statement Respecting the Earl of Selkirk's Settlement.*
 5 Robert Semple, Letter written at York Factory to Colin Robertson, Sept. 5, 1815. S.P.
 6 Duncan Cameron, Speech to Freemen. Copy taken from Fort Gilbralter Journal by Colin Robertson.
 7 Selkirk, Letter to Colin Robertson, March 30, 1816. S.P.
 8 Robert Semple, Letter to Duncan Cameron, March 31, 1816. S.P.
 9 Alexander Macdonell, Letter to Duncan Cameron, March 18, 1816, *Statement Respecting the Earl of Selkirk's Settlement.*

CHAPTER THIRTEEN   The Awful Day of Seven Oaks
 1 Francis Delorme, Declaration of a free Canadian, referring to speech by Duncan Cameron, June, 1815. Declared before Alex MacDonell, J.P., July 20, 1816.
 2 Alexander Macdonell, Letter to J. D. Cameron, March 13, 1816, *Statement Respecting the Earl of Selkirk's Settlement.*
 3 W. B. Coltman, Commissioner's Report, *Papers Relating to the Red River Settlement,* p. 183.
 4 *Ibid.*
 5 John Pritchard, Sworn statement made at Montreal, Feb. 18, 1817, *Papers Relating to the Red River Settlement,* p. 66.
 6 W. B. Coltman, Comissioner's Report, *Papers Relating to the Red River Settlement,* p. 186.
 7 John Pritchard, Sworn statement, *Papers Relating to the Red River Settlement,* p. 68.
 8 Proclamation, June 20, 1816. S.P.

CHAPTER FOURTEEN   Selkirk on the Way
 1 Joseph Berens, Jun., Letter to Lord Selkirk, Aug. 30, 1815. S.P.
 2 Selkirk, Letter to the Governor, Deputy Governor and Committee of the H.B.Co., Feb. 14, 1815, *Papers Relating to the Red River Settlement.*
 3 Lord Bathurst, Letter to Sir Gordon Drummond, Gov. Gen., March 18, 1815, *Papers Relating to the Red River Settlement.*
 4 J. Harvey, Sec. to Sir Gordon Drummond, Letter to Wm. McGillivray, June 8, 1815.
 5 William McGillivray, Letter to Lt. Col. J. Harvey, June 8, 1815, *Papers Relating to the Red River Settlement.*

6   J. Harvey, Letter to Messrs. Maitland, Gordon and Auldjo, *Papers Relating to the Red River Settlement.*
7   Sir Gordon Drummond, Letter to Lord Selkirk, April 13, 1816. S.P.
8   John Halkett, Letter to Lord Selkirk, April 17, 1816. S.P.
9   John Harvey, General Order, May 29, 1816. S.P.
10 Selkirk, Letter to Robert Semple, April 26, 1816. S.P.
11 Robert Murray, Instructions to Clark and Street, March 11, 1816. S.P.
12 Miles Macdonell, Letter written at Lac la Pluie to Lord Selkirk, July 7, 1816. S.P.
13 John Allan, Letter to Lord Selkirk at Sault Ste. Marie, July 31, 1816. S.P.

CHAPTER FIFTEEN   Flimflam at Fort William
1   Peter Fidler, Letter written at Jack River to Owen Keveny, Aug. 11, 1816. S.P.
2   *Statement Respecting the Earl of Selkirk's Settlement.* (The same declaration by McNabb appears in the Selkirk Papers.)
3   Selkirk, Letter to Att. Gen. D'Arcy Boulton, Aug. 17, 1816. S.P.
4   G. A. Fauché, Declaration, June 24, 1817, *Statement Respecting the Earl of Selkirk's Settlement.*
5   *Ibid.*
6   Samuel Gale, Letter to Lord Selkirk, Oct. 28, 1816. S.P.
7   Selkirk, Letter to Lt. Gov., Nov. 12, 1816. S.P.
8   Earl Bathurst, Letter to Sir John Sherbrooke, Gov.-in-Chief, Feb. 11, 1817.
9   Andrew Cochran, Sec. to Gov., Letter to Lord Selkirk, Oct. 28, 1816. S.P.
10 John Richardson, Letter to Sir John Sherbrooke, Nov. 9, 1816. S.P.
11 Samuel Gale, Letter to Lord Selkirk, Oct. 28, 1816. S.P.

CHAPTER SIXTEEN   The Silver Chief at Red River — At Last
1   Lady Jean Selkirk, Letter to Sir John Sherbrooke, Aug. 22, 1816. S.P.
2   Sir John Sherbrooke, Letter to Lord Selkirk, Oct. 30, 1816. S.P.
3   Daniel Mackenzie, Sworn Declaration, Drummond's Island, Nov. 11, 1816, *Papers Relating to the Red River Settlement.*
4   Miles Macdonell, Letter to Andrew Colvile, Feb. 1, 1822. S.P.
5   W. B. Coltman, Coltman Report, June 30, 1818, *Papers Relating to the Red River Settlement.*
6   W. B. Coltman, Letter to Sir John Sherbrooke, July 2, 1817, *Papers Relating to the Red River Settlement.*
7   W. B. Coltman, Coltman Report.
8   *Ibid.*
9   W. B. Coltman, Letter to Sir John Sherbrooke, May 20, 1818, *Papers Relating to the Red River Settlement.*
10 W. B. Coltman, March 28, 1818. S.P.
11 Samuel Gale, Letter to the Countess of Selkirk, May 26, 1818. S.P.

CHAPTER SEVENTEEN   The War of Words in the East
1   Selkirk, *A Sketch of the British Fur Trade in North America.*
2   Mercator, *Montreal Herald,* Feb. 8, 1817.
3   *Ibid.,* Nov. 2, 1816.
4   Correspondent, *Montreal Gazette,* Dec. 24, 1817.

5   John Strachan, *A Letter to the Right Honourable The Earl of Selkirk* (London, 1816).
6   John Strachan, Letter to Wm. McGillivray, May 2, 1815 (Ontario Historical Society, *John Strachan Letter Book,* ed. by George W. Spragge, 1946).
7   John M. Gray, *Lord Selkirk of Red River* (Toronto, Macmillans of Canada, 1963).

CHAPTER EIGHTEEN   The Distressing Year in Court
1   William McGillivray, Letter to the Duke of Richmond, Oct. 3, 1818, *Papers Relating to the Red River Settlement.*
2   N. F. G. Uniacke, Letter to Lord Selkirk, Feb. 9, 1818. S.P.
3   J. B. Robinson, Letter to Sir Peregrine Maitland, Lt. Gov., Dec. 5, 1818, *Papers Relating to the Red River Settlement.*
4   Selkirk, Letter to Sir P. Maitland, Oct. 21, 1818, *Papers Relating to the Red River Settlement.*
5   John Allan, Letter to J. B. Robinson, Sept. 16, 1818, *Papers Relating to the Red River Settlement.*
6   J. B. Robinson, Letter to Sir P. Maitland, Dec. 5, 1818, *Papers Relating to the Red River Settlement.*
7   *Montreal Gazette,* Nov. 17, 1818.

CHAPTER NINETEEN   Warfare Ended
1   George Bryce, *The Life of Lord Selkirk.*
2   Edward Ellice, Memorandum to Andrew Colvile, Dec. 2, 1819. S.P.
3   Selkirk, Letter to A. Colvile, Dec., 1819, as quoted by Chester Martin in *Red River Settlement, Canada and its Provinces* (Toronto, Glasgow Book Co., 1914).
4   Andrew Colvile, Letter to Edward Ellice, Dec. 31, 1819. S.P.
5   Andrew Colvile, Letter to Thomas Clark, April 28, 1820. S.P.

CHAPTER TWENTY   The Settlers Must "Walk Alone"
1   Miles Macdonell, Proclamation at Red River, April 6, 1819. S.P.
2   Miles Macdonell, Letter to A. Colvile, Feb. 1, 1820. S.P.
3   Andrew Colvile, Letter to Samuel Gale, Feb. 19, 1820. S.P.
4   Alexander MacDonell, Letter to A. Colvile, Nov. 13, 1821. S.P.
5   George Simpson, Letter to A. Colvile, May 20, 1822. S.P.
6   *Ibid.,* May 31, 1824.
7   Andrew Colville, Letter to R. P. Pelly, June 4, 1824. S.P.

CHAPTER TWENTY-ONE   The Hayfield Experimental Farm
1   William Laidlaw, Letter to Lord Selkirk, July 22, 1818. S.P.
2   Selkirk, Memorandum to Capt. Matthey, June 12, 1818. S.P.
3   William Laidlaw, Letter to Lord Selkirk, July 22, 1818. S.P.
4   *Ibid.,* Jan. 9, 1819.
5   George Simpson, Letter to A. Colvile, May 31, 1824. S.P.

CHAPTER TWENTY-TWO   The Buffalo Business
1   Selkirk, Letter to Miles Macdonell, June 5, 1813. S.P.
2   Miles Macdonell, Letter to Lord Selkirk, July 17, 1813. S.P.

3   Selkirk, Letter to Miles Macdonell, Dec. 21, 1814. S.P.
4   *Ibid.,* March 23, 1815.
5   William Laidlaw, Letter to Lord Selkirk, July 22, 1815. S.P.
6   Alexander MacDonell, Letter to A. Colvile, 1821, S.P.
7   John Pritchard, Letter to A. Colvile, Aug. 29, 1820. S.P.
8   *Ibid.,* June 9, 1821.
9   George Simpson, Letter to A. Colvile, Sept. 3, 1821. S.P.
10 Andrew Colvile, Letter to John Pritchard, March 11, 1824. S.P.
11 James Ogilvie, Letter to Lady Selkirk, Oct. 21, 1826. S.P.

CHAPTER TWENTY-THREE   Cows for the Colony
1   Colin Robertson, Letter to Lord Selkirk, July 18, 1818. S.P.
2   Alex Cuddie, Letter to Lord Selkirk, Sept. 7, 1819. S.P.
3   Thomas Clark, Letter to Robert Dickson, April, 1814. S.P.
4   Selkirk, Letter to Newport Kent, April 20, 1818. S.P.
5   Selkirk, Letter to Michael Dousman, Sept. 21, 1819. S.P.
6   Robert Dickson, Letter to Lord Selkirk, July 21, 1819. S.P.
7   Adam Stewart, Letter to Lord Selkirk, Aug. 13, 1819. S.P.
8   *Ibid.,* Jan. 30, 1820.
9   Alexander MacDonell, Letter to A. Colvile, Nov. 13, 1821. S.P.
10 A. Bulger, Letter to A. Colvile, Sept. 1, 1822. S.P.
11 *Ibid.,* Sept. 8, 1822.

CHAPTER TWENTY-FOUR   The Long Wait for Wool
1   Andrew Colvile, Letter to Alexander MacDonell, 1821. S.P.
2   Andrew Colvile, Letter to R. P. Pelly, March 11, 1824. S.P.
3   George Simpson, Letter to A. Colvile, June 4, 1829. S.P.
4   Robert Campbell, Diary, copy of which was loaned to the author by Mr. Harry
    Maltby.

CHAPTER TWENTY-FIVE   Oh for a Horse to Pull My Plow!
1   James Sutherland, Letter to Robert Semple, Dec. 16, 1815.
2   William Laidlaw, Letter to Lord Selkirk, July 22, 1818. S.P.
3   Alexander MacDonell, Letter to A. Colvile, Aug. 8, 1820. S.P.
4   George Simpson, Letter to the Governor and Committee of the H.B.Co., Aug.
    26, 1831, Published with permission of the Governor and Committee of
    the H.B.Co.
5   Nicholas Garry, Deputy Gov., Letter to George Simpson, Feb. 23, 1831,
    Published with permission of the Governor and Committee of the
    H.B.Co.
6   George Simpson, Letter to the Governor, Deputy Governor and Committee of
    the H.B.Co., Aug. 10, 1832, Published with permission of the Governor
    and Committee of the H.B.Co.
7   Eden Colvile, Acting Governor of Rupert's Land, Letter to Sir George
    Simpson, Aug. 24, 1851, Published with permission of the Governor and
    Committee of the H.B.Co.

CHAPTER TWENTY-SIX   How Are the Crops?
1   Sir George Simpson, Evidence before the Select Committee of the House of
    Commons, Feb. 26, 1857. British Parliamentary Papers, 1857.

2 Peter Fidler, Letter to Owen Keveny, Aug. 11, 1816. S.P.
3 Robert Semple, Letter to Lord Selkirk, Dec. 20, 1815.
4 Frederick Matthey, Letter to Lord Selkirk, Aug. 30, 1818. S.P.
5 *Ibid.,* Aug. 2, 1819.
6 John Pritchard, Letter to A. Colvile, Aug. 29, 1820. S.P.
7 Memorandum for Lord Selkirk's approval, July 23, 1819. S.P.
8 Alexander MacDonell, Letter to A. Colvile, Aug. 8, 1820. S.P.
9 George Simpson, Letter to A. Colvile, Sept. 3, 1821. S.P.
10 *Ibid.,* May 20, 1822.
11 *Ibid.,* June 24, 1823.
12 *Ibid.,* May 31, 1824.
13 *Ibid.,* June 14, 1826.

CHAPTER TWENTY-SEVEN   The End of a Chapter
1 Select Committee of the House of Commons, London, June 23, 1857.
2 George Simpson, Letter to A. Colvile, May 15, 1833. S.P.
3 *Ibid.,* Sept. 6, 1833.
4 Chester Martin, *Canada and Its Provinces,* Vol. XIX.

Reference Reading

Bell, C. N., *The Old Forts of Winnipeg,* Historical and Scientific Society of Man., May, 1927.

Bryce, George, *The Life Of Lord Selkirk,* Musson Book Co., Toronto.

Garrioch, A. C., *First Furrows,* Stovel Co., Winnipeg, 1923.

Gray, John Morgan, *Lord Selkirk Of Red River,* Macmillan Co. of Canada, Toronto, 1963.

Hargrave, J. J., *Red River,* 1869.

Lucas, Frederick C., *Historical Diary of Winnipeg,* Cartwright and Lucas, 1923.

Martin, Archer, *The Hudson's Bay Company Land Tenures,* William Clowes and Sons, London, 1898.

Martin, Chester, *The Red River Settlement, Canada and Its Provinces,* Vol XIX, Glasgow Book Co., Toronto, 1914.

MacBeth, R. G., *The Selkirk Settlers In Real Life,* William Briggs, Toronto, 1897.

Montreal Gazette, 1814 to 1820.

Montreal Herald, 1814 to 1820.

Morton, Arthur Silver, *A History of the Canadian West to 1870-71,* Thomas Nelson and Sons, Toronto, 1939; Second Edition, University of Toronto Press, 1973.

Morton, Arthur Silver, *Sir George Simpson,* J. M. Dent and Sons, Canada, 1944.

Oliver, E. H. (Editor) *The Canadian North-West, Legislative Records,* Government Printing Bureau, Ottawa, 1914 (Two volumes).

Papers Relating to the Red River Settlement, Ordered By The House of Commons, 1819.

Ross, Alexander, *The Red River Settlement,* Smith, Elder and Co., London, 1856.

Selkirk Papers.

The Beaver, Published quarterly by the Hudson's Bay Company.

Watson, Robert, *Lower Fort Garry,* Hudson's Bay Co., Winnipeg, 1928.

INDEX

DATE DUE
DATE DE RETOUR